THE CABINET OF LINGUISTIC CURIOSITIES

THE CABINET OF LINGUISTIC CURIOSITIES

A Yearbook of Forgotten Words

PAUL ANTHONY JONES

THE UNIVERSITY OF CHICAGO PRESS

The University of Chicago Press, Chicago 60637
© 2017 by Paul Anthony Jones
Published 2019
Printed in the United States of America

28 27 26 25 24 23 22 21 20 19   1 2 3 4 5

ISBN-13: 978-0-226-64670-1 (cloth)
ISBN-13: 978-0-226-64684-8 (e-book)
DOI: https://doi.org/10.7208/chicago/9780226646848.001.0001

First published in Great Britain by Elliott and Thompson Limited, 2017.

LIBRARY OF CONGRESS CATALOGING-IN-PUBLICATION DATA

Names: Jones, Paul Anthony, 1983– author.
Title: The cabinet of linguistic curiosities : a yearbook of forgotten words /
    Paul Anthony Jones.
Description: Chicago : The University of Chicago Press, 2019. | "First pub-
    lished in Great Britain by Elliott and Thompson Limited, 2017." | Includes
    bibliographical references.
Identifiers: LCCN 2019008167 | ISBN 9780226646701 (cloth : alk. paper) |
    ISBN 9780226646848 (e-book)
Subjects: LCSH: English language—Etymology.
Classification: LCC PE1574 .J668 2019 | DDC 422.03—dc23
LC record available at https://lccn.loc.gov/2019008167

♾ This paper meets the requirements of ANSI/NISO Z39.48-1992
(Permanence of Paper).

For Kevin, with thanks

INTRODUCTION:
A word for all occasions

London's Haymarket Theatre was packed to the rafters on the evening of 16 January 1749. An excitable audience had filled it to capacity after an advert in a local newspaper had promised a performance by a conjuror apparently able to transport himself from centre stage and into an empty wine bottle on a table nearby. The feat sounded too incredible to be true, for the very good reason that it was. The advertisement was a hoax.

Precisely who perpetrated it remains debatable, but when it became clear that a teleporting conjuror was not going to perform that night, one of the Haymarket's staff bravely came to the stage to explain that the performance would have to be cancelled – and in response the audience erupted into a furious riot that all but destroyed the theatre's interior. But this curious event did have a silver lining, at least: it is the origin of the bizarre and seldom-used word *bottle-conjuror*, which remains in place in the dictionary as a byword for a hoaxing prankster or charlatan.

The tale of the *bottle-conjuror* is just one of an entire year's worth of historical and etymological stories that fill the pages of this book: dip into this *Cabinet of Linguistic Curiosities* every day of the year, and you'll be met with a curious or meaningful historical anniversary and an equally curious or long-forgotten word of the day, picked from the more obscure corners of the dictionary.

On the day on which flirting was banned in New York City, for instance, you'll discover why to *sheep's-eye* someone once meant to look at them amorously. On the day on which a disillusioned San Franciscan declared himself Emperor of the United States, you'll find the word *mamamouchi*, a term for someone who considers themselves more important than they truly are. And on the day on which George Frideric Handel completed his 259-page *Messiah* oratorio after twenty-four days of frenzied work, you'll see why a French loanword, literally meaning 'a small wooden barrow', is used to refer to an intense period of work undertaken to meet a deadline. The English language, it seems, is vast enough to supply us with a word for all occasions – and this linguistic *Wunderkammer* (skip ahead to 7 June for that one . . .) is here to prove precisely that.

I have been raiding these troves of long-lost linguistic treasure since 2013, when the @HaggardHawks Twitter account tweeted its first few obscure words and language facts. And I've been tweeting daily nuggets of linguistic gold every day since, from random left-brain cluttering trivia (advance the letters of the word *oui* ten places through the alphabet and you'll arrive at *yes*) to bizarre etymological curiosities (because you have to straddle it, *bidet* means 'pony' in French). But alongside all those, Haggard Hawks tweets a daily Word of the Day: a typically strange or long-forgotten word that it's hoped you will never have heard of before and may, for whatever reason, wish to add to your daily vocabulary. And it is that which brings us to the book you're now holding in your hands.

Partly a yearbook of obscure language and partly an annual of events and observances, by opening this *Cabinet of Linguistic Curiosities* you'll find both a word and a day to remember, every day of the year. Each one has its own dedicated entry here, on which a curious or notable event and an equally curious or notable word are both explored. And because there really is a word for all occasions, all 366 daily doses of linguistic interest tie in with each daily event, and vice versa.

So whatever date this book has found its way into your hands, let's get right to it: there's a whole year's worth of linguistic curiosities waiting to be discovered.

quaaltagh *(n.)*   the first person you meet on New Year's Day

Proving there really is a word for everything, your *quaaltagh* is the first person you meet on New Year's Day morning.

If you think that word doesn't look even remotely English, you're right: *quaaltagh* (pronounced '*quoll*-tukh', with a rasping 'gh' like the sound in *loch*) was borrowed into English from Manx, the Celtic language of the Isle of Man, in the early nineteenth century. Its roots lie in a Manx verb, *quaail*, meaning 'to meet' or 'to assemble', as it originally referred to a group of festive entertainers who would come together to gambol from door to door at Christmas or New Year singing songs and reciting poems. For all their efforts, these *quaaltagh* entertainers would be invited inside for food and drink before moving on to the next house on their route.

If, as was often enough the case, all of that happened early on the morning of 1 January, then there was a good chance that the leader of the *quaaltagh* would be the first-footer of each household. As a result, a tradition soon emerged that the identity of the *quaaltagh* could have a bearing on the events of the year to come: dark-haired men were said to bring good luck, while fair-haired or fair-complexioned men (or, worst of all, fair-haired women) were said to bring bad luck – a curious superstition said to have its origins in the damage once wreaked by fair-haired Viking invaders.

Eventually, the tradition of door-to-door New Year's Day gambolling disappeared (presumably because everyone is feeling far too delicate the morning after the night before), but the tradition of the *quaaltagh* being your luck-bringing first encounter on the morning of New Year's Day, either inside or outside your house, has remained in place in the dictionary.

fedifragous *(adj.)*　　promise-breaking, oath-violating

If you made a New Year's resolution only to ditch the gym for a box of chocolates or an afternoon in the pub on 2 January, then the word you might be looking for is *fedifragous* – a seventeenth-century adjective describing anything or anyone that breaks an oath or a promise, or reneges on an earlier agreement.

Fedifragous combines two Latin roots: *foedus*, meaning 'treaty' or 'contract', and *frangere*, meaning 'to break'. *Foedus* is a common ancestor of a clutch of more familiar words like *confederate*, *federal* and *federation*, while it is from *frangere* that the likes of *fragment*, *fragile* and *fraction* are all descended – as well as an entire vocabulary's worth of more obscure and equally broken words:

- *confraction* (n.) a smashing or crushing, a breaking up into small pieces
- *effraction* (n.) a burglary, a house-breaking
- *effractive* (adj.) describing anything broken off something larger
- *irrefrangible* (adj.) incapable of being broken
- *ossifragous* (adj.) powerful enough to break bone

Along similar lines, *ossifrage* – literally 'bone-breaker' – is an old name for the lammergeyer, an enormous mountain-dwelling eagle known for its habit of smashing bones by dropping them from a great height and then devouring the shards. And even the humble *saxifrage* plant can take its place on this list: its name derives from the Latin *saxum*, meaning 'rock' or 'stone', and literally means 'stone-breaker'. The Roman scholar Pliny the Elder would have you believe that this refers to the plant's supposed effectiveness in treating kidney stones but, alas, it's more likely to be a reference to the plant's habit of growing in cracks and fissures in rocks.

eucatastrophe *(n.)*   a sudden and unexpected fortuitous event

If a *catastrophe* is an unexpected disaster, then a *eucatastrophe* is its opposite: using the same positive-forming prefix found in words like *euphoria* and *euphonious*, J. R. R. Tolkien coined the word *eucatastrophe* in 1944, defining it as 'the sudden happy turn in a story which pierces you with a joy that brings tears'.

As well as being the author of *The Hobbit* (1937) and the *Lord of the Rings* trilogy (1954–55), Tolkien – born on 3 January 1892 – was a professor of English at Oxford University and an expert philologist and etymologist. Alongside his fiction, he compiled a dictionary of Middle English, completed his own translation of the Anglo-Saxon epic *Beowulf* and, following active service in the First World War, worked for a time on the very first edition of the *Oxford English Dictionary*.

As an expert in Germanic languages, Tolkien was tasked with researching a clutch of Germanic-origin words falling alphabetically between *waggle* and *warlock* at the *OED* – *waistcoat, wake, walnut, wampum* and *wan* among them. The verb *want* ended up being the longest entry he assembled (Tolkien eventually identified more than two dozen different definitions and sub-definitions of it) but oddly it was the *walrus* that proved the toughest etymological challenge. He discovered that the walrus's original and long-forgotten English name, *morse*, is entirely unrelated to the word we use today, while the name *walrus* itself represents a metathesised (i.e. reordered) form of an Old Norse word, *hrosshvalr*, literally meaning 'horse-whale'. Why replace one word for the other? And why rearrange the Norse word we ended up using? No one is entirely sure, and in fact the word posed such a problem that Tolkien continued to study and lecture on its origins long after he left the *OED* in 1920.

spike-bozzle *(v.)*   to sabotage; to ruin or render ineffective

The longest workers' strike in history ended on 4 January 1961, when a band of disgruntled barbers' assistants in Copenhagen, Denmark, finally returned to work after thirty-three years. By 5 January, presumably, every man in Copenhagen was *imberbic* (that is, beardless).

The act of downing tools has been known as *striking* since the mid 1700s, when supposedly dissatisfied sailors would show their refusal to go out to sea by lowering or 'striking' their sails. Strikes have also been known as *steeks*, *stickouts*, *turn-outs* and *rag-outs* down the centuries, while those who cross the picket lines have been known by an array of depreciative nicknames including *dungs*, *scabs*, *ratters*, *snobs*, *knobs* and *knobsticks*.

Disgruntled workers have been *sabotaging* their equipment in protest since the early 1800s: the word comes from *sabot*, a type of French wooden boot, and although linguistic folklore will have you believe that the original *saboteurs* threw their shoes into their machinery in protest, sadly there's little evidence to back that story up. But why *sabotage* anything at all, of course, when you can *spike-bozzle* it?

A term originating during the First World War, *spike-bozzling* originally referred to the practice of scuppering or completely destroying enemy aircraft or equipment. In that sense, it probably derives from the practice of 'spiking' a gun – that is, driving a nail into its mechanism to render it useless – perhaps combined with *bamboozle* or *bumbaze*, an eighteenth-century Scots word meaning 'to confound' or 'to perplex'. By the mid 1900s, however, *spike-bozzling* was being used more broadly to refer to any attempt to ruin or render something ineffective, or else to upset another's work or plans.

pontitecture *(n.)*   the building of bridges

If etymological legend is to be believed, both *pontiff* and *pontifex* – titles held by and used of the Pope – derive from the Latin word for 'bridge', *pons*. If that's the case, then the *pontiff* is literally a 'bridge-builder' or 'bridge-maker', perhaps a figurative reference to his task of building spiritual bridges between heaven and earth, or else perhaps a literal reference to the papal blessings supposedly once bestowed on newly constructed bridges.

That Latin root, *pons*, crops up elsewhere in the dictionary in a handful of obscure words like *pontage* (a toll paid for the use or upkeep of a bridge), *ponticello* (the bridge of a stringed instrument), *pont-levis* (a drawbridge, or a term for a horse unseating its rider) and both *transpontine* and *cispontine* (adjectives describing things located on opposite sides of a bridge – flick ahead to 30 June for more on that).

Pons is also at the root of *pontitecture*, a term for the construction of bridges coined by a nineteenth-century Scottish scholar and businessman named Andrew Ure in 1853. 'There is perhaps no other form of pontitecture', Ure wrote in his *Dictionary of Arts, Manufactures & Mines*, 'which can compete with the wrought-iron girder when the clear space exceeds 70 feet.' Quite.

Ure's term *pontitecture* – which he based straightforwardly enough on the same template as *architecture* – is also a fitting word for today: it was on 5 January 1933 that work began on the construction of San Francisco's Golden Gate Bridge.

recumbentibus *(n.)* a powerful or knockout blow

The word *recumbent*, meaning 'lying down', derives from a Latin verb, *recumbere*, meaning 'to recline' or 'to rest'. The less familiar verb *recumb* – 'to rest', 'to rely upon' – derives from the same root, as does the superb word *recumbentibus*, which was adopted directly into English from Latin in the early 1400s.

In its native Latin *recumbentibus* was used merely of the act of lounging or reclining, but when the word was adopted into English it was given a twist: English writers, no doubt familiar with the word from its appearance in several early Latin translations of the Bible, began to use it to refer to forceful, knockout or knockdown blows, strong enough to knock someone off their feet.

> Had you some husband, and snapped at him thus, I wise he would give you a recumbentibus.
>
> John Heywood, *A Dialogue of Proverbs in the English Tongue* (1546)

The word remained in use in that sense through to the late seventeenth century, before largely falling out of use. Nowadays, we tend only to refer to *knockout* blows as precisely that, but a strike strong enough to knock someone off their feet can also be called a *purler* (literally a 'hurling' or an 'overturning'), a *stramazoun* (derived from an Italian word for a downward strike of a sword), and a *sockdolager* (flick ahead to 8 April for more on that).

With knockout blows in mind, the first documented boxing match in English history took place on 6 January 1681. According to a report in the *London Protestant*, Christopher Monck, 2nd Duke of Albemarle, arranged the fight between his butler and his butcher. The butcher, reportedly, was victorious.

translunary *(adj.)*   located beyond the moon

A *lunatic* was originally – and quite literally – someone whose bizarre behaviour was believed to be influenced by the moon: the word derives from the Latin word for 'moon', *luna*, which also crops up in *lunacy*, the deranged behaviour of a lunatic. Similarly, *lunambulism* is a nineteenth-century word for sleepwalking that supposedly is worsened by a full moon. A *lunarnaut* is an astronaut who has travelled to the moon, while an inhabitant of the moon, were one to exist, would be a *lunarian*. One *lunation* is the period of time between one full moon and the next. Anything described as *novilunar* or *plenilunar* takes place during a new or full moon, respectively. And while something that is *circumlunar* orbits or revolves around the moon, anything that is *translunary* is positioned beyond or on the other side of the moon.

Speaking of which, on 7 January 1610 the legendary astronomer Galileo Galilei wrote for the first time of a group of three 'fixed stars' he had observed close to Jupiter. In the weeks and months that followed, he not only discovered a fourth star to add to his list, but found that they were not 'fixed' as he had presumed, but instead appeared to be orbiting Jupiter. What he had observed were not stars, he finally determined, but the first natural satellites in astronomical history found to orbit a planet other than the earth.

sheep's-eye *(v.)*   to look amorously at someone

On 8 January 1902, it was reported that a bill had been tabled in the New York State Assembly that sought to punish 'any person who is intoxicated in a public place, or who shall by any offensive or disorderly act or language annoy or interfere with any person or persons'. Although the bill's impenetrable legalese kept its rulings fairly vague, its architect, State Assemblyman Francis G. Landon, was less ambiguous when it came to explaining who he intended it to target. As he explained to the *New York Morning Telegraph*, 'My bill is aimed at the flirters, gigglers, mashers, and makers of goo-goo eyes in public. We have all been disgusted with them . . . so they must be brought to their senses.' Anyone caught in violation of Landon's bill faced a $500 fine, or even up to a year in prison.

Remarkably, Landon's bill was passed the following day. Even more remarkably, it has never been repealed – meaning flirting has officially been illegal in New York ever since.

Long before Landon's *goo-goo eyes*, the flirters and romantics of sixteenth-century Europe had *sheep's-eyes*. According to the *Oxford English Dictionary*, *to cast* or *throw a sheep's-eye* has been used to mean 'to look lovingly, amorously, or longingly at someone' since the early 1500s; almost three centuries later, in 1801, the poet Samuel Taylor Coleridge coined the verb *sheep's-eye*, meaning to do precisely that. Sheep's eyes aren't especially romantic of course (although there's no accounting for taste) but the expression apparently alludes to the sheep's dopey, wide-eyed appearance – the same appearance that is at the root of the expression *to look sheepish*.

Looking sheepish in New York, incidentally, is entirely legal.

manatine *(adj.)*   resembling a manatee

On 9 January 1493, shortly before embarking on the return journey from the Americas to Europe, Christopher Columbus wrote in his journals that 'the admiral went to the Rio del Oro', on modern-day Haiti, where 'he saw three mermaids, which rose well out of the sea'.

'They are not so beautiful as they are painted,' Columbus continued, 'though to some extent they have the form of a human face.' As exciting a discovery as this would have been, unsurprisingly neither Columbus nor his admiral actually saw a mermaid that day. Instead, they saw a trio of manatees, the large plant-eating aquatic mammals that inhabit the warm seas and brackish rivers of the Caribbean and the Amazon.

In fact, the word *manatee* would not appear in English until almost fifty years after Columbus's death, when an account of 'those huge monsters of the sea' known to the inhabitants of Central America as the '*manati*' was published in 1555. Folk etymology would have you believe that the name derives from the Latin word for 'hand', *manus* – a reference to the manatee's surprisingly hand-like flippers, which contain five bony 'fingers' and end in a set of short semi-circular fingernails used to grip the seabed as it feeds. But the truth is that *manatee* is actually derived from a local Carib word, *manáti*, meaning 'breast' or 'udder', as female manatees feed their young with a rich milk produced from teats below each of their flippers. Their surprisingly human-like habit of appearing to 'cradle' their offspring in their 'arms' as they feed could only have helped fuel the myth that they were mermaids, but despite all their human-like characteristics – and despite Columbus's *manatine* description – the manatee's closest living relative is actually the elephant.

love-libel *(n.)*   a love letter, a love note

Libel is the crime of publishing a written statement that damages another person's reputation. A *love-libel* is a love letter or love note, the contents of which are hardly likely to be disparaging of the person on the receiving end. In both cases, *libel* is derived from *libellus*, a Latin word that literally means 'little book'. That meaning was essentially still intact when the word first appeared in English in the thirteenth century as another word for a handwritten statement or document, and from there it came to mean a leaflet or a widely distributed pamphlet, before the Elizabethan playwright Thomas Dekker coined the word *love-libel* – literally, 'a handwritten admission of someone's love' – in 1602.

The crime of *libel* took a different route. In the medieval legal system, a *libel* was a formal document outlining the allegations raised against a plaintiff, but by the seventeenth century things had changed: thanks to the use of *libel* to refer to a publicly distributed document or pamphlet, in legal contexts *libel* had come to refer to the crime of publishing or circulating a defamatory statement. As that meaning began to take hold, all other meanings of the word quickly drifted into obscurity – including Dekker's *love-libel*.

On the topic of which, on 10 January 1845 a brief letter was sent from Telegraph Cottage in Hatcham, Surrey, to 50 Wimpole Street in Marylebone, London. 'I love your verses with all my heart,' the letter began, 'and this is no off-hand complimentary letter that I shall write.' The note was the very first love letter sent by Robert Browning to his eventual wife Elizabeth Barrett, whose lengthy courtship via a total of 573 items of correspondence is one of English literature's most enduringly romantic tales.

great-go *(n.)*   a national lottery

The very first state lottery in English history – the brainchild of Elizabeth I, no less – was drawn before an eager crowd assembled outside St Paul's Cathedral on 11 January 1569. Ticket-holders had paid a whopping 10 shillings (equivalent to more than £100 today) to take part, but the prizes were incentive enough: £3,000 in cash, lush silken tapestries, huge quantities of gold and silver plate and 'good linen' were all up for grabs, while anyone lucky enough to afford a ticket was even granted temporary immunity from all but the most serious of crimes just for taking part. The stakes were considerable – but so was the debt Elizabeth's father, Henry VIII, had lumbered the country with, and her national lottery went some way towards plugging the hole in the national coffers.

By the seventeenth and eighteenth centuries, state lotteries known as *great-goes* – a reference to the earlier use of *go* to mean 'a thief's booty' or 'a prize catch' – had become fairly common. (Even the construction of the original Westminster Bridge was partly funded by the sale of £625,000 worth of lottery tickets.) But for every state-organised *great-go*, there was a *little-go* – a corrupt ploy practised in the shadiest inns and gambling houses of eighteenth-century England. Aimed at fleecing money from anyone too credulous or too trusting to notice, *little-goes* involved players placing money on numbers drawn at random from dozens of numbered tiles placed in a bag, with the player whose number was picked first winning a jackpot. Knowing that the poorer-educated and least numerate participants would likely opt for lower numbers, the organisers of these *little-goes* would typically neglect to put any single-figure tiles in the bag, ensuring that while there was always at least one winner, there were always many more losers.

unriddleable *(adj.)*   unsolvable

When it first appeared in the language back in the Old English period, the word *riddle* was used in a number of different ways to mean 'consideration', 'counsel' or 'discussion', 'interpretation', 'imagination', or 'conjecture'; despite appearances, it's actually a distant etymological cousin of *read*. But over time, *riddle* came to be attached almost exclusively to problems or issues that require consideration or imagination – and, eventually, to intentionally puzzling statements or enigmatic brain-teasers, designed to be deliberately confusing.

Although it is seldom used in the same way today, *riddle* can also be used as a verb meaning either 'to speak in or pose riddles', or oppositely, 'to solve puzzles' or 'to answer difficult questions'. It was this meaning that the English diarist John Evelyn had in mind when, in 1647, he wrote to a friend to discuss a meeting he had had with King Charles I. At the time the king was being held under house arrest by an increasingly powerful and belligerent parliament – and his trial and execution were two years away. 'The king's case', Evelyn wrote, 'is just like the disarmed man, who, whether he agrees that his antagonist shall keep his weapon or not, is forced to let him have it . . . I protest unto you, things were never more unriddleable than at this instant of time.'

Unriddleable ultimately means 'unsolvable', 'impossible' or 'inescapable' – and is an apt word for today, as it was on 12 January 1976 that crime writer and queen of the whodunnit Dame Agatha Christie died, aged eighty-five.

supervivant *(n.)*   a survivor

In January 1842, towards the end of the First Anglo-Afghan War, an eagle-eyed British Army officer stationed in Jalalabad, Afghanistan, watched in disbelief from the city walls as an exhausted, bloodstained man slowly emerged on horseback from a distant mountain pass. As his horse staggered closer to the city, it became clear that the man was wearing a British Army uniform, and a rescue party was promptly sent out to collect him.

The lone soldier was identified as thirty-year-old Scottish military surgeon William Brydon. He had set off from Kabul a week earlier as part of a vast assembly ejected from the city following a violent Afghan uprising. On the understanding that they would be guaranteed safe passage to Jalalabad, some 70 miles away, the group set off – but en route were massacred by Afghan tribesmen. Of the 4,500 soldiers and 12,000 civilians who departed Kabul, Brydon was the only survivor.

Brydon's story of survival is an astonishing one: he had somehow escaped encounter after encounter with Afghan fighters, one of whom had brought his sword down so sharply on to Brydon's head that a section of his skull had been cleaved clean away. Had he not stuffed a copy of *Blackwell's Magazine* into his cap as insulation against the bitter cold, the blow would have assuredly killed him.

Brydon reached the relative safety of Jalalabad on the morning of 13 January 1842, often claiming to be the only survivor – or *supervivant*, a sixteenth-century word that literally means 'one who outlives' – of a disastrous chapter in history known as the Retreat from Kabul.

proditomania *(n.)* the irrational belief that everyone around you is a traitor

Proditomania is the unnerving feeling that you're surrounded by people out to get you. Coined in the late 1800s, it derives from the Latin verb *prodere*, meaning 'to betray' – as do the likes of *prodition* (a fifteenth-century word for treason or treachery), *proditor* (a traitor) and *proditorious* (an adjective describing traitorous or perfidious actions, or someone liable to give away secrets).

Any one of these would make an apt word for today, as it was on 14 January 1741 that the infamous traitor Benedict Arnold was born. A general in the American Revolutionary War, Arnold planned to surrender his fort at West Point in New York to the British, but as soon as his intentions were discovered he quit his post and was drafted into the British forces. As a result of his actions, Arnold's name has entered the dictionary as a byword for anyone who commits equally treasonous or duplicitous actions – as have a handful of equally unsavoury characters:

- *Catiline* (n.) a word for a treasonous conspirator, named after a Roman senator who plotted to overthrow the Roman Republic in 63 BC
- *Delilah* (n.) a treacherous temptress, derived from the lover who betrayed Samson to the Philistines in the Old Testament
- *quisling* (n.), or *quislingite*, one who collaborates with an enemy, terms famously derived from Norwegian officer and Nazi collaborator Vidkun Quisling
- *Sinon* (n.) the name of the Greek warrior who coerced the Trojans into accepting the Trojan Horse has since become a byword for anyone who misleads others with lies or falsities

alamodic *(adj.)*   extremely fashionable, voguish

If something is *à la mode*, then it is in or of the very latest fashions or trends. Unsurprisingly that phrase is French, and was borrowed into English in the early 1600s – but it didn't take long for English speakers to begin to tinker with it to develop their own anglicised derivatives.

By the mid 1600s, for instance, an *alamode* was a fashionable person or a fashionable catchphrase or remark, and later the name of a type of glossy black silk. And in the mid 1700s, a Latin-influenced adjective, *alamodic*, emerged to describe anything that represented the epitome of the very latest fashion.

There's nothing wrong with being *alamodic*, of course – unless you happen to be luckless London haberdasher John Hetherington. On 15 January 1797, Hetherington wore a new black silk hat he had made that was noticeably and trend-settingly taller than any other. The *Hatter's Gazette* reported that Hetherington set off from his shop on The Strand wearing 'a tall structure having a shiny lustre, and calculated to frighten and intimidate people'. The report continued:

> Several women fainted at the unusual sight, while children screamed, dogs yelped, and a younger son of Cordwainer Thomas, who was returning from a chandler's shop, was thrown down by the crowd which had collected, and had his right arm broken.

Hetherington was arraigned before the Lord Mayor on a charge of breach of the peace and inciting a riot, but successfully defended himself by claiming he was merely 'exercising a right to appear in a head-dress of his own design – a right not denied to any Englishman'.

bottle-conjuror *(n.)*   a prankster, a charlatan

In 1749, a tantalising advertisement appeared in several London newspapers:

> At the New Theatre in the Hay-market, on Monday next, the 16th instant, to be seen, a person who performs the several most surprising things following, viz. . . . he presents you with a common wine bottle, . . .; this bottle is placed on a table in the middle of the stage, and he (without any equivocation) goes into it in sight of all the spectators, and sings in it; during his stay in the bottle any person may handle it, and see plainly that it does not exceed a common tavern bottle.

The theatre was packed to the rafters on the night of 16 January 1749 – but the conjuror failed to show up. The audience grew increasingly restless, and as an employee of the theatre bravely walked on to the stage to explain that everyone would be refunded, they erupted into a violent riot that gutted the theatre.

The identity of the conjuror who had claimed to be able to fit inside 'a common tavern bottle' is unknown, but popular legend claims that it was John Montagu, 2nd Duke of Montagu, a notorious practical joker of whom his mother-in-law once wrote, 'All his talents lie in things only natural in boys of fifteen years old – and he is about two and fifty.' Montagu, if legend is to be believed, entered into a bet with his friends that he could fill a theatre with people, and concocted the bottle illusion as a means of grabbing the public's attention.

No matter who the hoaxer was, however, the incident quickly led to the term *bottle-conjuror* becoming a byword for a fraudster or prankster in eighteenth-century English.

cadette *(n.)*   a younger sister or daughter

When the word *cadet* was first borrowed into English from French in the early seventeenth century, it originally referred to a younger son or brother. In that sense, it derives from *capitellum*, a diminutive of the Latin for 'head', *caput*, which literally makes a *cadet* a little or inferior leader – namely one forced to take a less important role than his superiors or older siblings. And if a *cadet* is a younger brother, then a *cadette* is a younger sister.

Appropriately enough, the youngest of the Brontë sisters, Anne, was born on 17 January 1820. Despite having a reputation as the quietest of the three girls, Anne was a fierce champion of her own work and fought against adverse circumstances her entire life. For one, it is believed that she likely suffered from a stammer or speech impediment: in 1848, she wrote to a friend that 'you must know there is a lamentable deficiency in my organ of language which makes me almost as bad a hand at writing as talking, unless I have something particular to say', while her older sister Charlotte expressed concern that it would be 'the talking part' that Anne would find difficult when she left home at nineteen to find work as a governess. Even once she had found employment, Anne found herself in charge of some appallingly spoiled and disobedient children, and was fired from her first job after raising concerns over the behaviour of the children in her care. Undaunted, she quickly found a second job (with twice the salary of her first) and channelled all of her experiences as a governess into her novels *Agnes Grey* (1847) and *The Tenant of Wildfell Hall* (1848), both now considered classics of English literature.

mauka *(adv.)*   inland, heading away from the coast

On 18 January 1778, part way through his third round-the-world voyage, the English explorer James Cook made landfall at an isolated group of islands in the middle of the Pacific Ocean. He named them the Sandwich Islands, in honour of John Montagu, 4th Earl of Sandwich – but today, we know them as Hawaii.

To English speakers, the native Hawaiian language probably seems a little bizarre. At the time of Cook's visit, it had no written form (and it took another five decades for American missionaries to develop a written Hawaiian alphabet so that they could publish a Hawaiian translation of the Bible). Even then, the Hawaiian alphabet only has thirteen recognisable letters: the consonants H, K, L, M, N, P and W; the five vowels A, E, I, O and U; and the *'okina*, an apostrophe-like symbol used to represent a unique sound made by stopping the airflow at the back of the throat. Those relatively limited resources mean that Hawaiian words – a handful of which have ended up in English dictionaries – can appear very peculiar indeed:

- *aa* (n.) a rough volcanic lava
- *heiau* (n.) a temple
- *humuhumunukunukuapuaa* (n.) a Hawaiian reef triggerfish
- *iiwi* (n.) a species of Hawaiian honey-creeper bird
- *pupu* (n.) a savoury appetiser

Hawaiian is also unusual in that it has no equivalents of *left* and *right* when giving directions. Instead, showing just how important the islands are to the islanders, Hawaiian directions are given using one of two words: *makai*, meaning 'seaward' or 'in the direction of the coast', and *mauka*, meaning 'inland', or 'in the direction of the mountains'.

raven-messenger *(n.)* someone who turns up too late to be of use

According to the Book of Genesis, the raven was the first animal released from Noah's Ark after the Great Flood. Although accounts of the story differ, the raven is typically said not to have returned to Noah immediately, but instead 'went forth to and fro until the waters were dried up from off the earth'. When the raven failed to return, Noah released a dove, which happily flew back to the Ark with an olive leaf in its bill to show that the floodwaters had finally abated.

This episode is the origin of *raven-messenger*, an ancient expression referring to someone – and, in particular, someone bearing news or an important message – who does not return when required, or arrives too late to be of any use. *Raven-messengers* like these are also known as *corbies* or *corbie-messengers*, a Scots dialect term derived from the French word for 'raven', *corbeau*.

The earliest *raven-messenger* we know about comes from the *Cursor Mundi*, an enormous Middle English account of the history of the world thought to have been written sometime around the early fourteenth century. According to its author, the reason Noah's raven failed to return was that it found some carrion floating on the surface of the water. As a result, 'that messenger', the *Cursor Mundi* explains, 'that dwells long in his journey . . . may be called, with reason clear, one of the raven messengers'.

And, fittingly, it was on 19 January 1809 that the American horror writer and author of 'The Raven', Edgar Allan Poe, was born in Boston.

antimetabole *(n.)*   the repetition, in a transposed
order, of words or phrases in
successive clauses

Derived from the Greek for 'turning in the opposite direction',
an *antimetabole* is a figure of speech in which a pair of words
or phrases is repeated in successive clauses, but in an inverted
order. So, 'when the going gets tough', as everyone knows, 'the
tough get going'.

A construction like this is also known as a *chiasmus*, a
similar figure of speech that takes its name from the X-shaped
Greek letter chi in reference to its criss-crossing structure. But
strictly speaking, in a *chiasmus* the elements being inverted do
not necessarily have to match: the structure and grammar of
the sentence, as well as the spelling or meaning of the words
involved, can all be played around with to create a rhythmic-
ally balanced and near parallel structure. Or, in the words of
George Carlin, 'Don't sweat the petty things, and don't pet the
sweaty things.'

Ultimately, an *antimetabole* is a stricter, more precise version
of *chiasmus*, but one that nevertheless produces very effective results. So, 'you can take the man out of the city, but you
can't take the city out of the man'. As the Three Witches in
Shakespeare's *Macbeth* have it, 'Fair is foul, and foul is fair.'
In the words of Benjamin Franklin, 'We do not stop playing
because we grow old; we grow old because we stop playing.'
And as President John F. Kennedy memorably said in his inaugural address, delivered on 20 January 1961: 'Ask not what your
country can do for you; ask what you can do for your country.'

Rasputinism *(n.)*   corrupting influence, especially over a government for political gain

The Russian mystic and itinerant monk Grigori Rasputin, known for his creeping influence over Tsar Nicholas II, was born in western Siberia on 21 January 1869.

Rasputin's involvement in the tsar's court began in 1906, when he was hired as a faith healer by Nicholas's wife Alexandra to help treat their young son Alexei's haemophilia. Out of gratitude, the emperor and his wife came to regard Rasputin as a prophet or mystic of extraordinary power, and as respect for him grew in the tsar's court, so too did the influence Rasputin could wield over the decisions made and enacted by Nicholas.

By the time Russia became embroiled in the First World War, however, Rasputin had come to be regarded with mounting suspicion, and when Nicholas left St Petersburg to direct the Russian army in the increasingly bloody conflict, the way was paved for Rasputin's downfall. Left to their own devices, he and Alexandra – a German-born granddaughter of Queen Victoria, accused by some of being a German double agent – became increasingly unpopular, and as the Russian war effort began to falter, Rasputin was assassinated on 30 December 1916 by a group of Russian noblemen who had come to violently oppose his influence.

Quite how much influence Rasputin genuinely had in Nicholas's court is debatable. Nevertheless, the stories that have since emerged of his supposed mystical corruption of the tsar and his family have led to the coining of the word *Rasputinism*, defined by the *Oxford English Dictionary* as 'the exercise of corrupting influence over a government or ruler'.

manubiary *(n.)* plundering

After the Roman army had finished plundering its way through its latest conquest, the time came to divide up the spoils of war. Those in charge were traditionally given their own share of the booty known as the *manubiae*, a word thought to derive from the Latin for 'hand', *manus*, in the sense that it was handed over to the triumphant generals personally.

Quite how much cash the *manubiae* corresponded to is unknown, but given that some commanders reportedly used the money to fund infrastructure projects, construct buildings or roads or even organise sporting events in their own honour, we can presume that it was often fairly sizeable. Either way, the generals were nevertheless permitted to do with it whatever they wished – with most opting simply to distribute small amounts of cash among the troops under their control. The custom eventually fell into disuse, and as the empire and the role and power of the emperor grew ever greater, it became customary for the spoils of war to come under the exclusive control of the emperor himself.

It's from the Ancient Roman *manubiae* that the English language has gained both the adjective *manubial*, describing anything that has been plundered or pillaged (in Roman architecture a *manubial column* was one on which the trophies and spoils of war could be displayed) and *manubiary*, a seventeenth-century word for the act of plundering or spoliation, or else for someone who makes a living by plundering or robbing. Case in point: Captain William Kidd, the Scottish sailor and pirate-hunter-turned-pirate, who was born on 22 January 1645.

ice-legs *(n.)*   the ability to keep your balance on ice

Sailors have been successfully earning their *sea-legs* since the early eighteenth century. Based on that, the ability to keep yourself upright while walking on ice or frozen ground has been known as your *ice-legs* since the mid nineteenth century, when the English journalist William Blanchard Jerrold, while on a trip to Sweden in 1854, wrote, 'It is difficult to gain sea-legs, but to accomplish ice-legs is yet more difficult'. *Ice-legs* is a perfectly suitable word for the middle of winter, but there's another reason why it should so suit today's date: the extraordinary Battle of Texel was fought on 23 January 1795.

A key engagement in the War of the First Coalition (a five-year conflict between France and much of the rest of Europe), the Battle of Texel began with a fleet of fourteen Dutch ships becoming trapped in sea ice off the coast of the Netherlands in the winter of 1795. Despite their precarious position, the fleet knew that the surrounding ice would protect them from attack – but late on the night of 23 January, a cavalry regiment of French Hussars decided to prove them wrong.

Muffling their horses' hooves with fabric, the Hussars made their way out into the middle of the frozen sea and launched a surprise attack, successfully taking all fourteen ships without the loss of a single man. The Battle of Texel remains perhaps the only example of a naval battle fought between warships and cavalry in all military history – and is an extraordinary testament to the French troops' *ice-legs*.

transmural *(adj.)*   situated beyond or on the other
side of a wall

A *mural* is an artwork painted directly on to a wall, while a *mural tree* is a fruit tree or vine that grows against a wall, and a *mural crown* was a trophy once bestowed on the first Roman soldier to scale the wall of the besieged city. For all those reasons, it's easy to see why the word *mural* itself should derive from the Latin word for 'wall', *murus* – but it's certainly not the only English word to share that derivation.

An *antemural*, for instance, is an outbuilding or fortification, lying outside the walls of a town or city; somewhere described as *intramural*, oppositely, lies inside a city's walls. The adjective *intermural* describes the space formed between adjacent walls, or else anywhere situated between or bounded by two walls. To *immure* someone is to imprison or confine them or, quite literally, to wall them up. And *murage* was a tax or levy once used to fund the building or upkeep of the walls of a town or city.

One final word for this list: *transmural*, an adjective describing anywhere lying beyond or on the opposite side of a wall. Coined in the mid nineteenth century, *transmural* was originally used specifically in reference to lands lying on the northern side of Hadrian's Wall, the 84-mile Roman wall constructed between the Tyne and the Solway Firth during the reign of the Roman Emperor Hadrian in the second century AD; it was on 24 January 76 AD that the future emperor Hadrian was born in Hispania, the Roman region corresponding to modern-day Spain.

syne *(adv.)*   since, thereupon

The Scottish poet Robert Burns was born in Alloway, Ayrshire, on 25 January 1759.

Burns's use of his native Scots vocabulary in his poetry – combined with the enormous popularity of his writing since the nineteenth century – has led to a number of the Scots dialect words he used being introduced to the English language. *Jaunter* ('idle chatter'), *blastie* ('an ugly little creature'), *forjeskit* ('tired out'), *crously* ('confidently, boldly'), *mixty-maxty* ('jumbled, muddled'), *blirt* ('an outburst of tears'), *drappie* ('a little drop') and *branky* ('gaudy, ostentatious') are just some of the terms Burns's poetry has helped to introduce to the dictionary. But of all his contributions, perhaps one word – or rather three – stands out above all others.

Burns wrote the Yuletide ballad 'Auld Lang Syne' in 1788, basing its lyrics on an earlier Scots folk song dating from the seventeenth century. The poem's retrospective theme celebrating enduring friendships and relationships soon made it popular around Christmas and New Year, and before long reciting the poem (or, rather, singing it to the melody of an old Scots folk tune) had become a New Year tradition. As well known as the poem is, however, Burns's often impenetrable Scots vocabulary means that many New Year revellers might not be too sure of what they're singing. *Auld* means 'old' of course, and *lang* simply means 'long' – but *syne*?

Essentially, *syne* means 'since', but from its earliest recorded appearance in the language in the fourteenth century it has been variously used to mean 'thereupon', 'immediately afterwards', 'subsequently' and even 'moreover' or 'furthermore'. Ultimately *auld lang syne* can be roughly said to mean 'old times' or 'times gone by'.

griph *(n.)*   a puzzle, a brainteaser

'Nothing is more attractive to intelligent people than an honest, challenging problem.' So wrote the Swiss mathematician Johann Bernoulli in 1696.

Bernoulli had devised a mathematical puzzle he hoped would challenge the greatest minds of the day: given two points, *A* and *B*, assign a path to a moving body, *M*, along which it will arrive at *B*, starting from *A* and falling by its own gravity, in the least possible time. To the not-so-mathematically-well-versed, Bernoulli's problem is best understood by imagining a ball rolling down the hypotenuse of a right-angled triangle. The ball will make it from one corner to the other by gravity alone – but there is a faster route.

Bernoulli originally set a six-month time limit on his challenge, but it soon proved so tricky that he was compelled to extend that by another year. It was in that time, on 26 January 1697, that a copy found its way to Sir Isaac Newton. He solved the puzzle that evening.

An especially challenging puzzle or riddle like this can be called a *griph*. That word dates from the early 1600s in English, but it has its origins in a Greek word for a fishing creel, *gryphos*, in an imaginative reference to the words of a riddle being intricately woven together like the reeds of a basket. One question remains, though: what was the answer to Bernoulli's *griph*?

As Newton realised, the fastest route from *A* to *B* is not a straight line but rather a curve sweeping steeply down from *A* and extending outside the bottom of the triangle before curving back to *B*. Mathematicians now know this type of curve as a *brachistochrone* – a name derived from the Greek for 'the shortest time'.

nyctograph *(n.)*   a device for writing at night

Lewis Carroll was born on 27 January 1832.

Well known for his playful and inventive use of language, Carroll is responsible for introducing a clutch of typically idiosyncratic words to the language, such as *unbirthday, manxome* ('fearsome, monstrous') and *snicker-snack* ('a snipping sound'). He also created a great many so-called 'portmanteau' words combining elements of two existing words, like *chortle* (*chuckle + snort*), *frumious* (*fuming + furious*) and *galumph* (*gallop + triumph*). And even the use of the word *portmanteau* (originally a type of suitcase) to describe words like these is Carroll's idea: as Humpty Dumpty explains to Alice in *Through the Looking-Glass, and What Alice Found There* (1871), 'You see it's like a portmanteau: there are two meanings packed up into one word.'

But not all of Carroll's inventions were quite so frivolous – and nor were they all linguistic.

In 1891, Carroll invented the *nyctograph*, a device consisting of a flat board with a series of quarter-inch squares cut into it that could be used, letter by letter, to guide his pen as he wrote in the dark. Carroll even invented an encrypted alphabet just for the purpose: 'I tried rows of square holes,' he wrote, 'but the letters were still apt to be illegible. Then I said to myself, "Why not invent a square alphabet, using only dots at the corners, and lines along the sides?"'

Carroll kept the device inside a notebook in his bed. 'If I wake and think of something I wish to record,' he later explained, '[I] draw from under the pillow a small memorandum book containing my nyctograph, write a few lines, or even a few pages . . . replace the book, and go to sleep again.'

mulctable *(adj.)*   punishable, deserving of a fine or penalty

As a noun, a *mulct* is a fine or penalty imposed for an offence. As a verb, it can be used to mean both 'to impose a financial penalty' and 'to extract money from someone by fraudulent means' – in other words, precisely the kind of behaviour that might deserve a penalty. So how did the word come to have two such opposing meanings?

Of the two, the sense of a fine or penalty is older: *mulct* derives from *multa*, a Latin word for a monetary penalty, and it's from there that the word was adopted into English in the early 1500s. This meaning remains in place in English (mostly in legal contexts), but it is the use of *mulct* to mean 'to swindle' or 'defraud' that is now the more established sense. It developed in the mid 1800s, perhaps merely as an extension of the original meaning (in the sense of obtaining money from someone), or perhaps through the influence of *milk*, which has been used figuratively since the sixteenth century to mean 'to defraud' or 'exploit'. Or perhaps this meaning developed because those on the receiving end of a fine or penalty are not always so agreeable, and might consider themselves the victim of an unduly harsh or even fraudulent system. Whatever the motivation for the change, behaviour that is *mulctable* is nevertheless deserving of a fine or penalty.

On 28 January 1896, appropriately enough, a gentleman named Walter Arnold found himself on the receiving end of the world's first speeding fine. According to a report in the *London Daily News*, Arnold had been caught driving his 'horse-less carriage' at 8 mph and for his recklessness was fined 4 pounds, 7 shillings.

zalabiya *(n.)*   an ancient Persian dessert of fried and sweetened batter

On 29 January 1924, an American inventor named Carl R. Taylor patented a device for, as he explained it, transforming 'thin, freshly baked wafers, while still hot, into cone-shaped containers': the ice-cream cone was born.

According to culinary folklore, however, the story of the ice-cream cone isn't quite as straightforward as Taylor's patent application might suggest – and, in fact, its origins lie in an ancient wafer-like pastry known as *zalabiya*.

The earliest recipe for making *zalabiya* has been unearthed in a medieval cookbook published in Baghdad sometime in the tenth century. From there, the recipe travelled far and wide across the Middle East and into Africa, central Asia and the Far East, so that today variations of *zalabiya* are one of the most popular sweet snacks everywhere from Tunisia (where they're known as *zlebia*) to Azerbaijan (*zülbiya*), India (*jilapi*) and the Philippines (*jalebie*). And from there the recipe finally made its way across the Atlantic Ocean.

Brothers Frank and Robert Menches were running an ice-cream stand at the 1904 St Louis World's Fair when they ran out of bowls in which to serve it. As luck would have it, just a few stands away a Syrian chef named Ernest A. Hamwi was selling *zalabiya,* and, spotting the brothers' predicament, began rolling his wafers into cones that could then be used to hold a single dollop of ice cream. As luck would have it, Carl R. Taylor was reportedly one of the Menches' customers – and the rest is ice-cream history.

acephalous *(adj.)*   leaderless

The Greek word for 'head', *kephale*, crops up in a number of English words, the vast majority of which are medical or biological terms like *cephalalgy* (a headache), *cephalopod* (a creature like a squid or octopus) and *encephalitis* (inflammation of the brain).

Elsewhere in the dictionary, something that is *cynocephalous* has the head of a dog; something that is *criocephalous* has the head of a ram; and a *cebocephalic* statue has the head of a monkey. An *anacephalaeosis* – literally 'back to the head' – is a recapitulation or restatement of the main points of an argument. A *polycephalist* is someone who acknowledges more than one ruler or superior. An *autocephalous* church or organisation is one that governs itself. And, should you ever need it, *cephalonomancy* was an ancient form of divination in which a donkey's head would be observed boiling over a fire: while the head boiled away, a list of phrases (or, as was often the case, the names of accused criminals) would be read aloud, and any cracking or movement of the skull while a name was spoken was taken as a sure sign of guilt.

One last 'head' word in the dictionary is *acephalous*. Although it literally means 'headless', when it was first borrowed into English from French in the early 1700s *acephalous* referred to a country or organisation that has no clear leader or chief. Oddly, both meanings come into play today: it was on 30 January 1649 that King Charles I was beheaded on a charge of treason, leaving Britain kingless and in the hands of Oliver Cromwell's Parliamentarians.

Euroclydon *(n.)*   a huge storm

It's fair to say that January isn't too well known for its good weather, but the hurricane-like storm that struck the North Sea on 31 January 1953 was almost unimaginably destructive. A combination of a spring high tide and an enormous cyclonic windstorm pushed sea levels along the coasts of the UK, Netherlands and Belgium to more than 18 feet above sea level in places, flooding an area of land the size of Cheshire and killing more than 2,500 people. The disaster led to all the nations involved greatly improving their coastal and flood defences, while the British investigation into the disaster eventually led to the construction of the Thames Barrier in London.

So great was the 1953 disaster that the word *storm* seems not to do it justice. Instead, it was a *Euroclydon* – a vast tempest named after just such a storm that, according to the New Testament, was encountered by St Paul on his journey from Jerusalem to Rome:

> And when the Southern wind blew softly, they supposing to attain their purpose, loosed nearer, and sailed by Crete. But anon after, there arose by it a stormy wind called Euroclydon. And when the ship was caught, and could not resist the wind, we let her go, and were carried away.
>
> Acts 25:13–15

The name *Euroclydon* (pronounced 'you-*rok*-li-don') combines Greek words meaning 'the east wind', *euros*, and 'a wave' or 'billow', *klydon*. Since its first appearance in English in the sixteenth century, it has come to be used allusively to refer to any great wind storm or gale.

calepin *(n.)*   a dictionary, a book of authority or reference

Ambrogio Calepino, known as 'Calepinus', was a sixteenth-century Italian friar and scholar who published a landmark dictionary of Latin in 1502. Calepinus' dictionary soon established itself as the go-to reference work for Renaissance writers, and over the years that followed, it was steadily expanded until an edition translating Latin words into eleven different languages was published in 1590. So important was Calepinus' work that, by the end of the century, the word *calepin* had been adopted into English as a byword for any reference book considered the best of its type.

Of similar importance, the very first volume of the *Oxford English Dictionary* went on sale on 1 February 1884. Work had started on the dictionary in 1879, when it was originally predicted that this new comprehensive dictionary of the English language would take ten years to complete and be published steadily across four individual volumes. Five years later, senior editor James Murray and his team of researchers had only reached the word *ant*. Clearly, this was to be a much larger project than they could ever have envisaged.

After the *A–Ant* volume of 1884, a further 124 individual instalments or 'fascicles' of the dictionary were published over the decades to come, not necessarily in alphabetical order, but rather in the order they were completed. The final instalment – covering all the words from *wise* to *wyzen* – appeared in 1928. A supplementary volume filling in any remaining gaps appeared in 1933 to complete the first full edition of the *Oxford English Dictionary*.

naufrague *(n.)*   a shipwrecked person, a castaway

On 2 February 1709, explorers William Dampier and Woodes Rogers were sailing their ships, the *Duke* and *Duchess*, through the seemingly uninhabited Juan Fernández Islands off the west coast of South America, when Rogers noticed a fire blazing on the cliffs of the easternmost island, Más a Tierra. He quickly assembled a landing party – who, to their surprise, were met by a Scottish man named Alexander Selkirk.

Selkirk explained that he had once been sailing master of a ship called the *Cinque Ports*, but after the ship's captain had died, Selkirk found himself at odds with his successor, twenty-one-year-old Lieutenant Thomas Stradling. The pair had argued over the seaworthiness of the ship, and once they had rounded Cape Horn, Selkirk refused to go on until the ship was repaired; Stradling took him at his word, and abandoned him on an island 400 miles off the Chilean coast.

Despite the punishment, Selkirk actually fared reasonably well on the island: he caught wild goats for food, and even helped restore the health of Captain Rogers' crew, who were beginning to suffer from scurvy after months at sea. (The *Cinque Ports*, meanwhile, went on to sink off the coast of Colombia just weeks later, with the loss of most of her crew.)

A shipwrecked person like Selkirk – or, ironically, Captain Stradling – is properly known as a *naufrague*, a seventeenth-century word borrowed from Spanish that has its roots in the Latin word for a shipwreck, *naufragium*. Sadly, that word did not appear in Daniel Defoe's *Robinson Crusoe* (1719), the story of a shipwrecked castaway that Selkirk's real-life experiences are said to have inspired.

twankle *(v.)*   to play idly on a musical instrument

If you've ever had a piano lesson, chances are you can still pick out a tune. But even if you haven't, you still might know how to play one piece of music in particular: 'The Celebrated Chop Waltz', better known as 'Chopsticks', was published for the first time on 3 February 1877.

Written by a British composer named Euphemia Allen – who was aged just sixteen at the time – the 'Chop Waltz' is a simple waltz for piano that Allen published under the pseudonym 'Arthur de Lulli'. No doubt thanks to its simplicity, its catchy but uncomplicated melody and the fact that Allen wrote both solo and duet arrangements of it, the 'Chop Waltz' soon proved immensely popular among piano players. Before long, composers as renowned as Franz Liszt and Nikolai Rimsky-Korsakov were writing their own variations of it, and 'Chopsticks' is now arguably one of the most recognisable of all easy piano pieces – the perfect piece to *twankle* with while casually sitting at a piano.

According to the *English Dialect Dictionary* (Vol. VI, 1905), to *twankle* is 'to twang with the fingers on a music instrument'. In fact, that's just one word for it: absentmindedly strumming or playing an instrument is also known as *twiddling*, *twangling*, *tootling*, *noodling*, *plunking*, *thrummling* and *tudeling* (the latter of which, perhaps rather aptly, has its origins in a German word, *dudeln*, meaning 'to perform badly').

luition *(n.)*   the payment of a ransom

When it first appeared in the language in the thirteenth century, the word *ransom* referred to a payment made to escape a penalty or else to secure a pardon for an offence. In that sense, it derives via French from the same Latin root as words like *redeem* and *redemption*; in fact, *redeem* once meant 'to save someone's life by paying a ransom'. It took almost another century for the more familiar meaning of the word *ransom* – a payment made to secure the safe release of something – to develop, with a reference to some houses in the city of Canterbury being seized and held to 'great ransom' listed in a document dating from the early 1300s.

The act of paying a ransom is called *luition*. It dates from the seventeenth century, and derives from another Latin root, *luere*, meaning 'to pay' or 'to recompense'. A *king's ransom*, meanwhile, has been a proverbially colossal amount of cash since the late 1400s – and, oddly, both of these relate to today's events.

On his way back from the Crusades in 1192, the English King Richard I was captured and then given to Henry VI of Germany, the Holy Roman Emperor, who had him imprisoned. Henry desperately needed cash to strengthen his armies and defences, so he held Richard to ransom for a colossal 150,000 marks – equivalent to almost three times the annual income of the English crown. Clearly, something drastic had to be done to secure the king's safe return, so back in England taxes were raised and gold and silver was seized – even from the churches – until finally, on 4 February 1194, the ransom was paid and King Richard was released to return home.

propinque *(adj.)*   approximate, approaching accuracy

There's a reason why the expression *to square the circle* is used to refer to tasks that are near impossible: in 1882, the mathematician Ferdinand von Lindemann proved that squaring a circle – that is, producing a square with the same area as a circle using only a compass and a straight edge – is literally impossible. But that didn't deter American physician and amateur mathematician Edward J. Goodwin, who in 1894 published a proof in which he claimed to have done the (quite literally) impossible. The only problem was that in solving the unsolvable, Goodwin had redefined the irrational constant *pi* as a simple and straightforward 3.2.

Goodwin copyrighted his proof in 1897, but not wanting to deprive the schoolchildren of his home state of Indiana the chance to use his (entirely flawed) calculation, he drew up a bill outlining both the details of his proof and the terms of a financial deal that would allow local schools the opportunity to use his proof free of charge. He presented it to the local state legislature: 'The ratio of the diameter and circumference is as five-fourths to four,' the bill explained, while 3.141 was 'wholly wanting and misleading in its practical applications'. Ultimately, on 5 February 1897, the state legislature of Indiana passed a bill redefining one of the most basic of all mathematical concepts.

Goodwin's 3.2 was a *propinque* value – a fifteenth-century word (literally meaning 'near' or 'neighbouring' in Latin) that can be used to describe what might otherwise be called an approximate or ballpark figure. Unfortunately for Goodwin, 3.2 was eventually considered a *propinque* value too far, and with mounting pressure (and incredulity) from the national press, Goodwin's bill was indefinitely postponed by the Indiana State Senate.

dyvoury *(n.)*   bankruptcy, financial ruin

The property-trading board game *Monopoly* went on sale for the first time on 6 February 1935. Produced by Massachusetts board-game manufacturers Parker Brothers, the original *Monopoly* was based on the streets of Atlantic City, New Jersey, but after the game proved an instant success, editions based on other cities were soon being made. A London version appeared shortly before the Second World War (whereupon the British Secret Service approached John Waddington, licensee of the British edition, to produce a compact version of the game containing real street maps and real cash that could be handed out to prisoners of war by relief charities). The game – and the act of bankrupting your opponents – has remained enduringly popular around the world ever since.

The word *bankrupt* literally means 'broken bench', a reference to early moneylenders having their financial market stalls overturned if they were unable to repay their creditors. Being bankrupt was also once known as being *on Carey Street*, a reference to the location of the Bankruptcy Department of the Supreme Court in London. *Bagwesh*, or *hagwesh*, is an old English dialect word for destitution or bankruptcy, although its origins are a mystery – as are those of *dyvoury*, a sixteenth-century word for beggary or total financial ruin.

One theory claims *dyvoury* could be a corruption of *devour*, in the sense that a bankrupt person has eaten up all their resources, or else is derived from a local pronunciation of *diver*, in the sense of someone being drowned in debt. The exact origins of the word are, however, unknown.

Tapleyism *(n.)*   extreme optimism, even in the face of desperate circumstances

Mark Tapley is a character in Charles Dickens' sixth novel, *Martin Chuzzlewit* (1844). Resolutely cheerful and brimming with positivity, Mark resolves to test his good humour by accompanying Martin on a journey to somewhere so unwelcoming and unpleasant it is sure to challenge even his unquenchable optimism: America.

After a hellish Atlantic crossing, the pair find themselves in Eden, a swampy, disease-ridden town populated by thieves and vagabonds, where both quickly succumb to a life-threatening fever. Despite being at death's door, however, Mark's natural positivity still shines through, and he memorably describes his bed-ridden malarial condition as 'Floored for the present, sir . . . but jolly!'

Mark Tapley's undying optimism, even in light of the appalling circumstances he and Martin find themselves in, is at the root of the word *Tapleyism* – which is just one of a number of words in the dictionary that derive from the names of Charles Dickens' characters.

Dickens – who was born on 7 February 1812 – is also responsible for endlessly useful and imaginative words like *Podsnappery* ('narrow-minded self-satisfaction', just like that shown by John Podsnap in *Our Mutual Friend*), *Chadbandism* ('toadyish sycophantic behaviour', named in honour of the Reverend Chadband in *Bleak House*) and *bumbledom* (a word for fussy pomposity, just like that displayed by Mr Bumble in *Oliver Twist*). In fact, such is the breadth of Dickens' contribution to our language that we can even credit him with a slang word for an umbrella: if you've ever called your brolly a *gamp*, then you've namechecked the alcoholic midwife Sarah Gamp, who is seldom encountered in *Martin Chuzzlewit* without her trusty battered umbrella.

degelation *(n.)*   the process of thawing

Should the weather take a turn for the worse at this time of year, it might be worth remembering that *gelation*, or *aggelation*, is the process of freezing or solidifying. At the root of both of these words is the Latin verb *gelare*, meaning 'to freeze'; despite appearances, both *jelly* and *gelato* derive from the same source, as do the likes of *gelatine* and *gelatinous*, *congeal* and *geal*, a fifteenth-century word meaning 'to stiffen with cold'. Something that is *gelable*, meanwhile, is capable of being frozen, while *recongelation* is the act of freezing or being frozen again. And should the weather happen to take a turn for the better, *degelation* is the act or process of melting or thawing.

That's certainly what happened on 8 February 1684, when the last of an intense frost that had gripped the City of London for fifty days finally disappeared. According to one account:

> the pools were frozen 18 inches thick at least, and the Thames was so frozen that a great street . . . was built with shops and all manner of things sold [on the ice]. Hackney coaches plied there as in the streets. There were also bull-baiting, and a great many shows and tricks to be seen.

The *degelation* of the river, however, seems to have been quick:

> This day the frost broke up. In the morning I saw a coach and six horses driven from Whitehall almost to the bridge (London Bridge) yet by three o'clock . . . the ice was gone, so as boats did row to and fro.

lunette *(n.)*   a small moon or natural satellite

On 9 February 1913, a peculiar series of meteor showers crossed the sky over a vast area of the globe from Canada to Brazil. The shower became known as the Great Meteor Procession, a name referring to the fact that, unlike most meteor showers that radiate from a single point, these appeared to move slowly across the sky in formation, each seeming to follow in the others' paths. According to one eyewitness account from northern Canada:

> A huge meteor appeared . . . which, as it approached, was seen to be in two parts and looked like two bars of flaming material, one following the other. They were throwing out a constant stream of sparks, and, after they had passed, they shot out balls of fire straight ahead that travelled more rapidly than the main bodies. They seemed to pass over slowly and were in sight about five minutes. Immediately after their disappearance in the southeast a ball of clear fire, that looked like a big star, passed across the sky in their wake. This ball did not have a tail or show sparks of any kind. Instead of being yellow like the meteors, it was clear like a star.

As reports of the shower began to appear in the press, the astronomer Clarence Chant mapped them and saw that they seemed to form a large arc across much of North America. The appearance of the meteors, and the line their reports formed on his map, led him to conclude that these had not been any ordinary rocks but instead the remnants of a short-lived rocky satellite of the earth, that had been pulled into our orbit and disintegrated in the sky. The rocks, Chant concluded, were the remnants of a tiny moon or – to use a word first coined in the mid 1600s – a *lunette*.

hubbleshow *(n.)* a noisy uproar, a riot

Hubbleshow is a sixteenth-century word for a noisy commotion or disturbance. Originally a Scots dialect term (as is the verb *hubble*, meaning 'to cause problems' or 'to incite anger or annoyance'), it is possible that *hubbleshow* is related to an old Flemish word, *hobbel-tobbel*, meaning 'tumultuously' or 'uproariously'. Another theory claims its etymology is intertwined with that of *hubbub*, which has its origins in an old Gaelic exclamation or war cry, *ababú*, essentially meaning 'forever' or 'victory'. But whatever its origins, it's a word worth recalling today thanks to one of the most unusual and unexpectedly violent *hubbleshows* in English history.

On 10 February 1355 – the feast day of St Scholastica, patron saint of studying – a group of Oxford University students drinking at the city's Swindlestock Tavern complained to the landlord, John de Bereford, about the quality of the liquor he was serving. De Bereford responded in typically diplomatic style with 'stubborn and saucy language', according to one account, and in response one of the students threw a quart pot at his head. The situation soon spiralled violently out of control and, showing no signs of calming down, the men of the city were called to arms while the entire student body of the university came out in retaliation. The fighting continued long through the night, and as word of the commotion spread as many as 2,000 men from the surrounding countryside joined the fray. University buildings were ransacked and burned out, and by the time the St Scholastica Day Riot ended, sixty-two scholars, students and townspeople had been killed.

insinuendo *(n.)*   an insinuated remark

An *insinuendo* is a combined *insinuation* and *innuendo*: an insinuated, thinly veiled remark carrying some kind of secondary meaning.

That combination of two pre-existing words makes *insinuendo* an example of a 'blended' or portmanteau word, and places it firmly in the same category as a quirky collection of words like *docudrama, infomercial, stagflation* and *prequel* – not to mention all the bizarre portmanteaux invented by Lewis Carroll (for more on which, flick back to 27 January).

Because of their fairly unsubtle construction and often somewhat clumsy sound, portmanteau words often raise the hackles of language purists; even *insinuendo*, coined way back in the mid nineteenth century, was disdainfully labelled 'a tasteless word' when it first appeared in the *Oxford English Dictionary* in 1976. But many portmanteaux do fall into popular use.

The original *motorcade*, for instance, was a 'motorised cavalcade' that drove through Rockford, Illinois, in 1910. *Newscasts* have existed since 1928; *brunch* even longer:

> To be fashionable nowadays, we must 'brunch'. Truly an excellent portmanteau word . . . indicating a combined breakfast and lunch.
>
> *Punch* (1869)

And on 11 February 1812, Massachusetts governor Elbridge Gerry stealthily redrew the boundaries of the state senate electoral districts to benefit his Democratic-Republican Party. When the *Boston Globe* happened to liken the shape of one of his redrawn districts to that of a monstrous salamander, the word *gerrymandering* was born.

evanidness *(adj.)*   short-lived, transitory

It was on 12 February 1554 that Lady Jane Grey, de facto Queen of England for just nine days, was executed. The eldest daughter of Henry Grey, Duke of Suffolk, Jane was the first cousin once removed of the young and sickly King Edward VI, the only son of Henry VIII. As Edward lay dying in 1553, aged just fifteen, he nominated Jane as his successor, thereby invalidating his half-sisters Mary and Elizabeth's claims to the throne. Shortly after the king's death, however, allegiances changed: Mary was proclaimed Queen Mary I, while Jane was deposed and imprisoned in the Tower of London on a charge of high treason. Although her life was initially spared, she was executed the following year.

Appropriate for the death of Britain's shortest-reigning monarch, the adjective *evanid* describes anything fleeting or short-lived, or else faint, weak or liable soon to collapse or dissolve. The word derives from the Latin verb *evanescere*, meaning 'to fade away' or 'to disappear', which is in turn based on a Latin word, *vanus*, meaning 'empty', 'idle' or 'vacant'. Both *vanish* and *evanescent* come from the same root – as do a host of equally transitory or empty words.

Vaniloquence, for instance, is empty, idle chatter or language, while to *vaunt* is to boast of your own accomplishments or speak of something in unduly high terms. Before it came to mean 'self-admiration', *vanity* originally meant 'futile' or 'of little profit' while something that was *vain* was originally worthless or valueless; and likewise, *vainglory* or *vaingloriousness* is empty, worthless or unwarranted glory or exaltation.

xenodochy *(n.)*   hospitality, the entertainment of strangers

The Greek word for 'stranger' or 'alien', *xenos*, is at the root of a number of English words including *xenophobia* (the fear or dislike of anything strange or foreign) and *xenon* (the noble gas isolated by William Ramsay and Morris Travers in 1898 and given a name referring to the fact that they had discovered a 'stranger' left over in a sample of liquid air). Much less familiar are the seventeenth-century word *xenodochy*, essentially meaning 'hospitality', and its related adjective *xenodochial*, meaning 'hospitable' or 'kind to strangers'. Even older still, a *xenodochium* is a hostel or guesthouse, or room in a house set aside for receiving visitors.

A fine example of misplaced *xenodochy* took place on the night of 13 February 1692. Forced to abandon their support for the deposed King James and instead sign an oath of allegiance to his successor, William III, the Clan MacDonald of Glencoe found themselves singled out by the Secretary of State, John Dalrymple, who had long been suspicious of the Highlanders' actions and was keen to show that any disloyalty to the king would not be tolerated. To that end, Dalrymple found an ally in the MacDonalds' enemies, the Clan Campbell.

The Campbells arrived at the MacDonalds' home in Glencoe seeking shelter from a snowstorm in early February. Thanks to the traditional hospitality of the Highland clans, they were duly invited in as guests. But after twelve days living with their unsuspecting hosts, late on the night of 13 February, the Campbell soldiers enacted a devastating order to 'cut off root and branch' the entire MacDonald clan. The Glencoe Massacre, as it later became known, claimed the lives of thirty-eight MacDonald clansmen.

limerence *(n.)* romantic infatuation, besottedness

Entirely suitable for Valentine's Day, the word *limerence* is defined by the *Oxford English Dictionary* as: 'the state of being romantically infatuated or obsessed with another person, typically experienced involuntarily and characterised by a strong desire for reciprocation of one's feelings'.

The word was coined as recently as the 1970s by the American professor of psychology Dorothy Tennov, who introduced it in her book *Love and Limerence: The Experience of Being in Love* (1979). Having collated anecdotes and testimonies from hundreds of volunteers asked to describe their romantic experiences, Tennov outlined her theory that being in love – or else experiencing a romantic infatuation – creates a distinct and wholly involuntary psychological state that occurs in precisely the same way among all people, regardless of their gender, race and other distinguishing factors. 'To be in the state of limerence', Tennov explained, 'is to feel what is usually termed "being in love".'

Although she originally called this state of infatuation *amorance*, Tennov eventually settled on the word *limerence* for her concept – and, in her writing, referred to anyone experiencing precisely that kind of romantic infatuation or desire as a *limerent*. As she later explained, both words were entirely her own invention:

> It has no roots whatsoever. It looks nice. It works well in French. Take it from me it has no etymology whatsoever.
> *The Observer* (September 1977)

corrumper *(n.)*   a corruptor, a destroyer

The Greek philosopher Socrates is generally said to have been sentenced to death by a jury of 500 Athenian men on 15 February 399 BC. After pleading his defence for several hours, Socrates lost his case by a margin of 280 votes to 220, at which point, after several further hours' deliberation, the jury decreed that the only suitable punishment was death, administered by drinking a cup of poisonous hemlock. Socrates' last words, as he stumbled to the floor and turned to a friend, were somewhat underwhelming: 'Crito, we owe a cock to Asclepius. Do pay it. Don't forget.'

The charges on which Socrates had been brought before the court were spurious: failing to recognise the gods recognised by the state, introducing new deities and – most famously of all – 'corrupting the youth of Athens'.

Corruption derives from the Latin verb *rumpere*, meaning 'to break', which makes it an etymological cousin of words like *rupture, interruption, bankrupt* and *erupt*. Its earliest meaning was a physical one, referring to the disintegration or putrefaction of something that has become spoiled or contaminated, but the modern meaning wasn't far behind: moral *corruption*, precisely like that of which Socrates was found guilty, emerged in the fourteenth century and has been the word's predominant meaning since the mid 1600s.

Corrump is a less familiar and long-forgotten synonym for *corrupt* that derives from the same root. It, too, originally meant 'to spoil' or 'to render useless' through decay or decomposition, before more figurative meanings emerged in the Middle Ages: by the mid 1300s, *corrump* was being used variously to mean 'to bribe', 'to spoil the language' and 'to make morally corrupt'. One who does precisely that, meanwhile, is a *corrumper*.

maledict *(n.)*   the victim of a curse

While a *malediction* is a curse or imprecation, the victim of a curse is a *maledict*. Both words derive from Latin, and have at their root Latin words meaning 'bad', *male*, and 'speak', *dicere*.

One of history's most famous *maledictions* – and, according to legend, perhaps one of history's most famous *maledicts* – was the curse of Tutankhamen and its supposed victim, English archaeologist Howard Carter. In 1922, amid the debris of an Egyptian tomb, Carter discovered a set of steps that led to a sealed doorway bearing Tutankhamen's name. Behind it was a series of hidden chambers, each containing dazzling treasures that had not been seen for 3,000 years. Over the months that followed, each chamber was carefully examined and its treasures catalogued until finally, on 16 February 1923, Carter opened the last door and entered Tutankhamen's burial chamber.

If legend is to be believed, in disturbing Tutankhamen's resting place Carter unleashed a millennia-old curse that brought on the demise of several members of his team and all those who subsequently came into contact with the king's mummified remains. Lord Carnarvon, Carter's financial patron, was one of the first to die, succumbing to an infected mosquito bite four months later. An early visitor to the tomb, the American railroad magnate George Jay Gould I, died of pneumonia in May. Carnarvon's half-brother, the diplomat Aubrey Herbert, died in the autumn after a botched dental procedure. And the radiologist who X-rayed Tutankhamen's mummy also died of a mysterious illness the following January.

Despite that cluster of fatalities, however, the curse of King Tut was apparently not powerful enough to claim the life of the man who started the entire affair: Howard Carter died sixteen years later, on 2 March 1939.

escry *(n.)*   a battle cry

Also used in a looser sense to mean simply a tumult or disturbance, an *escry* is a war cry – a loud, rousing exclamation
shouted by a body of fighters as a rallying call to a common
cause.

The war cry of choice for the Ancient Greeks was *alala*, a
word coined onomatopoeically to resemble the cry itself, but
which eventually came to be considered the name of a minor
goddess personifying the battle cry. The Romans preferred their
own call, known as a *barritus*, which was probably picked up
from warring tribes encountered in Germania. According to the
historian Tacitus, the *barritus* had a 'harsh tone' and sounded
like a 'hoarse murmur', and was made by the soldiers putting
'their shields before their mouths, in order to make the voice
swell fuller and deeper as it echoes back'.

During the American Civil War, Confederate troops developed a whooping battle cry known as the *rebel yell*, which was
likely based on Native American war cries the soldiers would
have been familiar with from before the war. The Japanese kami-
kaze cry *banzai* literally means '10,000 years', and was originally
part of a longer exclamation expressing loyalty to the Japanese
emperor. And since the mid 1940s at least, American paratroop-
ers – and now almost anyone jumping from a high point – will
shout *Geronimo*, the name of an Apache leader who died on
17 February 1909. Precisely why Geronimo's name has come
to be attached to such a niche activity is a mystery, with various
explanations pointing to either a film or a song that was popular
in America during the Second World War.

vinomadefied *(adj.)*   utterly soaked in wine

George Plantagenet was a son of Richard, the Duke of York, and a brother to two English kings, Edward IV and Richard III.

After Edward took to the throne in 1461, George became embroiled in an uprising against him in the north of England alongside his father-in-law, the Earl of Warwick. When his treachery was discovered he fled into exile in France. George reconciled with Edward on his return to England, but then fell out with Richard over his intention to marry George's sister-in-law, Anne, and thereby claim some of the Earl of Warwick's lands for himself. Edward stepped in to settle the dispute – but in the aftermath he became convinced that George had set his eyes on taking the throne for himself. George was arrested, brought before Parliament accused of slandering the king, and sentenced to death. On 18 February 1478, he was executed in secret in the Tower of London – supposedly by being drowned in a vat of Malmsey wine.

Mystery surrounds George's death: it is unclear what role, if any, the future King Richard III had in his downfall, and whether such a bizarre punishment as being drowned in wine was actually employed, or whether it was merely a slanderous myth concocted later. Either way, the story makes the seventeenth-century adjective *vinomadefied*, describing anything utterly soaked in wine, a fitting (if somewhat macabre) word for today.

anaphrodisiac *(n.)* anything that diminishes sexual appetite

If an *aphrodisiac* is a food or drug that increases sexual desire, then the opposite is an *anaphrodisiac*. Both words derive from the name of the Greek goddess of love and beauty, Aphrodite, whose name in turn is said to come from the Greek for sea foam, *aphros* – a reference to the legend of Aphrodite being born out of the waves.

Of the two terms, *aphrodisiac* is the older by more than a century, with talk of *anaphrodisiacs* beginning to emerge only in the more prudent nineteenth century. And another decidedly prudent nineteenth-century invention – with an unlikely *anaphrodisiacal* past – came into being on 19 February 1906.

John Harvey Kellogg was a physician and superintendent of a sanitarium in Battle Creek, Michigan, in the late 1800s. A member of the Seventh Day Adventist Church, Kellogg was obsessed with sexual abstinence: he wrote several books on the subject, reportedly never consummated his marriage, and through his work at the sanitarium looked to develop diets and medical treatments to aid his *anaphrodisiac* crusade. Meat, spicy food, alcohol and tobacco were all decidedly off limits, and in the interests of promoting as bland a diet as possible, John and his brother, Will Keith Kellogg, began experimenting with wheat and corn.

One day, when a tray of cooked wheat was accidentally left out to dry, the brothers struck on the idea to pass it through rollers, hoping to obtain flat sheets of wheaten dough; instead, the mixture shattered into individual flakes. A patent for 'Flaked Cereals and Process of Preparing Same' was granted, and on this day in 1906 the Kellogg brothers founded the Battle Creek Toasted Corn Flake Company.

pignoratitious *(adj.)*   pawned or pledged; referring to the act of pawning or pledging

To *pignorate* something is to pawn or pledge it, while the act of pawning is properly known as *pignoration*, and any property that has been pawned or pledged can be described as *pignoratitious*. All of these derive from a Latin word for a pledge or stake, *pignus*, which can also be used in English in its own right to refer to any property held as security for a debt, or else a contract organising just such an arrangement. And on 20 February 1472, an agreement to do precisely that was enacted that changed the geography of the United Kingdom forever.

In 1469, the Scottish King James III became betrothed to Margaret, the young daughter of Christian I of Norway and Denmark, in an effort to quell the diplomatic tension between the two kingdoms. A handsome dowry was brokered as part of the marriage, but unfortunately for King Christian the cash sum involved was just too great. Instead, he was forced to pawn the Northern Isles – now Orkney and Shetland – to the Scottish king.

Having been invaded and settled by Vikings as early as the ninth century, the Orkney and Shetland Islands had long been under Norwegian rule, but King Christian's financial situation was such that he had little choice but to return the islands to Scottish rule. Beginning in September 1468, Christian pawned his lands in Orkney for 50,000 guilders; his Shetland claims, pawned for a more conservative 8,000 guilders, followed in May 1469; in 1470, the ancient title of Earl of Orkney was ceded to the Scottish king; and on 20 February 1472 both sets of islands were finally annexed to Scotland. The islands, with their distinct and decidedly Nordic-influenced culture, have remained a Scottish possession ever since.

auto-burglar *(n.)*   a burglar who burgles their own home

On 21 February 1858, a Massachusetts businessman named Edwin Holmes installed the very first electronic burglar alarm at his home in Boston. Its design was rudimentary but effective: based on the existing telegraph system, Holmes connected the doors and windows of his house by wires to an electromagnet linked to a bell. Whenever a door or window was opened, a jolt of electricity was sent down to the wire and the bell rang.

Holmes's business initially struggled (not least because household electricity was still in its infancy at the time) but in 1859 he relocated to New York – a city he later described as being 'where all the country's burglars made their home' – and within a matter of years had installed more than 1,000 of his alarms.

The word *burglar* derives from a Latin word for a fortress, *burgus*, and shares a common ancestor with the likes of *borough* and *burgh*. But elsewhere in the dictionary, all manner of housebreakers are accommodated:

- *clank-napper* (n.) a burglar who specialises in stealing and pawning silverware
- *home barnacle* (n.) a burglar who consistently preys on the same house
- *morning-sneak* (n.) a thief who robs shops while their shopkeepers are setting up for the day
- *star-glazer* (n.) a thief who cuts the glass out of windows to reach the goods displayed in shops

Of all the burglars in the dictionary, perhaps the most hapless is the *auto-burglar* – a word coined by the novelist Charles Reade in 1884 to describe a burglar who burgles their own home.

camisado *(n.)* a surprise invasion or attack carried out at night

Derived from the Spanish for 'shirt', *camisa*, the word *camisado* originally referred to a surprise military attack carried out at night, in which the invading forces wore matching shirts over their armour so that they could recognise one another in the dark. That original (and fairly specific) meaning slowly broadened over time; by the time the word was adopted into English in the mid 1500s, a *camisado* was merely any attack or invasion carried out under cover of darkness. And a perfect – if somewhat hapless – example took place on this day in 1797.

Amid rising tensions between Britain and France, Napoleon's French Revolutionary government decided to launch a three-pronged attack against Britain and in support of an Irish independence organisation known as the Society of United Irishmen. Some 15,000 French troops were dispatched in the campaign, the majority to Ireland and a further two parties to mainland Britain. Unfortunately, bad weather forced two of the three contingents to turn back, while a third – intending to land as close to Bristol as possible and take the city by force – went ahead. At 2 o'clock in the morning on 22 February 1797, they landed near Fishguard on the Pembrokeshire coast.

On their arrival, however, discipline among the French troops quickly broke down, and many of the irregulars that had been drafted into the company deserted. Those who remained were soon confronted by a large assembly of British militia – bolstered by hundreds of furious locals. After two days of sporadic fighting, the French side surrendered, and the last invasion of British soil by a hostile foreign power was over almost as quickly as it had begun.

hemerology *(n.)*   a diary, a record of the day's events

Derived via Latin from a Greek word meaning 'an account of the day', *hemerology* is a seventeenth-century word for a diary or journal – or, as the English lexicographer Thomas Blount defined it in his 1656 dictionary *Glossographia*, a 'register declaring what is done every day'.

A diary can also be known as an *ephemeris* (which once referred to a chart for calculating the positions of heavenly bodies), a *diet-book* (*diet* originally meaning a way of life or course of events, not just what is eaten) and a *noctuary* (which is literally a record of a night's events, not just a day's), while the act of recording daily events in a diary has been known both as *journalising* and *diarising* since the mid 1800s.

One of the English language's most famous journalisers, Samuel Pepys, was born on 23 February 1633. He kept his daily journal from 1660 to 1669, recording in it all manner of day-to-day activities, including nursing a hangover ('Waked in the morning with my head in a sad taking through the last night's drink, which I am very sorry for') and attending the theatre ('We saw [*A*] *Midsummer's Night's Dream*, which I had never seen before, nor shall ever again, for it is the most insipid ridiculous play that ever I saw in my life'). Pepys's diary also provides an important eyewitness account of several major historical events, including the Great Fire of London and the events of the Great Plague. As a linguistic resource, it provides us with the earliest known record of an array of words, including *housewarm*, *mantelpiece*, *nepotism* and *youngish*.

Undecimber *(n.)*   an extra month added to a calendar

Unlike the calendar we use today, the Roman calendar only had 355 days, and because it was a full ten days short of the length of time it takes the earth to revolve around the sun, it quickly fell out of sync with the solar year. Before long, festivals and harvests were being celebrated entirely out of season.

The Romans' solution to this was to insert an extra month into their calendar – known as *Mercedonius*, or the 'work month' – that divided February in two. Roughly every two years, 23 February (the date of *Terminalia*, the Roman festival of boundaries) was followed by the entire month of *Mercedonius*, which was itself followed by 24 February (the date of a Roman festival known as *Regifugium*, or 'the flight of the king'). If that system seems unnecessarily complicated, you're right – and if you think that system could be easily manipulated, you'd be right again.

Whether or not *Mercedonius* was added to the Roman calendar was a decision left to a high priest known as the *pontifex maximus*, who would occasionally base his decision not on the needs of the city, but on keeping his friends and acquaintances in office for longer. Ultimately, *Mercedonius* was eliminated from the Roman calendar by Julius Caesar, who introduced his reformed Julian calendar in 46 BC.

Extra months that are added to calendars are properly known as *intercalary* months, but the name *Undecimber* has been in use in English since the mid nineteenth century as a placeholder name for any additional thirteenth calendar month. (Oddly, the name *undecimber* derives from the Latin for 'eleven', *undecim*, in deference to the fact that the twelfth month of the year, December, was originally the tenth month of the Roman calendar and took its name from the Latin for 'ten'.)

twarvlement *(n.)* circuitous, long-winded speech

According to the *English Dialect Dictionary* (Vol. VI, 1905), *twarvle* is a Yorkshire dialect word meaning 'to walk with an unsteady, tottering gait', or else 'to twist', 'to twirl' or 'to sway'. In the extended sense of a meandering, tortuous route, the word *twarvlement* refers to what the dictionary defines as 'circumlocution in narration' – or, put another way, long-winded, rambling talk.

An infamous example of political *twarvlement* took place on 25 February 1820, when US congressman Felix Walker delivered an impossibly lengthy speech. Walker spent six years as the representative of Buncombe County, North Carolina, during which time Congress was tasked with debating the so-called Missouri Question – namely, whether the state of Missouri should be admitted to the Union as a free or slave state. The matter had already been rumbling on for several months when finally, hours before a decisive vote was due to be taken, Walker stood to address the house – and delivered a rambling, utterly unnecessary 5,000-word speech. Walker's speech (which, as a comparison, was a full 1,000 words longer than the entire role of Hamlet) exasperated his already exhausted colleagues, but amid calls to stop his address and retake his seat, Walker called out that he was not 'speaking to the House, but to Buncombe', the name of the North Carolina county he had been elected to represent.

Before long, *speaking for Buncombe* had dropped into nineteenth-century political slang to mean 'doing something purely for the sake of other people', and by the mid 1800s had become so widely used that *Buncombe* gained a newly simplified spelling, *bunkum* – and the English language had gained another word for empty chatter or complete and utter nonsense.

anacronym *(n.)* an acronym or initialism the full meaning of which is little known or unfamiliar

Coined in the 1970s – and explained by the *Oxford English Dictionary* as likely a combination of *anachronism* and *acronym* – an *anacronym* is an acronym formed from the initial letters of a phrase or series of words that is mostly unknown or has long been forgotten. Examples of *anacronyms* are few and far between in the dictionary (and depend entirely on how familiar you are with the words themselves), but among the most famous are:

- *base jump* (n.) parachuting from a fixed point – literally a 'building, antenna, span or earth' – has been known as *base jumping* since the early 1980s
- *care package* (n.) the original *care packages* were humanitarian aid parcels delivered in the aftermath of the Second World War by an organisation known as the 'Cooperative for Assistance and Relief Everywhere'
- *laser* (n.) stands for 'light amplification of stimulated emission of radiation'
- *scuba* (n.) perhaps most famously of all, scuba technology dates back to 1952, and stands for the considerably less pronounceable 'self-contained underwater breathing apparatus'

One more *anacronym* to add to this list came into being on 26 February 1935, when two men – Robert Watson-Watt and Arnold Wilkins – demonstrated that reflected radio waves could be used to detect aircraft flying overhead. The rudimentary technology they were testing eventually became known as *radar* – or, in full, 'radio detection and ranging'.

anepronym *(n.)*   a trademarked name that has come
to be used generically

Following on from the *anacronym* comes the *anepronym*, a term
used to refer to a trademark or brand name that, for one reason or another, has come to be used as a generic term in the
language.

While some of these words are still familiar as brand names
today – like *Kleenex*, *Elastoplast* and *Hoover*, used as generic
words for disposable tissues, sticking plasters and vacuum clean-
ers – a great many more have long since lost their connections
with the proprietary brands from which they developed. *Jacuzzi*
baths, *minicoms*, *cellophane* plastic, *dayglo* paints or dyes, *laun-
dromats* and even *decaf* coffee have all been (or still remain)
proprietary terms in English-speaking territories, as have *jet
skis*, *Popsicles*, *Filofaxes* and *Rolodexes*, *identikit* pictures, *bubble
wrap*, *growbags* and even *Exocet* missiles.

Muzak is not just a generic term for background music,
but a trademarked brand that was sold for $345 million in
2011. *Spandex* fabric was given a name that is an anagram of
'expands' when it was invented in 1958. *Biro* pens are not only
named after their Hungarian inventor, László Bíró, but remain
a trademark registered by the BIC stationery company. And,
so widespread was the use of the name *Aspirin* as a generic
name for the painkiller acetylsalicylic acid, that Germany's Bayer
pharmaceutical company was forced to rescind its trademark
on the name in the Treaty of Versailles. *Aspirin* – patented by
the German chemist Felix Hoffman on 27 February 1900 – has
remained a generic name in many countries ever since.

mountweazel *(n.)*   a fictitious entry added to a book to prevent plagiarism

On 28 February 1939, an editor casually flicking through the second edition of *Webster's New International Dictionary* (1934) noticed that a peculiar word was missing an etymological explanation. In its entirety, the entry read:

> **dord** *(dôrd)*, *n. Physics & Chem. Density.*

An investigation was launched and eventually the error was uncovered. The letter *D* could be used as an abbreviation of 'density' in a scientific context, but the index card on which that was written had been misread and misfiled not as the upper or lower case letter 'D or d', but as a word, *dord*. The oversight somehow managed to slip through the editorial cracks, and *dord* was given a part of speech and even a suggested pronunciation before being alphabetised, typeset and added to the dictionary.

It may have proved an embarrassing blunder for the dictionary's editors, but the accidental inclusion of *dord* had an unexpected advantage: should it ever crop up in any rival publication, the editors would know that the entry must have been copied directly from theirs. By adding a fake word to their dictionary, they had unwittingly set a trap for would-be plagiarists.

Fake words like these are also known as *nihilartikels* (literally 'nothing-articles') or *mountweazels*, the name of an Ohio-born fountain designer and photographer named Lillian Virginia Mountweazel who was listed in the 1975 edition of the *New Columbia Encyclopedia*. Regrettably, despite her renowned photographs of rural American mailboxes and her tragic death in an explosion while on an assignment for *Combustibles* magazine, Ms Mountweazel never actually existed.

bissext *(n.)*   the extra day added to a leap year

When Julius Caesar reorganised the Roman calendar in 46 BC (for more on which, flick back to 24 February), he added an extra day to each of the Roman months and decreed that a further additional day should be added to February every third, and eventually every fourth, year. That decision not only did away with the older, messier system of adding an entire month to the calendar every two years to keep the days in line with the seasons, but paved the way for what we now call a leap year.

The extra day we add to the calendar every leap year is properly known as a *bissext* or *bissextus*, a name derived from the Latin *bis*, meaning 'twice', and *sextus*, meaning 'sixth'. Originally, using Julius Caesar's system, this leap day was added to the calendar after 24 February – six days before the first day, or *calends*, of the following month. But rather than consider this additional day as a new day in its own right, it was instead considered a continuation of the previous day, making it literally the 'second sixth-day' before the first of the month – hence, it became the *bissext*.

This term remained in occasional use in English through to the seventeenth century, when the more usual word for this kind of arrangement, *leap*, became the standard name. Although no one is quite sure why we call these bissextile years *leap years*, it's thought that it might refer to the fact that each date after February in a leap year occurs on the next-but-one weekday to the previous year.

cacafuego *(n.)*   a blustering braggart

There's no polite way of putting this, but the word *cacafuego* literally means 'fire-shitter': borrowed into English from Spanish, it combines an old Spanish word, *cacar*, meaning 'to produce excrement', with the Spanish word for 'fire', *fuego*.

Despite that fairly unpleasant etymology, *cacafuego* ended up in use in seventeenth-century English thanks to the somewhat unlikely-sounding involvement of Sir Francis Drake. Sailing up the east coast of South America during his circumnavigation of the world in the late 1500s, Drake found himself tailing a grand Spanish galleon, *Nuestra Señora*, that he had heard was laden with a rich cargo of treasure from the Spanish colonies. Drake caught up with the ship off the coast of Ecuador, but knowing that an attack made under cover of darkness was his best bet he slowed his progress, so that by the time the *Hind* reached alongside early on 1 March 1579 it was the middle of the night. After a brief skirmish the Spanish crew surrendered, leaving Drake to take control of the ship and its cargo before heading off once more to complete his journey.

Drake's captured galleon might have been officially known as the *Nuestra Señora de la Concepción*, but to her crew she was the *Cacafuego*, or 'fire-shitter' – a nickname likely referring to her impressive weaponry and blazing cannon fire. When news of Drake's plundering of the ship broke back in England, that word quickly dropped into use in seventeenth-century English as a byword for a blustering, swaggering braggart – a meaning perhaps influenced by the fact that, despite her impressive armoury, the *Cacafuego* had proved no match for Drake.

pantagruelian *(adj.)*   gigantic, comically or grotesquely oversized

The iconic horror movie *King Kong* had its world premiere at New York's Radio City Music Hall on 2 March 1933. The film was met with near universal acclaim, and over the four days that followed it set a new record when all its first forty showings sold out. In total, it went on to gross more than $3 million.

The extraordinary success of *King Kong* soon led to its title character's name falling into figurative use in American slang as a nickname for what the *Oxford English Dictionary* calls 'a person or thing of outstanding size or strength'. But Kong isn't the only oversized character to have found his way into the dictionary as a byword for any equally gigantic or oversized person.

The name of *Gogmagog*, a legendary giant from early British folklore, has been used to describe any man of immense stature or strength since the early thirteenth century, while the Elizabethan poet and pamphleteer John Taylor coined the adjective *Gogmagogian* in 1612. The enormous inhabitants of the imaginary country of Brobdingnag in Jonathan Swift's *Gulliver's Travels* (1726) have led to the word *Brobdingnagian* being used to describe anyone of enormous size. The name of the biblical giant *Goliath* has been used allusively of tall or enormous people since the mid seventeenth century. And from a collection of bawdy tales about two giants, Gargantua and his son Pantagruel, written by the French Renaissance writer Rabelais in the sixteenth century, come the everyday adjective *gargantuan* and its less familiar cousin *pantagruelian* – both of which can be used to mean 'gigantic', 'monstrous' or 'comically or grotesquely oversized'.

epistolophobia *(n.)*   the fear of receiving correspondence

Of all the countless phobias that have been given names, among the most curious are those relating to the most innocent of everyday activities. *Eisoptrophobia*, for instance, is the fear of looking in mirrors. *Haphephobia* is the fear of being touched. *Koumpounophobia* is the fear of holding or fastening buttons. And *epistolophobia* – derived from the Greek *epistole*, meaning 'letter' or 'message' – is the fear of receiving post.

It could be said that fear of what might be in the mail led to the enactment on 3 March 1873 of the Act of the Suppression of Trade in and Circulation of Obscene Literature and Articles of Immoral Use – an American federal statute better known as the Comstock Act. Born in Connecticut in 1844, Anthony Comstock was the founder the New York Society for the Suppression of Vice. He spent much of his life campaigning and protesting against what he saw as the increasingly lax morals of nineteenth- and twentieth-century America. To that end, he was extraordinarily successful: his Comstock Act made it illegal for what he termed 'obscene, lewd, or lascivious' material from being couriered by the US mail, and he was officially given the title of United States Postal Inspector. Although Comstock initially wished to ban only information regarding contraception and abortion, his rules eventually became so chokingly restrictive that the United States Postal Service was even banned from delivering anatomical textbooks to medical students. As a result of his moral crusade, the term *Comstockery* eventually came to refer to any excessive or overly prudish censorship.

breviloquent *(adj.)*   pithy, succinct; characterised by brevity of speech

Derived from a Latin word meaning 'short speaking', *breviloquence* is a seventeenth-century word for conciseness or brevity, while someone known for just such a pithy and succinct manner of speaking could be described as *breviloquent*. That was certainly the case on 4 March 1793, when George Washington delivered his second presidential inaugural address.

When Washington was first sworn in as president in New York on 30 April 1789, his debut inaugural address had been a relatively lengthy affair, running to just over 1,400 words. In it he had spoken of the 'great anxieties' he had in becoming president, his renouncement of all 'pecuniary compensation' that would otherwise come with him taking office, and his hope that as president he might help in 'the advancement of [the] happiness' of the American people.

Things were vastly different when, a little under four years later, Washington again found himself elected as president and obliged to serve a second term. This time the inauguration took place in Philadelphia (by now the national capital) and Washington delivered an inaugural address of just 135 words.

Beginning with a simple 'Fellow citizens', Washington mentioned the 'confidence which has been reposed in me' by the American people, and his wish that if he were to fail in his supporters' eyes, he might be 'subject to the upbraidings of all who are now witnesses of the present solemn ceremony'. The *breviloquent* speech was – and remains to this day – the shortest inauguration speech in American presidential history.

zawn *(n.)*   a fissure or cave in a coastal cliff

The feast day of the patron saint of Cornwall, St Piran – or *Gool Peran* in the native Cornish language – is 5 March.

Piran is believed to have been born in Ireland sometime in the mid fourth century, but according to legend he fell out of favour with the Irish clergy and was thrown into the Irish Sea with a millstone tied around his neck. Miraculously, he somehow survived and floated across the sea to a new life in Cornwall.

The Cornish language predates English and is descended from the ancient Celtic languages. Throughout that lengthy history, Cornish has faced considerable difficulties: it suffered a devastating setback in the Prayer Book Rebellion of 1549, which imposed the English Book of Common Prayer on the Cornish-speaking population, of whom more than 5,000 lost their lives in the bloody skirmishes sparked by the revolt. The language continued to dwindle through to the eighteenth century, with the last native Cornish speaker, Dolly Pentreath, dying in 1777. Happily, the scholars and linguists of the nineteenth century refused to let the language die with her, and efforts were made to maintain it in grammars and dictionaries. Their publication sparked a resurgence in interest in the twentieth century, and the language now boasts several hundred fluent speakers.

Among the Cornish words adopted into English are:

- *bucca* (n.) a hobgoblin or sprite said to live below ground; figuratively, a foolish, empty-headed person
- *guag* (n.) an area of land that has already been mined
- *muryan* (n.) a species of fairy said to dwindle in size throughout its life before finally transforming into an ant
- *vug* (n.) a cave or natural cavity in a rock
- *zawn* (n.) a fissure in a coastal cliff

obsidion *(n.)* a siege; the state of being besieged

Obsidian with an 'a' is the name of a black volcanic glass, allegedly derived from the name of a Roman explorer, Obsius, who brought a sample of the stone back to Europe from Africa. *Obsidion* with an 'o' is a seldom-used fifteenth-century word for a siege or a besieged state, which is derived from a Latin word, *obsidere*, meaning 'to surround or beset on all sides'.

Appropriately enough, today marks the date on which one of the most famous sieges in history came to an end. The Alamo, in San Antonio, Texas, began life as a former Catholic mission before it was abandoned in the late 1700s and occupied by a company of Spanish militiamen in 1803. After the outbreak of the Texas Revolution in 1835, the mission was surrendered and taken over by a small number of revolutionary troops who occupied the site until early the following year. Then, in late February 1836, the Mexican army arrived in San Antonio de Béxar and for the next thirteen days laid siege to the Alamo.

At long last, on 6 March 1836, the invading Mexicans over-ran the Alamo walls. The Texan troops inside fell back and barricaded themselves in some of the interior rooms, but the Mexican forces used an abandoned cannon to destroy the doors and easily defeated the remaining defenders. After almost two weeks, the bloody siege – or *obsidion* – of the Alamo was over.

gobble-pipe *(n.)*   a saxophone

The very first jazz record, *The Dixie Jass Band One-Step/Livery Stable Blues*, was released on 7 March 1917. Recorded just a fortnight earlier by the Original Dixieland Jass Band, the record proved wildly successful and served to usher in the jazz age of the following decade. Before long, jazz music had become the defining sound of the early 1900s, popularised by contemporary stars like Cab Calloway, Louis Armstrong and Benny Goodman.

It was Goodman who, in 1937, released *The Camel Caravan*, an album of jazz and swing numbers popularised by an NBC radio show of the same name. The original album was released with a booklet of notes that included a guide to 'The Language of Swing', among which were a selection of jazz-age phrases and terms:

- *alligator* (n.) bandleader Cab Calloway's term for a devotee of swing music who does not play an instrument themselves
- *gobble-pipe* (n.) a saxophone
- *gutbucket* (n.) a style of 'low down swing', or a term for the swinging rhythm of blues music
- *paperman* (n.) a musician who cannot improvise and can play only from sheet music
- *sugar band* (n.) a group of musicians specialising in schmaltzy, sentimental music

As well as *gobble-pipe*, Goodman's vocabulary included such evocative nicknames as *rock crusher* (a concertina), *grunt-horn* (a tuba), *agony-pipe* (a clarinet) and *wood pile* (a xylophone), while a *paperman* who specialised in classical music would be a *long-hair*, and a band who played anything but swing were a *long underwear gang*.

Zenobia *(n.)*   a powerful, determined woman

8 March is International Women's Day, which makes *Zenobia* a fitting word for today.

Zenobia was a third-century queen of Palmyra, which at that time was a grand city and province of the eastern Roman Empire. Her husband Odaenathus was the founder of the Palmyrene Kingdom and ruled an impressive stretch of the Middle East between the Black, Red and Mediterranean seas. All that came to an end in 267 AD, when Odaenathus was assassinated along with his first-born son and heir, Hairan I. Next in line to the throne was his second son, Vaballathus, but as he was just ten years old Zenobia was left to take de facto control – and soon proved a more than capable leader.

Over the years that followed, Zenobia greatly expanded her kingdom to establish a vast Palmyrene Empire. As empress, she stood up to the might of Rome and in 271 AD proclaimed Palmyra independent of the Roman Emperor Aurelian – but it wasn't to last. The following year, Aurelian's army headed east and defeated Zenobia's forces at Antioch. Palmyra was besieged, and Zenobia and Vaballathus were captured. Their fates are unknown, but in their absence Palmyra fell and by 273 AD was once more under Roman control.

Zenobia's place in history was assured nevertheless: she had taken control of a vast kingdom at a critical point in its history – and at a time when it was all but unheard of for a woman to wield such power – and succeeded in extending its range and influence to the greatest extent in its history. Quite rightly, she now is commemorated in the dictionary as a fitting byword for any powerful, determined woman.

poppin *(n.)*   a child's doll

A *poppin* is a child's doll or puppet, a word that dates back to the fifteenth century in English and has its origins, via the French *poupine*, in the Latin word for 'doll', *puppa*. Oddly, that's also the origin of the word *pupil*, both in the sense of a school student and the black circular centre of the eye – although how all three are related takes a little imagination.

The Latin words for 'girl' and 'boy' were *pupa* and *pupus*. Derived from those came the diminutive forms *pupilla* and *pupillus*, which, as well as meaning 'little girl' and 'little boy', could also be used to mean 'orphan' or 'ward', 'doll' or 'puppet' (in the sense that they are an effigy of a little person) and ultimately 'school student'.

If you look very closely into someone's eyes, however, you'll also see a *pupilla* or *pupillus* – that is, a diminutive version of yourself reflected back at you. Because of that, the black centre of the eye itself also came to be known as the *pupilla*, and eventually the *pupil*, as it appeared (albeit with a bit of imagination) to contain a tiny person.

As etymologically related words go, school pupils, eyeballs and dolls are probably among the most unusual. How those words are related to today, however, is more straightforward: it was on 9 March 1959 that the very first Barbie dolls went on display at the American Toy Fair in New York.

telepheme *(n.)*   a message sent by telephone

On 10 March 1876, Alexander Graham Bell picked up his prototype telephone and summoned his assistant with the words, 'Mr Watson, come here – I want to see you.'

'To my delight,' he later wrote in his journal, 'he came and declared that he had heard and understood what I had said.' The world's first telephone call had been made.

Bell might be credited with inventing the telephone, but he certainly didn't invent the word itself. In fact, the word *telephone* made its first appearance in English way back in 1832 (a full decade before Bell was even born) when it originally referred to a contraption consisting of a piece of packthread attached to a tuning fork used to transmit a tone from one end of the string to the other. Earlier still, in 1827 the French inventor Jean-François Sudre had used the name *téléphone* for an elaborate communication system that allowed messages to be transmitted using musical notes. In all instances of the word, however, the derivation is the same: *telephone* combines two Greek roots meaning 'far', *tele*, and 'sound', *phone*.

The former is also present in the word *telepheme*, which was coined in 1852 as a word for a message sent by telegraph, and thereafter applied to a message sent by telephone in the 1880s. As the *Universalist Quarterly* explained in 1882:

> To 'telegraph' is to write from a distance; a 'telegram' is the message itself; to 'telephone' is to make a far-away sound; and the term 'telepheme' has been proposed for . . . the oral message sent.

Unfortunately, while the telephone caught on, the *telepheme* did not.

XYZ *(n.)* a hack journalist, a writer who takes on any work for cash

On 11 March 1702, the *Daily Courant* – England's first daily newspaper – was published for the first time. The work of Edward and Elizabeth Mallett, the *Courant* comprised a single sheet of newsprint divided into two columns of almost unbroken text, with advertisements on the reverse. There were no headlines, but a single masthead gave the paper's name and the date of the latest edition.

Published from the Malletts' offices on Fleet Street, the *Courant* was essentially a digest of material from other existing periodicals, but set out to provide just the facts. As the Malletts explained in the first edition, the *Courant* was not there 'to give any comments or conjectures of his own, but will relate only matter of fact; supposing other people to have sense enough to make reflections for themselves'. The paper remained in print until 1735.

Over the centuries since the *Courant*'s debut in the early eighteenth century, journalists and writers have been known by all manner of (often not particularly complimentary) nicknames, including *quill-drivers, adjective-jerkers* and *yarn-choppers*. A *penny-a-liner* was a journalist paid per line in Victorian slang, while the earliest meaning of the word *spaceman* was a journalist paid by the amount of space their work took up in a newspaper. But of all the journalistic nicknames, perhaps the strangest is *XYZ*: according to an 1889 *Dictionary of Slang, Jargon and Cant*, an *XYZ* was a 'common literary caterer', so called as this was the pseudonym of a writer who advertised in the back pages of *The Times*, 'offering to perform all descriptions of literary work at very moderate and unprofessional prices'.

sonrock *(n.)*   a fireside seat

According to the *English Dialect Dictionary* (Vol. V, 1904), *sonrock* is an old Irish word for 'a soft seat to lie or lean upon near the fire'.

Precisely where the word comes from is unclear, but it likely has an etymological cousin in *sonkie* or *sunkie*, an old Scots dialect word for a low bench or milking stool. That in turn is a derivative of another Scots word, *sonk* or *sunk*, which was variously used to mean a pad of straw used to cushion a saddle, a bank of earth or turf, and a seat of turf or sods constructed, according to the *Scottish National Dictionary*, 'at the fireside or against a sunny gable'.

Wherever its origins may lie, *sonrock* is the perfect word for today: it was on 12 March 1933 – just eight days after his inauguration – that President Franklin D. Roosevelt gave the first of a series of radio addresses that became known as his 'fireside chats'. A supreme communicator, Roosevelt was quick to embrace the power of radio, and when a banking crisis threatened to cripple his presidency before it had begun, he took to the airwaves to explain to an audience of 60 million listeners 'what has been done in the last few days, why it was done, and what the next steps are going to be'. The result was an overwhelming boost in public morale.

Roosevelt went on to deliver a total of thirty of these 'fireside chats' – a name based on a statement by Roosevelt's press secretary, who said the president liked to imagine himself speaking to a few people around a cosy fireplace – throughout his presidency.

ecdysiast *(n.)*   a striptease artiste

On 13 March 1898, a dancer named Blanche Cavelli performed what is credited with being the world's first public striptease on stage in a Paris nightclub.

The act – entitled *Le Coucher d'Yvette*, or 'Yvette Gets Ready For Bed' – was advertised as a 'pantomime' on the playbill of Le Divan Fayonau nightclub on rue des Martyrs, not far from the Moulin Rouge. Entering a stage set with just a chair and a bed, Cavelli danced to a live piano accompaniment while removing as many layers of clothing as the censors of the day would allow. Nevertheless, by modern standards the performance was relatively tame: the curtain fell on Cavelli, still dressed in a silk nightgown, merely climbing into bed.

The proper term for a striptease artist like this is an *ecdysiast* (pronounced 'eck-*dizzy*-ast'), while *ecdysiasm* is the act of removing one's clothes. Both terms have their roots in a Greek word, *ekdysis*, meaning 'to shed' or 'to cast off', which also survives in English in the considerably less provocative process of *ecdysis* – a zoological term for the shedding or sloughing off of an outer skin or covering, a phenomenon associated with the likes of snakes, lizards, spiders and crabs.

pericranics *(n.)*   intelligence, wits, mental faculties

If you're *eagle-witted*, then you're extremely clever. A *dapperwit* is a smart, quick-minded young man. *Sharpshins* is an old dialect word for an intelligent child (as well as for someone fleet of foot), while the old Yorkshire word *head-languager* refers to a scholar or schoolmaster, or else someone who is highly intelligent or well educated. And likewise, if you're gifted in your *pericranics*, then you're extremely smart.

The English essayist and writer Charles Lamb – best known for *Tales from Shakespeare* (1807), his and his sister Mary Lamb's retelling of Shakespeare's plays as children's stories – is credited with inventing the word *pericranics* in a letter in 1800. He presumably based the word on the *pericrane* or *pericranium*, the anatomical name for the thin membrane that envelops the outside of the skull, and which has been variously used as a nickname for the head, the brain or the seat of a person's intelligence since the late sixteenth century. But why should a collection of words referring to supreme intelligence be particularly appropriate today?

Well, it was on 14 March 1879 that Albert Einstein was born in the city of Ulm in southern Germany. Einstein's groundbreaking work, most notably his theory of relativity, changed the course of science in the twentieth century and earned him both the 1921 Nobel Prize for Physics and a place in the dictionary: as well as giving his name to both a unit of light energy and chemical element number 99, *einsteinium*, the *Oxford English Dictionary* lists Einstein's name as a byword for 'a mathematical or scientific genius'.

sicarian *(n.)*   an assassin

It was on 15 March 44 BC, the notorious Ides of March, that Roman Emperor Julius Caesar was assassinated by a group of rebels from his own senate, led by co-conspirators Brutus and Cassius. Although Caesar's last words are popularly said to be 'Et tu, Brute?', that phrase was merely popularised by Shakespeare's portrayal in *Julius Caesar* (in which they are followed by the less well-remembered, 'Then fall, Caesar.') In fact, many contemporary accounts report that Caesar said nothing at all as he was killed: Plutarch merely records that he pulled his toga over his head in dismay when he saw that Brutus was among his assassins.

The word *assassin* itself derives via French from an Arabic word, *hashishin*, that literally means 'hashish-eaters'. It originally referred to a group of Nizari Shia Muslims living in Persia and Syria during the time of the Crusades, who would reputedly consume vast quantities of hashish before embarking on rampaging attacks aimed at murdering opposition leaders or high-ranking elites. In reference to these attackers, the word *assassin* first appeared in the English language in the fourteenth century, before the more general sense of someone who murders a prominent figure in a planned attack developed in the mid 1500s.

Assassins and killers can also be known as *murdermongers*, *sword-takers*, *braves* and *bravos*, as well as *sicarians* – a fifteenth-century word derived from the Latin word for a dagger, *sica*.

daedal *(adj.)*   skilful, displaying great artistic craft or shrewdness

On 16 March 1900, the archaeologist Sir Arthur Evans completed the purchase of a vast site on the island of Crete surrounding the ancient city of Knossos. Although the ruins of the city had been discovered the previous century, Evans' purchase allowed for an extensive examination of the site. Within months, they had uncovered a colossal Bronze Age palace of 1,000 interconnected rooms unlike anything that had ever been found before, and as the dig continued it became clear that this palace had once been the centre of a vast and surprisingly advanced city. Evans' work eventually led to the discovery of the Minoan civilisation.

So complex was the vast Palace of Minos that tales of its intricate design are thought to have been the inspiration for the myth of the Labyrinth, the enormous maze-like structure supposedly constructed for King Minos of Crete to house the Minotaur, a monstrous half-man, half-bull hybrid. And, according to the myth, the Labyrinth was the work of a masterful Cretan architect named Daedalus, whose name – derived from a Greek word meaning 'cunning' or 'skilful' – can be used allusively of any equally skilful artist or craftsman.

Derived from the same root, the sixteenth-century adjective *daedal* can be used to describe any particularly expert piece of craftsmanship; to *daedalise* is to make something intricate or complicated; a *logodaedalus* is someone who is particularly cunning in their use of words; and every part of something that is *pandaedalian* is ingeniously made or expertly designed.

cudeigh *(n.)*   a gift given as a bribe

Today is St Patrick's Day, the feast day of St Patrick, a Christian missionary and bishop who died on 17 March 461, and the national day of Ireland.

The Irish language has contributed a vast number of words to English over the centuries, including an array of surprisingly familiar terms:

- *galore* (adv.) derives from the Irish *go leór*, which, unlike the English meaning of 'in abundance', is used to mean 'just sufficient' or 'just enough'
- *slob* (n.) originally meant 'mud' or 'marshland', and derives from an Irish word, *slaba*, meaning 'ooze' or 'slime'
- *smithereens* (n.) has been used to mean 'shards' or 'small pieces' in English since the early nineteenth century, and derives from its Irish equivalent *smidirín*
- *trousers* (n.) take their name from *triubhas*, an Irish word for breeches or loose-fitting shorts

Among the less familiar Irish words used in English is the fifteenth-century word *cuddy* or *cudeigh*. Derived from a corruption of the Irish *cuid oidhche*, literally meaning 'evening portion', *cudeigh* originally referred to the custom of a tenant putting on a supper or a night of entertainment for his lord, or else a rent or payment made in lieu of this custom. By the nineteenth century, however, that meaning had begun to drift into obscurity along with the custom itself, but the word *cudeigh* remained in place as another word for a gift or present, and in particularly one given as a bribe or 'sweetener'.

asmatographer *(n.)*   a dealer or writer of songs or sheet music

The word *asmatographer* was listed in Thomas Blount's *Glossographia*, an early English dictionary published in the mid seventeenth century, and defined as a word for 'they who sell or make songs, or lessons for any instrument'. The art of writing or composing songs or pieces of music, likewise, is known as *asmatography*. Both words have at their root a Greek word for a song, *aisma*, and both have remained little used in the language ever since their first appearance in Blount's dictionary in 1656. They are, however, both very apt for today.

On 18 March 1911, the songwriter Irving Berlin copyrighted one of the most famous songs of the early twentieth century: 'Alexander's Ragtime Band'. Originally an instrumental piece for solo piano that found limited success, the song found its audience when Berlin added lyrics ('Come on and hear, / Come on and hear, / Alexander's Ragtime Band!') and successfully pitched the piece to the producer of a Broadway revue entitled *The Merry Whirl*. Within eighteen months, the sheet music for the song had sold a staggering 1.5 million copies.

Although by this time Berlin was already a very prolific composer and songwriter (he published more than forty songs in 1911 alone) it is likely that without this early success, many of his later hits – 'White Christmas', 'There's No Business Like Showbusiness' and 'What'll I Do' among them – would have struggled to have found such an appreciative audience.

absconsion *(n.)* an escape

Derived from a Latin verb, *abscondere*, meaning 'to hide' or 'to keep secret', when it first appeared in the language in the mid seventeenth century the word *absconsion* was likewise used to mean a hiding or a concealment. By the nineteenth century, however, that meaning had changed: by then, the word referred to an escape, a flight, or a disappearance – and, in particular, an escape from police custody or from some kind of otherwise inescapable circumstances.

Fittingly, it was on this day that the escapologist Harry Houdini performed one of his most audacious and memorable escape acts. By the turn of the twentieth century, Houdini was already world renowned for his ability to escape from the most impossible of situations, and had earned a reputation for publicising his act by challenging the local chief of police in whatever town he was performing to lock him in one of the local jail cells. True to form, on 19 March 1906 Houdini was stripped naked, manacled, locked into cell number 60 of the Boston Tombs jail complex (while his clothes were locked in cell 77) and left alone. The next that Boston police superintendent William Pierce heard was a telephone call: Houdini was calling from the local theatre, half a mile away, where he was due to go out on stage. He had successfully escaped his cell, collected his clothes, scaled the prison wall and hitched a ride in a passing car all inside just sixteen minutes. Struck dumb by Houdini's extraordinary escape, all Pierce could reply was simply, 'I have nothing to say.'

Houdini staged numerous jail escapes like these throughout his performing life. Reportedly, he was never locked in a cell from which he could not escape.

siderism *(n.)*   the belief that the stars and heavens have an influence on life on earth

The Latin word for 'star', *sidus*, is the origin of a number of little-used words like *siderosous* ('star-struck'), *intersidereal* ('located among or between two stars') and *siderate* ('to blast with lightning'), as well as the much more familiar verb *consider*, which is believed to have originally meant 'to scrutinise the heavens' or 'to carry out an astrological investigation'. The belief that astrological phenomena can influence terrestrial activities is known as *siderism*, a term coined in the mid nineteenth century – and anyone signing up to that theory would believe today's date to be a particularly inauspicious one.

When the Black Death was at the height of its devastation across medieval Europe in the mid fourteenth century, desperate attempts were made to try to figure out the cause of the pestilence. Everything from earthquakes to witchcraft was blamed for a disaster that eventually led to the death of a third of the entire population of Europe. But scholars at the University of Paris had a different theory. At the request of the French King Philip VI, the university's medical faculty launched an investigation into the cause of the plague – and blamed the disaster on a 'triple conjunction' of the planets Mars, Jupiter and Saturn that had taken place on 20 March 1345.

It would be another six centuries before the true cause of the plague – a bacterium, *Yersinia pestis*, borne by fleas and in turn by rats – would be discerned.

Lob's pound *(n.)*   a prison

In his *Dictionary of the Vulgar Tongue* (1785), the English lexicographer Francis Grose defines *Lob's pound* as another word for a prison, giving this anecdote of the word's origin:

> [It alludes] to one Doctor Lob, a dissenting preacher, who used to hold forth when conventicles were prohibited, and had made himself a retreat by means of a trap door at the bottom of his pulpit. Once being pursued by the officers of justice, they followed him through divers subterraneous passages, till they got into a dark cell, from whence they could not find their way out, but calling to some of their companions, swore they had got into Lob's Pound.

It's a neat story. It's just a shame probably none of it is true. *Lob* in this sense is probably nothing more than an old sixteenth-century word for a clownish fool or a country bumpkin. Presumably as those kinds of loutish or dim-witted characters were once so likely to fall foul of the law, *Lob's pound* became a slang term for a prison.

From there, use of the word dwindled throughout the nineteenth century, but it apparently remained locally in a broader or more figurative sense: *A Glossary of Words Used in East Anglia* (1895), for instance, lists the word *lobspound* as meaning 'to be in any difficulty or perplexed state', while a guide to *The Folk-Speech of South Cheshire* (1887) defines it as 'difficulty, equivalent to *lumber*'.

It's the earlier punitive meaning of the word that comes into play on this day, however: on 21 March 1963, the notorious prison on Alcatraz Island in San Francisco Bay closed its doors after almost sixty years' use (for more on which, skip ahead to 11 June).

rampire *(n.)*   a dam, a barrier to water

When it first appeared in the language in the mid sixteenth century, the word *rampire* was essentially used to mean what we would now call a *rampart*: a raised defensive wall or walkway, typically around a fort or castle. In that sense both *rampire* and *rampart* derive from a French word meaning 'to fortify'. But while the meaning of *rampart* remained in place, the meaning of *rampire* began to change.

Before long, *rampire* was being used to refer to any protective or blockading barrier or raised wall, and in that sense eventually came to refer to a dam or barrier – either artificial or natural, like a mound of earth – for holding back water. And it was on this day that an extraordinary natural *rampire* was formed over one of the world's most famous natural landmarks.

On 22 March 1903, an enormous ice jam blocked the American side of Niagara Falls between the New York mainland and Goat Island, the wooded islet that splits the Niagara river into two cascading arms. The jam forced all of the water over to the Canadian side of the waterfall, which swelled enormously, while the US side ran dry enough to walk across the exposed riverbed. As the *Chicago Tribune* reported at the time:

> The ice started to dam in the rapids above the falls this afternoon, and tonight only a few small rivulets of water flow over the American side of the falls. The park was crowded with people watching the unusual sight, while the people on the Canadian side were attracted by the thunder of three-times the normal amount of water passing over the brink of the Horseshoe Falls.

hell-kettle *(n.)*   a deep gulf or abyss

Just outside Darlington in County Durham is a series of deep freshwater pools known locally as 'Hell Kettles'. The pools are the result of massive subterranean subsidence caused by vast deposits of gypsum being eroded underground. Local folklore has it that the pools are bottomless (they are said to have inspired Alice's tumbling descent into Wonderland in Lewis Carroll's stories) but unsurprisingly that legend is untrue. The pools' reputation was nevertheless enough to inspire the term *hell-kettle*, which has been used to refer to any bottomless pit or gulf in English since the late sixteenth century.

And the deepest of all the world's *hell-kettles* was charted for the first time on this day.

The HMS *Challenger* expedition, brainchild of Scottish naturalist Charles Wyville Thomson, set sail from Plymouth in 1872 and spent the next four years exploring 70,000 miles of the world's oceans. During that time hundreds of deep-sea trawls and depth and temperature readings were taken, so that by the time the expedition returned home in 1876 more than 4,000 new species had been identified and a vast body of oceanographic data had been collected.

On 23 March 1875, the *Challenger* crew took a depth sounding of 4,475 fathoms (equivalent to 5 miles) off the coast of the Mariana Islands in the western Pacific. The result so staggered the crew that they rounded the ship and took a second reading, only to have their original result confirmed. The crew had discovered the Mariana Trench, the deepest part of the earth's surface.

Modern technology has since recorded a depth of 35,184 feet at the deepest part of the trench – which, fittingly, is now named Challenger Deep.

patt *(n.)*　a stalemate

The Oxford and Cambridge Boat Race was first held in 1829 and has been an annual event – held every year except during the First and Second World Wars – since 1856.

Only once in that time has the competition ended in a tie: on 24 March 1877 the race was controversially declared a dead heat after strong winds and a patch of rough water that snapped the blade of one of Oxford's oars scuppered their lead and allowed the trailing Cambridge team to take advantage. Somehow, Oxford managed to keep up, so that by the end of the race both teams were alongside one another in the water. After an inquiry that went as far as a debate in a local law court, the thirty-fourth Oxford and Cambridge Boat Race was announced as a tie. The following day, the entire affair was summed up by the satirical magazine *Punch*, which ran the headline: 'Oxford won, Cambridge too'.

Games or races in which there is no clear winner have been known as *ties* since the late seventeenth century, and *dead heats* – originally a term from horse racing – since the late eighteenth century. The chess term *stalemate* (technically a misnomer, as in chess terms it is not an actual 'mate') has been in figurative use in English almost as long.

A *patt*, too, is a stalemate: derived via French from an Italian word for a vote that ends in a tie (which likely comes from the same Latin root as the word *pact*), *patt* dates back to the eighteenth century in English but, unlike its more familiar equivalent *stalemate*, has long since fallen into disuse.

meiosis *(n.)* a figure of speech that deliberately understates something truly serious

In biology, *meiosis* is a type of cell division. In rhetoric, *meiosis* is a figure of speech in which something is intentionally understated. In either case, the word appropriately derives from a Greek word meaning 'less'.

Rhetorical *meiosis* is often employed ironically or euphemistically, so use of 'The Pond' to refer to the Atlantic Ocean or the 'The Troubles' to refer to decades of unrest in Northern Ireland both qualify as examples. But *meiosis* can also be used with the intention of either belittling something that might otherwise appear daunting, or dismissing something that is actually potentially very serious: to paraphrase *Monty Python*, like dismissing a mortal wound as a nothing more than a scratch. And oddly, that brings us to today's date.

On 25 March 1199, Richard I and his army were besieging Château de Châlus-Chabrol near Limoges, France, when a stray crossbow bolt fired from the castle ramparts struck the king just above his shoulder blade. In typically lionhearted fashion, Richard simply retired to his quarters to remove the bolt, but when it proved too difficult to dislodge a surgeon was called and the seriousness of the situation soon became apparent.

The initial wound may have been survivable, but the surgeon's clumsy attempt to remedy it – and the infection that followed – were not. By 6 April, the king was dead.

As for the bolt that had brought down a king, it was found to have been fired by a boy whose father and elder brother had both been killed in the siege. To this day, 6 April is known in France as 'the day on which an ant killed the lion king'.

antichthon *(n.)* a hypothetical planet hidden from
our view on the opposite side of
the sun

The term *antichthon* – literally 'opposite earth' – was introduced
by the poet and scholar Thomas Stanley, who wrote of an earth-
like planet on the opposite side of the sun in his *History of
Philosophy* (1655). Those who followed the Greek philosopher
Pythagoras, Stanley explained, believed that there were ten solar
bodies: seven planets, the sun and moon, and a tenth planet or
antichthon, described as 'an earth above, opposite ours'.

No such planet actually exists, but the idea that there may
be a 'counter-earth' or similar extraneous planet somewhere in
our solar system has long captivated astronomers – and took a
bizarre step forward on 26 March 1859, when French astronomer Edmond Modeste Lescarbault noticed that a sunspot he
had been observing appeared to be moving across the surface
of the sun. Lescarbault immediately presumed that he was in
fact observing Vulcan, a hypothetical so-called 'intermercurial'
planet, believed to exist between Mercury and the sun. Urbain
Le Verrier, a mathematician and champion of Vulcan's existence,
was quick to seize on Lescarbault's discovery and announced
the discovery of a tenth planet to the Académie des Sciences.
Lescarbault, for his part, was awarded the *Légion d'honneur*.

Over the years that followed, Le Verrier collated dozens of
reported sightings of Vulcan to produce a detailed account of
the planet's predicted size and orbit. But as technology improved
and the number of sightings dwindled – and after Le Verrier's
death in 1877 – it became clear that no such planet existed. To
this day, the existence of neither an intermercurial nor *antich-
thonic* planet has any evidence to support it.

vinipote *(n.)*   a wine drinker

On 27 March 1860, an application by an 'M. L. Byrn of New York' was received by the US patent office for a device 'combining with [a] gimlet screw a T-handle'. In short, it was a corkscrew.

Byrn may have patented the corkscrew, but he certainly hadn't invented it: in 1795, an Oxford scholar named Samuel Henshall had designed a corkscrew based on a device for cleaning rifle barrels. But Byrn's patent nevertheless made it clear that his design was superior in 'strength and cheapness' and would 'serve both for cutting the wire from bottles requiring wire to keep the corks in place, and for drawing the corks out'. *Vinipotes* clearly have much to thank M. L. Byrn for.

The word *vinipote* means 'a drinker of wine, a wine-bibber, [or] a drunkard' according to the *Glossographia* (1656), an early dictionary of English by the seventeenth-century lexicographer Thomas Blount. Wine drinkers can also be known as *clareteers* and *grape-mongers*, while wine connoisseurs are properly known as *oenophiles* or *oenologists*.

Elsewhere in the wine-lovers' dictionary:

- *gardevine* (n.) an early nineteenth-century word for a wine bottle, derived from the French for 'wine-keeper'
- *Bacchant* (n.) another word for a lover of wine or a drunken reveller, derived from Bacchus, the Greek god of wine and revelry
- *oenomel* (n.) a mixture of wine and honey
- *merobibe* (n.) someone who drinks unadulterated or undiluted wine
- *punt* (n.) the dint in the bottom of a wine bottle; in eighteenth-century slang, *to drink out the island* meant 'to drink a bottle of wine until the dint becomes visible'

Barnumism *(n.)*   exaggerated, overblown promotion

On 28 March 1881, P. T. Barnum's Greatest Show On Earth opened in New York. The grandest circus of its day, the enterprise was a collaboration between the American showman Phineas Taylor Barnum and ringmaster James Bailey, two former adversaries who, after years of battling with one another to put on the most extravagant show possible, had finally set aside their differences and pooled their resources.

By working together, Barnum and Bailey delivered an extraordinary spectacle. A torchlit parade through downtown Manhattan was followed by a near non-stop performance in New York's Madison Square Garden: more than 600 performers and a vast menagerie including 300 horses, a troupe of performing monkeys and no fewer than 20 elephants performed simultaneously across three circus rings. The show was a resounding success. 'A man must have three pairs of eyes,' wrote a reviewer in the *Washington Post*, or else, 'think that while he is looking at one good thing he missed another'.

Even before the Barnum and Bailey circus had opened in 1881, P. T. Barnum had already cemented his reputation as a consummate showman and publicist, and his notorious rabble-rousing, self-promotional style was already legendary. As a result, the term *Barnumize* – defined by the *Oxford English Dictionary* as 'to exhibit with a lavish display of puffing advertisements' – had appeared in print as early as 1851, and was followed by the term *Barnumism*, coined in 1862, to refer to any kind of equally exaggerated or boastful promotion.

Aceldama *(n.)*   a place of great slaughter or bloodshed;
a battlefield

On 29 March 1461 the bloodiest battle ever fought on British soil took place outside a tiny rural village in North Yorkshire. The Battle of Towton, one of the most significant encounters of the Wars of the Roses, was played out during a blinding snowstorm by perhaps as many as 60,000 soldiers from the Houses of York and Lancaster. Some 28,000 men are supposed to have been killed in this one battle alone; if so, the Battle of Towton would have singlehandedly wiped out one per cent of the entire population of England at the time.

Well suited for such a bloody day in Britain's history, an *Aceldama* is a place of great slaughter or bloodshed. That word is believed to derive, via Greek, from an ancient Aramaic phrase literally meaning 'field of blood', and first appeared in English in early translations of the Bible written in the tenth century AD. According to the New Testament, *Aceldama*, or *Hakeldama*, was the name of the potter's field outside Jerusalem purchased by Judas Iscariot using the money he accepted to betray Jesus to the Romans; its name supposedly alludes to the fact that it was purchased with literal 'blood money'.

From there, the word dropped into figurative use in English to refer to any scene or location of great slaughter or bloodshed, or else any wretched or despicable place, and has remained in infrequent use ever since.

lickpenny *(n.)*   a costly enterprise, something demanding great expenditure

At 4 o'clock in the morning on 30 March 1867, an exhausting all-night negotiation between the American Secretary of State William H. Seward and the Russian diplomat Edouard de Stoeckl concluded with the agreement that the United States would purchase Alaska from Russia for a price of $7.2 million – equivalent to well over $100 million today.

The US Senate approved the purchase a little over a week later. President Andrew Johnson signed the ratifying treaty the following May, and by October Alaska had been formally handed over to the United States. The deal added 586,000 square miles of territory to the US at a cost of 2 cents per acre – but not everyone was pleased. Although public opinion was mostly in support of the deal, for some the price tag was too great. Before long, the Alaska Purchase was being dismissed as 'Seward's Folly', while Alaska itself was 'Seward's Icebox' and 'Johnson's Polar Bear Garden'.

Any purchase that demands great expenditure is a *lickpenny*, a word coined in a fifteenth-century ballad, *London Lyckpeny*, attributed to the English poet John Lydgate. The ballad satirises a journey into London taken by a Kentish man who has lost all his money and tries vainly to have his case heard in the courts. Once in London, however, the man finds it impossible to achieve anything without spending what little money he has left: even when he tries to leave and return home, the ferryman he approaches explains that he cannot escape London for anything 'under two pence'. Ultimately, in Lydgate's eyes, London was a city that essentially 'licks up' all your pennies until you are left with none.

dissight *(n.)*   an eyesore, anything unpleasant
to look upon

The Eiffel Tower officially opened on 31 March 1889. Designed by architect Gustave Eiffel, the 1,000-foot wrought-iron tower was built as the centrepiece of the 1889 *Exposition Universelle*, a grand world's fair held to celebrate the centenary of the French Revolution. On its completion, the tower became the world's tallest man-made structure, a title it held for the next forty-one years.

Although it has since become one of the world's most visited attractions, at the time not everyone was so pleased. Barely a fortnight after work began, an open letter by the Committee of Three Hundred – an alliance of writers and artists from the Paris arts scene, including Guy de Maupassant and the composer Charles Gounod – appeared in *Le Temps* newspaper:

> We writers, painters, sculptors, architects and passionate devotees of the hitherto untouched beauty of Paris, protest with all our strength, with all our indignation in the name of slighted French taste, against the erection . . . of this useless and monstrous Eiffel Tower . . . The Louvre, the Dome of les Invalides, the Arc de Triomphe, all of our humiliated monuments will disappear in this ghastly dream.

To the Three Hundred, the Eiffel Tower was a *dissight*, a term dating from the eighteenth century for anything unsightly or unpleasant to behold.

Luckily, tastes have since changed and the Eiffel Tower has since become an iconic addition to the Paris skyline. Guy de Maupassant, however, remained unconvinced: he reportedly ate lunch every day at the restaurant at the base of the tower as it was the only place in the city from which he could not see it.

dorbellist *(n.)*   a fool, a dull-witted dolt

The 'fool' of April Fool's Day is thought to derive from a Latin word for a blacksmith's bellows, *follis*, and probably originally referred to a chattering windbag before it came to mean an empty-headed dolt. According to etymological folklore, *nincompoop* comes from a corruption of the Latin phase *non compos mentis*, or 'not of sound mind' (but in truth is more likely to be little more than a nonsense invention). *Moron* is a Greek word literally meaning 'dull', and was once specifically defined by the short-lived American Association for the Study of the Feeble-Minded as someone with an IQ of between 51–70, while an *imbecile* had an IQ of 26–50 and an *idiot* 0–25; all three of these terms were quickly adopted as insults shortly after their introduction into psychological literature in 1910, and ultimately lost their technical connotations. And a *dunce* was originally a follower or advocate of the work of a Scottish scholar and philosopher named John Duns Scotus, whose once popular but soon out-dated theories saw his name become a byword for a nit-picking sophist or pretender to knowledge in the sixteenth century, and eventually a slow-witted fool or dullard.

A *dorbel* or *dorbellist* too is a fool or blockhead. It derives from the name of Nicolas d'Orbellis, a fifteenth-century French theologian and philosopher who was one of John Duns Scotus' most famous supporters. And just like Scotus himself, it was d'Orbellis' championing of old-fashioned reasoning that led his name to become associated with foolishness and dull-wittedness in the sixteenth and seventeenth centuries.

eluscate *(v.)*   to close or blind one eye

The adjective *louche* literally means 'squinting' in its native French, and was originally used to mean 'oblique' or 'not straightforward' when it was first borrowed into English in the early nineteenth century. It derives ultimately from a Latin adjective, *luscus*, meaning 'one-eyed', 'half-blinded' or, by extension, 'dimly lit', from which the little-known seventeenth-century words *luscition*, a long-forgotten word for poor-sightedness or purblindness, and *eluscate*, a verb meaning 'to close or blind one eye', such as when taking aim or using a telescope, are also descended.

Horatio Nelson was famously *eluscated* at the Siege of Calvi, on Corsica, in 1794 when he was struck with debris in his right eye and blinded. But seven years later he memorably used this *eluscation* to his advantage – and in doing so claimed a place in linguistic history.

According to legend, on 2 April 1801, Nelson was laying siege to a fleet of Danish ships in Copenhagen harbour when the signal came from the British flagship HMS *London* to cease firing and leave off action. Never one to back away from a fight, Nelson famously turned to his ship's captain, Thomas Foley, and exclaimed, 'Foley, I have only one eye – and I have the right to be blind sometimes', before raising his telescope to his blind eye and muttering that, 'I really do not see the signal.' The British ultimately continued with their onslaught and eventually claimed a decisive victory in what would become known as the Battle of Copenhagen.

Whether or not this event truly occurred is debatable, but Nelson's famous *eluscating* dismissal soon became a popular naval legend – and to this day we still talk of *turning a blind eye* to pressing or problematic issues.

traditor *(n.)* a traitor, one who betrays another

Traitor derives via French from a Latin word, *tradere*, literally meaning 'to hand over' or 'to deliver'. *Trade, tradition* and *treason* all derive from the same root, as does *traditor* – a fifteenth-century word for one who betrays another. Speaking of which, on this day in 1882 the American outlaw Jesse James was shot and killed by a member of his own gang.

Born in Missouri, James fell into a life of outlawry alongside his brother and two cousins in the aftermath of the Civil War, and for the next sixteen years he and his accomplices committed robberies and murders across the Midwest. Despite the reputation of the James gang, public sympathy – bolstered by a bungled attempt on their lives by the Chicago Pinkerton Detective Agency in 1875 that horrifically injured Jesse's mother – helped them to evade the authorities for more than a decade, but a brazen daylight bank robbery in 1876 eventually led to their downfall: in the shambolic escape, Jesse's cousins, the Younger brothers, were shot by police and the Jameses were forced to return home to their family farm to hide out.

With a reward now placed on his life, Jesse tentatively began to organise a new gang but failed to find accomplices as loyal to him as his cousins had been. On the morning of 3 April 1882, he invited his new recruits to the James family home to arrange their next robbery, but as he turned to adjust a picture on the wall, Robert Ford, one of the gang's newest members, shot him in the back. The cash reward on Jesse's life had, it seemed, been too enticing.

imprevision *(n.)*   lack or disregard of foresight, improvidence

In 1840, William Henry Harrison was elected the ninth President of the United States, having narrowly defeated the incumbent, Martin Van Buren, by 1.2 million votes to 1.1 million.

Harrison's victory was unique in a number of ways. For one, this marked the first election in US history in which either candidate had polled more than a million votes. At sixty-seven, Harrison was also the oldest president yet elected to office, and the first Whig candidate. At his inauguration, he set the record for the longest inaugural address – a rambling 8,445-word speech, full of classical allusions and anecdotes, which he had written himself. And when he died of pneumonia just thirty-one days later on 4 April 1841, Harrison became the shortest-serving president in American history.

Although the precise cause of Harrison's untimely death continues to be debated (more recently it has been suggested that an enteric fever caused by contaminated water might in fact have been to blame) the popular theory is that the president caught the cold that eventually killed him while he delivered his one-and-three-quarter-hour inaugural speech. The weather that day was windy and cold, and Harrison refused to wear a hat, gloves or overcoat. He also travelled to and from the ceremony on horseback, refusing to ride in the closed carriage that had been offered to him. Was this chain of poor decisions and lack of foresight really enough to bring down the president? It's possible – and makes *imprevision*, a nineteenth-century coinage for improvidence or a lack of foresight, a suitably ill-advised word for today.

95

dactylology *(n.)*   finger-speech

Born in Alabama in 1880, Helen Keller was left deaf and blind by an outbreak of scarlet fever when she was just nine-teen months old. That start in life led to an unruly childhood, and when her behaviour became too much for her parents to deal with they sought the help of a young tutor named Anne Sullivan.

Sullivan joined the Keller family on their farm in Alabama and over the months that followed painstakingly worked with Helen to help her understand words, language and the world around her. The breakthrough finally came on 5 April 1887, when Helen, helping Sullivan fetch water from the farmyard pump, connected the letters *W-A-T-E-R* that Sullivan was trac-ing on to the palm of her left hand with the fresh water that was running over her right. Keller later wrote in her autobiography:

> As the cool stream gushed over one hand, she spelled into the other the word 'water' . . . Suddenly I felt a misty consciousness as of something forgotten – a thrill of returning thought; and somehow the mystery of lan-guage was revealed to me. I knew then that 'w-a-t-e-r' meant the wonderful cool something that was flowing over my hand. That living word awakened my soul, gave it light, hope, joy, set it free!

Dactylology, also known as *chirology*, is another name for 'finger-speech' – either as sign language, or the tracing of letters using the hands and fingers. Both terms were coined in the seven-teenth century, and both have at their roots an Ancient Greek word: *dactylology* comes from the Greek word for 'finger', *dac-tylos*, while *chirology* comes from *chiros*, meaning 'hand'.

periscian *(n.)*   an inhabitant of the polar regions

On 6 April 1909, the American explorer Robert Peary became the first person in history to reach the North Pole.

Peary's claim to that title was later challenged (a former associate, Frederick Cook, maintained that he had reached the pole by dogsled the previous year), and the accuracy of his navigational readings has also been questioned (in all likelihood, Peary's expedition fell a few miles short of the actual pole). But nevertheless his achievement was an extraordinary one – and makes *periscian*, a word for an inhabitant of the polar regions, an apt word for today.

Periscian was coined in the second century BC by an Ancient Greek geographer named Posidonius. He developed a system of dividing the earth into three latitudinal zones based on the shadows of the people who lived there. As Strabo, a fellow geographer and advocate of Posidonius' system, explained:

> Amphiscians are those who at midday have their shadows sometimes projecting this way, to the north . . . [and] sometimes in the opposite direction . . . This happens only to those who live between the tropics. Heteroscians, on the other hand, are either those whose shadow falls to the north, like us, or . . . whose shadow falls to the south, like the inhabitants of the southern temperate zone.

The *Periscians* ultimately were those who dwelt at latitudes where uninterrupted sunlight in summer caused their shadows to move around them in a circle, like the spike on a sundial. So while the *Amphiscians* were given a name derived from the Greek for 'both', and the *Heteroscians* given a name derived from the Greek for 'other', Posidonius took the word *Periscian* from the Greek for 'encircling', *peri*, and 'shadow', *skia*.

crack-halter *(n.)* a 'gallows-bird', someone liable one day to be hanged; a habitual troublemaker

A *halter*, a word in use since the Old English period, is a rope by which horses are led or restrained. But the halter's similarity to a noose has meant that the word has been in use since the fifteenth century in English to refer to the rope used to hang criminals and troublemakers – and someone whose criminal behaviour makes them appear destined to one day 'crack' the hangman's noose makes *crack-halter* a sixteenth-century word for a 'gallows-bird' or habitual troublemaker.

In fact, the dictionary abounds with words for criminals and ne'er-do-wells whose shady lifestyle seems destined to lead them to the gallows. As well *crack-halter*, there are *crack-ropes* and *crack-hemps*, *stretch-halters*, *wag-halters* and *halter-sacks*, *slip-strings*, *hang-strings* and *hempstrings*, *hang-ups*, *gallows-clappers* and *gallows-climbers*. A group of gallows-birds is a *gallows-brood*, and in the Scots dialect, a *crack-halter* might be a *widdieneck*, a sixteenth-century term derived from a local term for a rope or loop made from twisted willow branches.

But if you manage to escape your fate (or, failing that, the authorities) you'll become a *rope-runner*, a *slip-halter*, a *gallows-scape* or a *slip-gibbet* – that latter a word listed in Francis Grose's *Dictionary of the Vulgar Tongue* (1785) as 'one for whom the gallows is said to groan'. No such last-minute escape was forthcoming for the infamous English highwayman Dick Turpin, however, who was hanged for the crime of horse theft at the gallows of the City of York on 7 April 1739.

sockdolager *(n.)*   something of exceptional size or
extraordinariness; a knockout blow

On 8 April 1838, the SS *Great Western* set sail on her maiden
voyage from Bristol to New York. The brainchild of engineer
Isambard Kingdom Brunel, the *Great Western* was a wooden-
hulled steamship that at more than 2,000 tons was the largest
passenger ship in the world at the time. Remarkably, Brunel
would go on to break his own record with two more ships, the
SS *Great Britain* (1843) and the SS *Great Eastern* (1859).

Fitting for the day on which the first of his record-breakers
set sail, the dictionary has a heady supply of words for things
considered the largest, grandest or most exceptional of their type:

- *ruby-dazzler* (n.) *dazzler* has been used to mean anything impressively showy or ostentatious since the early
  1800s, and both *bobby-dazzler* and *ruby-dazzler* are
  simply random extensions of that
- *rumptydooler* (n.) an excellent or outstanding person or
  thing has been known as a *rumptydooler* in Australian
  slang since the mid 1900s; like *ruby-dazzler*, it represents
  a random extension of the older eighteenth-century
  word *rumti*, or *rumtitum*, which in turn derives from
  the use of *rum* as an adjective meaning 'excellent'
- *sockdolager* (n.) probably derived from the use of *sock* to
  mean a knock or blow, a *sockdolager* was originally a knockout punch in nineteenth-century slang before it came to
  describe anything considered exceptional or sizeable
- *Typhon* (n.) the name of a colossal monster from Greek
  myth supposedly buried beneath Mount Etna, *Typhon*
  can be used allusively of anything of extraordinary size
  or power

lamprophony *(n.)* clearness of voice

In 1857, twenty years before Thomas Edison invented his phonograph, a French bookseller named Édouard-Léon Scott de Martinville patented the earliest known device for recording the human voice. Named the *phonautograph*, it consisted of a rudimentary stylus held against a rotating glass cylinder coated in a thin layer of plaster of Paris. The sound waves produced by someone speaking would ultimately cause the stylus to vibrate, tracing the waveform on to the cylinder.

Originally de Martinville intended his device to be used solely in laboratories for the study of acoustics and sound patterns. But as the vogue for recorded sound gathered pace in the late nineteenth century, it became clear that de Martinville's extraordinary *phonautograph* and the recordings it produced – known as *phonautograms* – could be used to play back the sounds they had recorded at a later date. And for that reason, it now holds a very special place in the history of recorded sound.

On 9 April 1860, de Martinville is believed to have recorded himself slowly reciting the French folksong 'Au Clair de la Lune'. The twenty-second recording may not be as impressive as Thomas Edison's first wax cylinder recording (a performance of Handel's oratorio *Israel in Egypt*, no less), but it nevertheless predates Edison's work by almost two decades, and remains the earliest known intelligible recording of the human voice.

An apt choice for today's word is *lamprophony*, a nineteenth-century term for clarity or clearness of voice, derived from a Greek word, *lampros*, meaning 'bright' or 'shining'; a voice as clear or intelligible as de Martinville's extraordinary recording, ultimately, might be described as *lamprophonic*.

centiday *(n.)* one one-hundredth of a day

Fittingly for this, the hundredth day of the year, one one-hundredth of a day is known as a *centiday* or *centid*, a seldom-called-upon unit of time equal to precisely fourteen minutes and twenty-four seconds.

As units of measurement go, the *centiday* is arguably not among the most useful – but compared to some of the units that lie elsewhere in the dictionary, it seems entirely reasonable:

- *barn* (n.) as barn doors are proverbially sizeable, researchers working on the Manhattan Project in the 1940s coined this term to refer to the relatively large (but still extraordinarily tiny) cross-section of a uranium nucleus: 0.000000000000000000000001 square centimetres
- *beard-second* (n.) based on the same template as *light-year*, one *beard-second* is the approximate length a man's beard hair grows in one second: 5 nanometres
- *microfortnight* (n.) equal to 1.2 seconds (1,000,000th of a fortnight), *microfortnight* is a unit taken from the so-called Furlong–Firkin–Fortnight system of weights and measures, devised for no reason other than to illustrate how impractical non-decimal systems can be
- *swath* (n.) one *swath* is a measure of farmland equal to the breadth of one sweep of a thresher's scythe; although the term has been in use since medieval times its precise size has never been standardised, although most definitions place it somewhere around 8 square feet

(For one more ridiculously precise measurement, flick ahead to 4 October and the story behind the *smoot* . . .)

copesmate *(n.)*   an adversary; a partner or colleague in power, an associate

As well as meaning 'to deal with' or 'to manage', *cope* can also be used to mean 'to strike' or 'to come to blows', an ancient and seldom-used form of the word that derives from the French *couper*, meaning 'to hit' or 'to cut'. Add to that the same *mate* used in chess, and you'll have a word that originally meant an adversary when it first appeared in the English language in the mid 1500s.

Before long, however, that meaning had begun to change. By the seventeenth century, *copemate* or *copesmate* (an 'S' added via influence from words like *craftsman* and *tradesman*) was being used to refer to anyone with whom you have an association or partnership, and in particular a colleague or companion with whom you share power. As the word continued to develop, lovers and paramours, partners in marriage, accomplices in plots and scams, and even two people who merely share the same job could all be *copesmates*, as could any two bonded or co-dependent things:

> Misshapen Time, copesmate of ugly Night
> > William Shakespeare,
> > *The Rape of Lucrece* (1594)

A true pair of *copesmates* – partners in power as well as husband and wife – were crowned joint King and Queen of England, Scotland and Ireland on 11 April 1689. William III and Mary II had swept to power the previous year in the Glorious Revolution that had deposed James II and firmly established William, the Dutch Prince of Orange's claim to the throne. At the couple's request, they ruled equally until Mary's death five years later. William then continued his reign alone until his death in 1702.

circumbilivagination *(n.)*   a circular motion,
a movement around

To *circumbilivaginate* is to circle or move around something, or, more figuratively, to speak in a roundabout way. It was in this figurative sense that the word was first used (and likely coined) by the French Renaissance writer François Rabelais in the early 1500s, and through translations of his work *circumbilivagination* – the act of *circumbilivaginating* – began to appear in early English dictionaries in the seventeenth century. As the English lexicographer Randle Cotgrave defined it in his *Dictionarie of the French and English Tongues* (1611), a *circumbilivagination* is a 'circular motion; going around, wheeling about'.

One of the most famous *circumbilivaginating* journeys took place on 12 April 1961. The cosmonaut Yuri Gagarin, aboard Soviet spacecraft *Vostok 1*, took off from Baikonur Cosmodrome in Kazakhstan at a little after 6 o'clock in the morning. By 6.17 he had reached orbital height, skimming the earth's upper atmosphere at more than 100 miles, and as the flight continued *Vostok 1* headed across Siberia, down across the Pacific Ocean and past the southern tip of South America to the Atlantic Ocean and back across Africa, Turkey and the Caucasus Mountains. Gagarin then returned to an altitude from which he was able to parachute safely to the ground.

Despite having encircled the globe, he landed just under two hours after lift-off – becoming the first human being in space, and completing the first manned orbit of the earth.

pugnozzle *(v.)*   to move the nose and lips like a
pug dog

The Nobel Prize-winning playwright, poet and novelist Samuel Beckett was born in Foxrock in Dublin, Ireland, on 13 April 1906. Through works like *Molloy* (1951) and *Waiting for Godot* (1953), Beckett established himself as one of the most influential modernist writers of the twentieth century. His linguistic creativity led to the invention of a host of peculiar words:

- *athambia* (n.) Beckett rescued this Greek term for imperturbability or unflappability from obscurity and included it in a speech in *Waiting for Godot*
- *panpygoptosis* (n.) strung together from Greek elements meaning 'all' (*pan*), 'rump' (*pygo*), 'sight' (*opto*) and 'condition' (*osis*), Beckett coined the term *panpygoptosis* in his novel *Murphy* to mean 'the condition of having short legs'
- *plutolater* (n.) derived from the same root as words like *plutocrat* and *idolater*, a *plutolater* is someone who worships wealth
- *vermigrade* (adj.) moving in a worm-like manner, a term Beckett coined in 1938
- *wantum* (n.) a blend of *want* and *quantum*, Beckett used *wantum* to mean 'a quantifiable deficiency or desire'

Of all of Beckett's motley contributions to the language, perhaps the strangest is *pugnozzle*. In his 1934 anthology of short stories, *More Pricks Than Kicks*, Beckett described the 'wretched little wet rag of an upper lip' on a pug dog 'pugnozzling up and back, in what you might call a kind of a duck or a cobra sneer to the nostrils'. To *pugnozzle*, ultimately, is to snort or move the nose and mouth like a pug.

bucklebuster *(n.)*   a line in a play that elicits a laugh from an audience

On 14 April 1865, Abraham Lincoln was shot in Washington DC; he died the following day, becoming the third US president to die in office, and the first to be assassinated. But despite this being such an infamous date in history, today's word is *bucklebuster* – a term from vaudeville slang for the punchline at the end of a gag or anecdote. So what's the connection?

Famously, President Lincoln was attending a performance of *Our American Cousin* in Ford's Theatre on the night that he was killed by an actor named John Wilkes Booth. Booth had become embroiled in a conspiracy to revive the Confederate cause in the closing months of the Civil War, and so, while his co-conspirators were elsewhere in Washington (two had been assigned to kill the Secretary of State, another to kill the vice president), Booth was tasked with assassinating the president.

Less well known, however, is the plan Booth formulated. Having found his way into the president's box, he waited for a line in the play he knew elicited a belly-laugh from the audience: on stage, actor Harry Hawk delivered the *bucklebuster*, 'Don't know the manners of good society, eh? Well, I guess I know enough to turn you inside out, old gal; you sockdologizing old man-trap!' As gales of laughter erupted from the auditorium, Booth took his chance and shot a single bullet, hitting the president in the back of the head. He then vaulted down on to the stage and fled.

President Lincoln died the following morning. Booth, meanwhile, escaped the theatre on horseback, but was tracked to a remote farmhouse in Virginia and killed twelve days later. Four of his co-conspirators were hanged the following July.

naufragous *(adj.)*   causing a shipwreck

Whereas a *naufrague* is a shipwrecked person (turn back to 2 February for more on that), something that is *naufragous* causes a shipwreck. To *naufragiate*, likewise, is to cause a shipwreck, while something that is *naufrageous* is in a dangerous or precarious position, or in a state of total ruin or destruction.

All these words date from the early seventeenth century and have at their root the Latin word for a shipwreck, *naufragium*, which itself combines the Latin for 'ship', *navis* (as in *navy*, *navigate* and the hull-shaped *nave* of a church), with the same Latin verb meaning 'to break' as in words like *fragment* and *fedifragous* (turn back to 2 January for that one). Any one of these words could also apply to today's date, as it was early on the morning of 15 April 1912 that RMS *Titanic* foundered and sank in the mid Atlantic Ocean, having been struck by an iceberg late the previous evening.

The *Titanic* had left Southampton on 10 April, and had stopped in Cherbourg and Queenstown (now Cobh, in southern Ireland) before setting sail for New York. She was four days into her maiden voyage when she hit an iceberg roughly 370 miles from Newfoundland at 11.40 p.m. on 14 April.

The iceberg collided with the *Titanic*'s starboard side, shattering the hull and bursting six of the ship's sixteen watertight holds. At 2.20 a.m. the following morning, what remained of the ship above the water buckled and broke in half – with over 1,000 people still on board – and sank into the ocean. Of the 2,200 passengers and crew on board, barely 700 survived.

tête-bêche *(n.)*   a pair of stamps wrongly printed with one upside down relative to the other

On 16 April 1900, the US Post Office released its first ever book of stamps, selling books of 2-cent stamps in sets of twelve, twenty-four or forty-eight.

Stamp collecting has been known as *philately* since 1864, when a French stamp enthusiast named Georges Herpin coined the word from a combination of two Greek roots meaning 'fondness' or 'attraction', *phil*–, and, bizarrely, 'exemption from tax', *ateleia*. That second root was the closest classical equivalent Herpin could find to the concept of the postage stamp as it was in the mid nineteenth century: previously, the cost of posting a letter was borne by the recipient, but by attaching a postage stamp to the envelope this cost could be paid in advance by the sender, and hence the letter was effectively exempt from postage 'tax' from the recipient's point of view.

Besides the word *philately* itself having a colourful etymology, stamp collectors have amassed a surprisingly detailed vocabulary all their own, with several unique philatelic terms having found their way into the dictionary. *Burelage*, for instance, is a fine network of lines or crosshatchings imprinted into the background of the design on a stamp to prevent counterfeiting. *Deltiology* is the specific collecting of postcards, derived from a Greek word for a writing tablet. *Indicia* are postage marks or printing labels other than postage stamps, such as airmail or bulk mail stamps and tags. And a *tête-bêche* – literally a 'head-to-tail' – is a pair of stamps in which one has been accidentally printed upside down relative to the other; rare *tête bêche* pairs are considered collector's items to many enthusiastic philatelists.

Pisgah *(n.)*   a view or glimpse of something
ultimately unobtainable or unreachable

According to the Old Testament, *Pisgah* – a Hebrew word meaning 'peak' or 'height' – was the name given to the mountaintop
from which Moses was granted a view of the Promised Land:

> Moses went up from the plains of Moab . . . to the top of
> Pisgah . . . And the Lord said unto him, This is the land
> which I sware unto Abraham, unto Isaac, and unto Jacob,
> saying, I will give it unto thy seed: I have caused thee to
> see it with thine eyes, but thou shalt not go over thither.
>
> Deut. 31:1–4

Because Moses was permitted to see the Promised Land but not
go there, the name *Pisgah* – or more specifically, a *Pisgah view*
– has been used allusively since the mid seventeenth century to
refer to a tantalising view of something ultimately unobtainable.
A *Pisgah Hill*, likewise, is a point from which some currently
unattainable future situation can be glimpsed.

A prime example of a *Pisgah view* took place in April 1970.
Two days after take-off, an oxygen tank on the *Apollo 13* spacecraft exploded, causing an array of technical problems that
affected the craft's power and air supplies. Makeshift repairs
salvaged the operation and the crew returned to earth on
17 April 1970. The closest *Apollo 13* ever came to the moon was
a distance of 137 miles – close enough to take tantalising photographs of the lunar surface – but by then the state of the craft
made landing an impossibility. Nevertheless, *Apollo 13* uniquely
skirted the far side of the moon during its flight, reaching a
point almost 250,000 miles from the earth – further than any
other manned spacecraft has ever reached.

terremotive *(adj.)*   seismic; as powerful as an earthquake

At 5.12 a.m. on 18 April 1906, the city of San Francisco was struck by an immense earthquake that remains one of the United States' most devastating natural disasters.

A vast stretch of the California coastline was affected by the quake, but it was San Francisco – by then a major West Coast trade port – that bore the brunt of the damage. The quake brought down buildings and tore up roads, and in its aftermath fires raged through what little of the city remained standing. In all, four-fifths of San Francisco was destroyed, while 250,000 people were left homeless and at least 3,000 were killed. Although the quake pre-dated the development of the Richter scale now used to measure the force of earthquakes, the 1906 quake is estimated to have had an intensity of 7.8 – powerful enough, unbelievably, to move the mouth of the nearby River Salinas six miles further south.

Something that has the same power or intensity as an earthquake, either literally or figuratively, can be described as *terremotive*, a nineteenth-century adjective introduced by the English scientist and theologian William Whewell in 1837. Writing in his *History of the Inductive Sciences*, Whewell described the 'frequent sympathy of volcanic and terremotive action in remote districts of the earth's surface', which suggested to him and others before him that the two natural phenomena were related; it would be several decades before the science of plate tectonics would be devised and accepted as the cause of both.

principiate *(v.)*   to cause to begin, to set in motion

To *principiate* something is to instigate it or set it in motion. First used in English in the seventeenth century, the word comes from the Latin *principium*, meaning 'beginning' or 'origin', which in turn is descended from the Latin *princeps*, meaning 'first' or 'foremost'. *Principiate* is ultimately a none-too-distant cousin of more familiar words like *principle* and *principal*, as well as *prince* – a title that literally refers to the firstborn son of a king, and ultimately the first person in line to succeed him.

One of history's most significant events was *principiated* on 19 April 1775, with what the poet Ralph Waldo Emerson would later refer to as 'the shot heard round the world':

> By the rude bridge that arched the flood,
> Their flag to April's breeze unfurled,
> Here once the embattled farmers stood,
> And fired the shot heard round the world.
>
> Concord Hymn (1837)

Emerson's poem famously refers to the very first gunshot of the American Revolutionary War.

Amid escalating tensions between the British and Colonial factions, at around 5 o'clock on the morning of 19 April several hundred British troops marched into Lexington, Massachusetts, and were met by seventy-seven armed Colonial minutemen assembled on the town common. Major John Pitcairn, head of the British troops in the area, is believed to have ordered the Patriot soldiers to disperse, which after a moment's hesitation they willingly did. Suddenly, a shot fired from an unknown gun rang out across the common, sparking the brief but momentous Battle of Lexington: the American Revolution had begun.

murdermonger *(n.)*   a writer of murder stories

Seldom encountered as a word in its own right in English today, *monger* derives from an Old English word for a trader, seller or pedlar of goods. In that sense, it survives almost nowhere else in the language today except for in the compound names of various traditional jobs and trades – like *fishmonger*, *ironmonger* and *costermonger* (literally an 'apple-seller', or 'seller of costards') – as well as in a looser sense in words like *warmonger*, *scaremonger* and *gossipmonger*, referring to people who provoke, incite or publicise.

In the sense of a pedlar or dealer of gruesome crime stories, the word *murdermonger* was coined in the late eighteenth century to refer to a writer of murder mysteries. By the turn of the twentieth century, however, that meaning had changed: although still infrequently used, the term *murdermonger* now typically applies to someone who incites, commits or deals professionally in murderous actions.

Of these two meanings, happily it is the first that links this word to today, as Edgar Allan Poe's 'The Murders in the Rue Morgue' was published for the first time on 20 April 1841. The tale of a French gentleman, C. Auguste Dupin, who becomes embroiled in the brutal murder of two young women in a Parisian apartment, Poe's 'Rue Morgue' is now widely recognised as the first modern detective story in English literature.

miscounsel *(n.)*   bad advice

Charlotte Brontë was born on 21 April 1816. Although best known today as a novelist, Charlotte – like her sisters – began her literary career writing poetry, and in 1836 sent some of her work to the poet laureate, Robert Southey. His reply arrived three months later:

> The daydreams in which you habitually indulge are likely to induce a distempered state of mind . . . Literature cannot be the business of a woman's life, and it ought not to be. The more she is engaged in her proper duties, the less leisure she will have for it, even as an accomplishment and a recreation. To those duties you have not yet been called, and when you are you will be less eager for celebrity.

Happily, Charlotte ignored his advice. The Brontë sisters self-published a collection of their poetry in 1846, while Charlotte went on to write the novels *Jane Eyre* (1847), *Shirley* (1849) and *Villette* (1853).

An instance of bad advice can be known as *miscounsel*, a word dating back to the late fifteenth century. Originally borrowed from French, *counsel* has been used to mean 'deliberation' or 'consultation' since the Middle English period, but it didn't take long for that meaning to broaden. By the end of the fourteenth century, *counsel* was being variously applied to someone who gave advice or information (particularly on legal matters), a confidential matter or secret, and a personal opinion or ulterior motive. The first *counsellors* arrived around the same time, before the first legal counsellors emerged in the mid 1500s – and the first psychiatric *counsellors* in the mid twentieth century.

solastalgia *(n.)*   mental distress or nostalgia sparked by environmental change

Earth Day is on 22 April, an annual event founded in 1970 to raise awareness of the pressing environmental issues and ecological problems facing the planet.

Originally celebrated only in the United States, since the early 1990s Earth Day has been observed worldwide and is now celebrated annually in almost every country on the planet: the Paris Climate Accord, the result of the 2015 United Nations Climate Change Conference, was signed in New York City on Earth Day, 22 April 2016, by delegates from 175 countries.

Solastalgia is a word fully suited for a day on which the world's environmental concerns are given centre stage. Coined in 2003 by the Australian philosopher and academic Glenn Albrecht, it refers to a kind of mental or existential distress caused by environmental change.

Unsurprisingly, *solastalgia* is modelled on the more familiar term *nostalgia*, which is itself built from a combination of two Greek roots meaning 'homecoming' and 'pain' or 'anguish'. But while *nostalgia* refers to an often sentimental longing for home by someone who has since departed, *solastalgia* – which also derives from a Latin word for 'solace' or 'comfort', *solacium* – describes the unease or distress experienced by someone whose home has changed around them as a direct result of environmental change, like rising sea levels, desertification, or catastrophes like oil spills or pollution. Someone experiencing *solastalgia*, ultimately, need not have left their home in order to experience a longing for the past.

G. H. *(n., int.)*   old news

St George's Day, feast day of the patron saint of England, is on 23 April. The name *George* is derived from a Greek word literally meaning 'earth-worker', and despite appearances is an etymological cousin of a diverse set of words including *geology* and *geography*, *allergy* and *synergy*, *energy* and *ergonomics*.

Elsewhere in the dictionary, however, *George* has gained an array of often quite bizarre alternative meanings. A *yellow George* was a golden guinea minted during the reigns of George I, II and III. In US slang, a *George* can be either a 25-cent piece or a dollar bill, both of which bear a portrait of George Washington. A *George* is also a loaf of brown bread, a name derived from an old naval slang term, *brown George*, for the poor-quality bread doled out in military rations. And *let George do it!* is an old American expression meaning 'let someone else take the blame' – which, according to linguistic folklore, derives from Louis XII of France entrusting much of the day-to-day running of his country to his prime minister, Georges d'Amboise.

George Horne, or more snappily *G. H.*, is another George to have found his way into the dictionary, in this instance as a means of pointing out to someone that they're telling you old news. According to the *Dictionary of Slang, Jargon and Cant* (1889):

> These initial letters owe their origin to a certain Mr George Horne, a typographer, who was in the habit of retailing stale news. If a workman repeats a story already known, an intimation to hold his tongue is conveyed by uttering the ominous letters 'G. H.'

bibliothetic *(adj.)*   pertaining to the arrangement of
books in a library

Signed by President John Adams on 24 April 1800, the same
Act of Congress that transferred the American capital from
Philadelphia to Washington DC also set aside a sum of $5,000
'for the purchase of such books as may be necessary for the
use of Congress . . . and for fitting up a suitable apartment for
containing them'.

The library that Adams founded was originally a fairly humble affair, consisting of little more than a handful of maps and a
few hundred books – most of which were destroyed by fire during the war of 1812. Happily, three years later former president
Thomas Jefferson offered his personal library of 6,500 books to
Congress as a replacement, and from there America's Library
of Congress steadily grew to become what is now the world's
largest, housing a collection of some 23 million books and
160 million individual items.

The books in Jefferson's library (and ultimately those in the
first Congressional library) were organised using a complicated
system inspired by the philosopher Francis Bacon: titles were
arranged under vague headings considered the 'faculties of the
human mind', like memory, reason and imagination. It wasn't
until the late nineteenth century that the library adopted a more
straightforward subject-by-subject cataloguing system.

The arrangement of books in a library can be described
as *bibliothetic*, an adjective – combining Greek roots meaning
'book', *biblios*, and 'arrangement' or 'setting', *thesis* – introduced
to the language by an American librarian and scholar named
E. C. Richardson in 1901.

arsefoot *(n.)* a penguin; any squat, short-statured waterbird

Apparently even penguins deserve their time in the spotlight, and so 25 April is World Penguin Day. Unfortunately, penguins don't fare too well in the dictionary, where they're left with a fairly unflattering etymology and an even more unflattering nickname.

Etymologically, *penguin* is something of a mystery. One very plausible theory claims that the birds take their name from the Welsh *pen gwyn*, literally meaning 'white head': indeed, the earliest mention of the birds in English, from the logbook of Sir Francis Drake's *Golden Hind* (1577–80), refers specifically to 'the foul which the Welsh men name Pengwin'.

Unfortunately, Drake's logbook goes on to explain that the birds are also 'so fat that they can but go [to the sea] and their skins cannot be taken from their bodies without tearing off the flesh because of their exceeding fatness'. And it's that cumbersome corpulence that has led to an alternative derivation from the Latin word *pinguis*, literally meaning 'fatty' or 'greasy', being proposed.

But why call penguins *penguins* at all, when you can also call them *arsefeet*? In his seven-volume *History of the Earth and Animated Nature* (1774), the Irish writer and scholar Oliver Goldsmith described how penguins suffer from an 'awkward position of the legs, which so unqualifies them for living on land', but makes them perfectly adapted for a life in the water. 'Our sailors, for this reason,' he continued, 'give these birds the very homely, but expressive, name of *arse-feet*.'

ceraunite *(n.)*   a meteorite

Ceraunite is another word for a meteorite, a piece of rocky debris originating in outer space that smashes through the earth's atmosphere and, surviving intact, impacts on to the earth's surface. Originally, however, meteorites were believed to be a weather-related phenomenon, believed by some to be created by the tumultuous action of thunder and lightning; even some of the greatest minds in history, from Aristotle to Isaac Newton, refused to believe that rocks could indeed fall from outer space, and thought instead that meteorites must somehow have terrestrial or meteorological origins. Ultimately, the word *ceraunite* literally means 'thunder-stone'.

All that began to change at around 1 o'clock in the afternoon on 26 April 1803, when a shower of some 3,000 fragments of rock rained down on the town of L'Aigle, 80 miles west of Paris. When news broke of the bizarre phenomenon, the French Academy of Sciences dispatched a keen young scientist named Jean-Baptiste Biot to L'Aigle to investigate.

Biot's research was meticulous: he interviewed locals who had witnessed the shower first-hand, collected a total of 82 lbs of meteoritic rock from the surrounding fields and mapped out where every single fragment he discovered had landed. The passionate and comprehensive report he compiled proved a landmark in astronomical history: Biot's exhaustive work led him and his colleagues to conclude for the first time that the rocks that had fallen on L'Aigle – like all those that had fallen in meteor showers before – were without doubt of extra-terrestrial origin.

cosmogony *(n.)*   the creation of the universe

Derived from two Greek roots – *cosmos*, meaning 'world' or 'universe', and *gonos*, meaning 'creation' or 'production' – *cosmogony* is a term used either for the creation of the universe and all things in it, or else a treatise written to explain the universe's origins.

Cosmos itself, of course, remains in use in English today to refer to the entirety of the universe, whereas *gonos* is found only in a handful of fairly obscure words like *zoogony* ('the development of animals'), *theogeny* ('the birth of gods') and *hippogony* (a nineteenth-century word for the pedigree of a horse).

Cosmogony, meanwhile, was coined in the late seventeenth century – not long after a curious theory was put forward by the German astronomer Johannes Kepler.

Kepler was an assistant to the Danish astronomer Tycho Brahe and a contemporary of Galileo, who inspired him to invest in (and ultimately improve the design of) a refracting telescope. His work helped to reinforce the theory that the sun, not the earth, lay at the centre of the solar system, and advanced the idea that the planets move, at varying speed, around elliptical rather than circular orbits.

But it was with the publication of his *Harmonices Mundi*, 'The Harmony of the World', in 1619 that Kepler advanced perhaps his most bizarre theory: the universe, he had calculated, had come into existence on 27 April 4977 BC. We now know Kepler to have been somewhere in the region of 13.7 billion years out with this estimate, but his contribution to our understanding of the world around us – at a time when the widespread understanding was still hopelessly misguided – is nevertheless remarkable.

mutine *(adj.)*   rebellious, threatening mutiny

Mutiny derives from an Old French word, *meute*, meaning a riot or uprising – or, because of their bloodthirsty volatility, a pack of hunting hounds. Derived from the same root is the long-forgotten word *mutine*, which first emerged in English in the mid 1500s as a noun, meaning a mutiny or uprising; a verb, meaning 'to revolt'; and later an adjective, describing any turbulent situation likened to a mutiny, or anyone or anything that is rebellious or mutinous.

All those meanings are appropriate today, as on 28 April 1789, the crew of HMS *Bounty* erupted into a mutiny led by the shipmaster's mate, Fletcher Christian.

The *Bounty* had left England under the command of Captain William Bligh one and a half years earlier, on a trip to collect breadfruit from Tahiti. The ship arrived in the autumn of 1788 and remained there for five months, but the lengthy layover ultimately proved detrimental to discipline and after three weeks back at sea Christian and twenty-five fellow crew-members revolted. Along with eighteen other crewmembers, Bligh was cast adrift in a 23-foot rowing boat in the middle of the Pacific – but what should have proved a death sentence was nothing of the sort.

Through expert seamanship, Bligh and his crew managed to reach Timor, some 4,000 miles west, and from there returned safely to England. As for the mutinous crew of the *Bounty*, several were captured on Tahiti and hanged, while Christian went on to establish a new community in the uninhabited Pitcairn Islands along with nine mutineers. Infighting and suspicion quickly consumed the group, however, and Christian was reportedly shot and killed in 1793.

apodeictic *(adj.)*   demonstrated to be
incontrovertibly true

Apodeixis is absolute proof, while so-called *apodeictic* state-ments are those that are unquestionably and demonstrably true. Both derive from a Greek word essentially meaning 'capable of demonstration', and were first adopted into English in the seventeenth century in discussions of Aristotelian logic. In more general use, however, they refer to statements of fact established with indisputable evidence – a memorable example of which occurred on 29 April 1974.

It was on this day that President Richard Nixon announced the release of the Watergate tapes – a total of forty-six tape recordings of conversations between him and members of his administration dating back almost three years. The White House had initially tried to suppress the release of the tapes in the aftermath of the Watergate affair, when five members of Nixon's Committee to Re-Elect the President (appropriately known as CREEP) were caught breaking into the Democrat Party headquarters in the Watergate building, Washington DC. But a unanimous Supreme Court ruling and growing public pressure forced the president's hand: 1,200 pages of transcribed conversations were made public the following day, with copies of the tapes following shortly after.

On one of the tapes, the president can be heard arranging to call on the FBI to cease its investigation of the break-in just six days after it occurred – incontrovertible proof that he had essentially entered into a criminal conspiracy tantamount to obstruction of justice. Nixon's presidency never recovered from the discovery of this 'smoking gun' and, faced with the prospect of an impeachment trial, he resigned from office the following August.

paragrandine *(n.)*   a device for protection against hail

We might be more used to using them to protect us from the rain, but an *umbrella* was originally a parasol: borrowed into English from Italian in the early 1600s, *umbrella* derives from the Latin for 'shade' or 'shadow', *umbra*. But scorching heat and driving rain aren't the worst that the weather can throw at us – so for protection against hailstorms, you'll need a *paragrandine*.

First used in English in the nineteenth century, *paragrandine* derives from the Latin word for 'hailstone', *grando*. Added to that is the prefix *para–* (a derivative of the Latin *parare*, 'to prepare'), which is used in English to form words bearing some sense of protection or defence. That makes a *parasol* literally a 'sun-protector'; a *parachute* a 'protector against a fall'; and a castle's *parapet* a 'breast-guard', so called because it covers the chest of anyone standing behind it.

If ever a *paragrandine* were to be useful, it would have been on 30 April 1888. At around midday, thick clouds gathered above the town of Moradabad, India, that were so dense it reportedly made the daytime as dark as the night. Then, without warning, hailstones the size of oranges began to rain down on the town in astonishing numbers: reports claim that in some places, the hail accumulated into piles 2 feet high. More than 200 people, and over 1,000 livestock, lost their lives in what is perhaps the most devastating hailstorm in history.

tandle *(n.)*   a bonfire

Beltane Day is an ancient Celtic festival still observed in parts of
Scotland and Ireland, most commonly on 1 May, to mark the
start of the summer. Historically, Beltane was the date on which
cattle would be driven out to summer pasture, but according
to ancient folklore they would first be made to walk between
two ritual bonfires that were supposed to safeguard the livestock
from disease and ensure that they remained protected for the
following season.

The origins of this festival are largely shrouded in mystery
– even the origin of the name *Beltane* itself is unsolved. One
theory suggests that it might have its roots in the name of some
ancient Irish deity, but it is more likely that it can be traced back
to an ancient word root meaning 'blazing hot' or 'bright fire', a
reference to the pair of bonfires that lit the animals' departure.

Celebratory or ritual bonfires like these can also be known
as *tandles* or *taunels*:

> Any large fire made out of doors is so designated. It is
> often an amusement to boys in rural districts to go out
> into the fields and collect the cuttings of hedges, dried
> grass, &c. into a heap, for the purpose of making a taunel.
> Great is their delight, when, having struck a match, and
> 'kennelt' [kindled] their fire, the flames begin to rise.
> *Notes & Queries*, 1868

Tandle is old English and Scots dialect term thought to have
its origins in *tandr*, an Old Norse word for a fire. In English,
tandle has been traced back to the eighteenth century in print,
but as with most dialect speech was probably in use locally far
earlier than that date might suggest.

cryptobiont *(n.)* an animal that lives out of sight, or in a concealed or hidden habitat

On 2 May 1933, the *Inverness Courier* ran a story about a local couple who had reportedly seen 'an enormous animal rolling and plunging on the surface' of Loch Ness. Although reports of a monster inhabiting the hidden depths of Loch Ness date back as far as the sixth century, the 1933 account soon sparked a flurry of renewed interest in the phenomenon, and before long reports were coming in with surprising frequency. The Loch Ness Monster has remained one of the world's most famous *cryptobionts* ever since.

The Greek word *kryptos*, meaning 'hidden' or 'secret', is the origin of a number of English words like *cryptography* ('the writing of coded language'), *cryptogram* ('an enciphered text or coded symbol') and *krypton*, so named by its discoverers because it remained so difficult to trace for so long. Elsewhere in the dictionary, *cryptolalia* is the use of obscure language, or a language indecipherable to outsiders. *Cryptomnesia* is that recollection of a long-forgotten memory mistakenly interpreted as a new thought or experience. A *cryptonym* is a code name, or a pseudonym used for clandestine purposes. And a *cryptobiont* is an animal that lives wholly out of sight.

As an ecological term, *cryptobiont* dates from the mid twentieth century and is typically used of creatures that inhabit caves, cavities, holes or concealed lairs, and so remain largely unseen to the outside world – which could also include the creatures studied in *cryptozoology*, the study of creatures not proven to exist.

transnate *(v.)*   to swim across something

The Latin word for 'swim', *natare*, crops up in a handful of suitably aquatic words in the dictionary:

- *circumnatant* (adj.) swimming around
- *enatant* (adj.) floating up to the surface
- *innatable* (adj.) unswimmable, unsuitable or unable to be swum in
- *natatile* (adj.) able to swim
- *supernatant* (adj.) floating on the surface of a liquid

The act of swimming, meanwhile, is properly called *natation*, while water that cannot be swum across is *intransnatable*. And residing somewhere between those two is the word *transnate*, a seventeenth-century word meaning 'to swim across'.

On 3 May 1810 the English poet Lord Byron completed his famous swim across the Hellespont, the 4-mile stretch of water separating the European side of Turkey from the Asian side, Anatolia. He had decided to attempt the crossing in emulation of Leander, the legendary character from Greek myth who supposedly swam the Hellespont every night to meet with his lover, Hero. Byron was twenty-two years old at the time and not yet famous for his poetry (nor, for that matter, his licentiousness) but he later immortalised his experience in a poem, 'Written After Swimming from Sestos to Abydos':

> For me, degenerate modern wretch,
> Though in the genial month of May,
> My dripping limbs I faintly stretch,
> And think I've done a feat today.

paronomasia *(n.)*   wordplay based on words that sound alike

Albeit somewhat unofficially, 4 May is *Star Wars* Day. Not because George Lucas's sci-fi epic *Star Wars* was released on that date (it was actually released on 25 May 1977). Nor because it was set, filmed or completed on that date. Instead, 4 May is *Star Wars* Day because 'May the fourth' sounds remarkably similar to 'may the force be with you', one of the franchise's most memorable lines.

This kind of play on words is properly known as *paronomasia*, a term from rhetoric that refers to a joke or witticism built around two or more words that sound alike. But like a lot of terms from rhetoric, there are many different types and subtypes of *paronomasia*. *Agnomination*, for instance, is a sound-alike wordplay focused on two neighbouring or consecutive words, while punningly reusing the same word twice in two different forms (like 'the punner has become the punee') is called *polyptoton*.

Also like the majority of rhetorical terms, *paronomasia* is constructed from Greek word roots. The first half, *para*, is a Greek word meaning 'beside', or 'by the side of', which also crops up in words like *paranormal*, *paragraph* and *parasite* (and which is different from the *para–* of the *paragrandine* we encountered on 30 April). The second half derives from the Greek *onomasia*, which literally means 'naming', and which crops up in fairly esoteric terms like *onomasticon* ('a list of names'), *onomastics* ('the study of place names and proper nouns') and *onomasiology* ('the branch of linguistics dealing with names and naming').

dactylogram *(n.)*   a fingerprint

On 5 May 1905, brothers Alfred and Albert Stratton were found guilty of murder at the Old Bailey in London and sentenced to be hanged. The crime the brothers had committed was violent but in itself no different from many others like it: on the evening of 27 March, they had forced their way into a shop in Deptford, south-east London, and bludgeoned to death both the shop's seventy-one-year-old owner, John Farrow, and his wife Ann, before making off with £13 cash from the till. What was unusual, however, was how the brothers' guilt had been proven.

One of the brothers had left a right-hand thumbprint on the underside of the cash box. Following police interviews with locals living in the Farrows' neighbourhood, the Stratton brothers were flagged as possible suspects, and after samples of their fingerprints were matched with those on the box, a conviction was all but guaranteed. In 1902 the newly formed Scotland Yard Fingerprint Bureau had successfully convicted a burglar, Harry Jackson, using fingerprint evidence, but the Stratton case marked the first time in British legal history that a fingerprint had secured a conviction for murder.

According to *The American Illustrated Medical Dictionary* (1913), a fingerprint taken for the purposes of identification is called a *dactylogram*, a word derived from Greek roots literally meaning 'finger-letter'. The science of comparing fingerprints, incidentally, is called *dermatoglyphics* – which, at fifteen letters, is also one of the longest English words with no repeated letters.

whipmegmorum *(n.)*   a noisy quarrel about politics

When the Fixed-term Parliaments Act was passed in 2011, legislation was introduced that stated general elections in the UK must be held every five years on the first Thursday in May. The act was introduced by David Cameron's Conservative–Liberal Democrat coalition government, which was formed as a result of the election held on 6 May 2010.

Suitable for a day (or, as the case may be, a week) on which political wrangling will take centre stage every half-decade, a *whipmegmorum* is a noisy quarrel about politics.

Whipmegmorum is a Scots dialect word dating from the mid seventeenth century that is thought to have begun as the name of a Scottish folk dance or folk tune; etymologically, its fairly fanciful spelling might well put it in the same category as the likes of *hey-nonny-nonny* and *fol-de-rol-de-rol* as little more than a nonsense string of filler syllables used as the refrain of a song. In that context, the earliest record of a *whipmegmorum* comes from an old Scots broadside, 'The Life and Death of the Piper of Kilbarchan, or The Epitaph of Habbie Simpson', written in the mid 1600s:

> So well's he keeped his decorum,
> And all the steps of Whip-meg-morum,
> He slew a man and wae's me for him,
> And bare the feed [put up with the fiend].

That song didn't have much of a political or satirical angle at the time, but around a century later its refrain gained one thanks to a (we can presume deliberate) confusion with the name of the ruling British Whig Party. Ultimately, *whipmegmorum* or *whigmigmorum* punningly came to refer to what the *Scottish National Dictionary* calls 'a noisy altercation or dispute, especially about politics'.

dedititious *(adj.)*   surrendering, yielding to another

Early on the morning of 7 May 1945, the chief of staff of the German Armed Forces High Command, General Alfred Jodl, signed the German Instrument of Surrender – the document securing the unconditional surrender of all German forces, thus ending the European side of the Second World War after six years' fighting. A tentative ceasefire began the following day, and hostilities officially ended one minute after midnight on 9 May.

The act of yielding or surrendering has also been known as *dedition* since the fifteenth century, while an act or person who is *dedititious* concedes or capitulates to another. Both of those words derive ultimately from the Latin *dedere*, meaning 'to surrender' or 'to hand over' – but as that extra syllable in the middle of *dedititious* suggests, there's one more piece to the puzzle.

The Latin verb *dedere* in turn produced an adjective, *dediticius*. It literally meant 'surrendered' or 'capitulated', but was also used as a noun in Latin to mean a prisoner of war, a foreign soldier or army who had offered an unconditional surrender, or else a freed slave who, due to some misdemeanour committed during their confinement, was not granted full citizenship on their release (an unfortunate figure known as a *deditician*). It's from *dediticius* that the English adjective *dedititious* ultimately developed and, along the way, gained its extra middle syllable.

Shadrach *(n.)* someone close to a source of heat

On 8 May 1902, Mount Pelée, a volcano on the Caribbean Island of Martinique, erupted with astonishing violence. As the upper side of the mountain ruptured, two dense clouds of ash, steam and volcanic gas – reaching more than 1,000°C – were thrown across the island. The capital, Saint-Pierre, bore the brunt of the eruption: the city was completely destroyed, and almost its entire population, perhaps as many as 40,000 people, were killed. But one man had a particularly lucky escape.

Ludger Sylbaris, a travelling performer with the Barnum & Bailey circus, had been arrested the previous night after a bar brawl and placed in solitary confinement in the Saint-Pierre jail. His cell, ironically, was the most sheltered building in the city: partly sunk into the ground, it had no windows but was ventilated from an opening facing away from the volcano, saving Sylbaris from the eruption the next day.

Someone who stands close to a source of heat but seems to be unaffected by it is a *Shadrach*, a term alluding to a story in the Old Testament in which King Nebuchadnezzar commanded that three men – Shadrach, Meshach and Abednego – be thrown into a 'fiery furnace' for refusing to worship a golden idol:

> Nebuchadnezzar came near to the mouth of the burning fiery furnace . . . and said, Shadrach, Meshach, and Abednego . . . come hither. Then [they] came forth of the midst of the fire. And the princes, governors, and captains . . . saw these men, upon whose bodies the fire had no power, nor was an hair of their head singed, neither were their coats changed, nor the smell of fire had passed on them.
>
> Daniel 3:26–7

mainour *(n.)*   a stolen object found in a thief's
                      possession when they are caught

On 9 May 1671, Thomas Blood – better known as 'Captain'
or 'Colonel' Blood – made an audacious attempt to steal the
Crown Jewels. Disguised as a parson, Blood had spent several
weeks befriending the newly appointed Master of the Jewel
House, Talbot Edwards, and arranged for a private viewing of
the jewels along with three accomplices whom he claimed were
his nephew and two friends. On entering the Jewel House, the
four men turned on Edwards, who was struck with a mallet,
bound and gagged. Somehow, however, the alarm was raised.

Amid the commotion that ensued, Blood used the mallet
to flatten St Edward's crown (the crown used in the coronation
ceremonies of British monarchs) and hid it under his surplice,
while another man stuffed the coronation orb down his trousers. Having made their escape, they were quickly apprehended
and in the struggle that followed the crown fell from Blood's
cloak. 'It was a gallant attempt,' he reportedly shouted as he was
arrested, 'however unsuccessful!'

Stolen property found in the possession of a thief when
they are apprehended is properly known as *mainour*, a French
loanword adopted into English in the fifteenth century that
derives from a corruption of *main oeuvre*, or literally 'handi-
work'. To be taken or found with *mainour*, ultimately, is to be
caught red-handed.

As for Blood, despite risking a potential charge of treason,
his crime was pardoned by none other than King Charles II
himself. Precisely why the king was so lenient remains a mystery
– although he is popularly said to have been overwhelmed by
the sheer audacity of Blood's crime.

orchestic *(adj.)* of or relating to dancing or a dance sequence

We might only associate orchestras with music today, but the word *orchestra* itself literally means 'a place for dancing'. Adopted into English from Latin, it has at its root the Greek verb *orkheisthai*, meaning 'to dance', as the original Ancient Greek *orkhestra* was a semi-circular space in front of a theatrical stage where the chorus would perform their songs and dances.

In Roman theatres, this space was reserved for senators and other dignitaries as it contained the seats closest to the stage. But over time the space came to be taken up by the various musicians accompanying the action on stage. And that change in meaning had apparently taken place by the time the word *orchestra* was adopted into English in the late sixteenth century:

> *Orchestra*. A theatre or scaffold whereon musitians, singers, and such like shew their cunning.
>
> Thomas Thomas, *Dictionarium linguae Latinae et Anglicanae* (1587)

The original choreographic meaning of *orchestra* survives intact in English in a handful of its (albeit fairly obscure) etymological cousins. *Orchestics*, for instance, is the art or theory of dancing. *Orchesography* is the use of diagrams or demonstrative symbols to notate dance steps. And the adjective *orchestic* is used to describe anything that resembles a dance, or else belongs to or is suitable for a theatrical dance sequence.

Any one of these words could be a pertinent choice for today, as it was on 10 May 1899 that the Hollywood dancer, singer, actor and choreographer Fred Astaire was born Frederick Austerlitz in Omaha, Nebraska.

twindle *(n.)*   a twin sibling

First recorded in English in the early 1500s, *twindle* is an old dialect word for a twin sibling. Apparently the word is little more than a diminutive of *twin* – and so could be literally interpreted as a 'little' or 'baby twin'.

Twins Chang and Eng Bunker were born on 11 May 1811 in Samut Songkhram, Thailand. At the time Thailand was still known as Siam, and as Chang and Eng were conjoined – linked by a strip of cartilage in their chest – the pair were the original *Siamese twins*. (Ironically, as both of their parents were half-Chinese, in their native Siam the Bunkers were known as the 'Chinese twins'.)

In 1829, the Bunkers agreed to tour the world with a Scottish merchant named Robert Hunter, who saw potential in exhibiting them as a curiosity. When their contract ended in 1839, they left showbusiness and settled in America, where they married two sisters, Adelaide and Sarah-Anne Yates, and had twenty-one children. (Initially, both couples lived together in rural North Carolina, but after the sisters fell out they moved into separate houses, with Chang and Eng spending three days alternating between the two.)

Financial difficulties forced the Bunkers to return to showbusiness after the Civil War, firstly exhibiting themselves in their own travelling exhibition and then accepting an invitation from showman P. T. Barnum to tour Europe in 1868. Chang – a heavy drinker, unlike his teetotal brother – suffered a devastating stroke in 1870 from which he never recovered, and on 11 January 1874, Eng woke to find his brother dead. With a cry of, 'Then I am going!' he asked for his brother's body to be placed in his arms. Three hours later, he too died.

word-grubber *(n.)* someone who uses obscure
or difficult words in everyday
conversation

The lexicographer and antiquarian Francis Grose died on
12 May 1791. Born in London in 1731, Grose originally sought
a career in the army, but when the militia he was enrolled with
disbanded in 1762 he turned his attention to draughtsmanship,
and began to exhibit drawings he had made of medieval ruins
in galleries across the capital. In 1772, he collected his artworks
in a book, *The Antiquities of England and Wales*, which was
quickly expanded into a four-volume series. In the 1780s, Grose
branched out into writing dictionaries, and published the first
edition of his most famous work – *A Classical Dictionary of the
Vulgar Tongue* – in 1785.

Focusing on slang, colloquialisms and thieves' cant, Grose's
dictionary included a great many informal (and often fairly
bawdy) terms that were overlooked by the more scholarly dictionaries of the time – often for good reason. A *thorough cough*,
for instance, Grose defined as 'coughing and breaking wind
backwards at the same time'. A *fire ship* is 'a wench who has the
venereal disease'. An *admiral of the narrow seas* is 'one who from
drunkenness vomits into the lap of the person sitting opposite
to him', while his friend, the *vice admiral of the narrow seas*, is 'a
drunken man that pisses under the table into his companions'
shoes'.

Not all of Grose's words were quite so unpleasant, however, and some would remain useful if revived today: given a
vocabulary as rich as Grose's, it might be worth remembering
that *word-grubbers* are, in Grose's terms, 'persons who use hard
words in common discourse'.

rag-manners *(n.)* bad manners

If you're *rag-mannered*, then you're uncouth or unmannerly, while *rag-manners* is a seventeenth-century word for bad manners or rude behaviour.

It was on this day that – apparently incensed by the *rag-manners* of his dining companions – one of the most famous figures in European history invented one of the most familiar pieces of culinary equipment.

By the mid 1630s, Cardinal Richelieu had risen to substantial power both in the French government and the Catholic Church. Consecrated as a bishop in 1607, he was raised to cardinal in 1622, and having been appointed Foreign Secretary in 1616 became Louis XIII's chief minister in 1624. He used his considerable influence to consolidate French royal power and champion French arts and culture; in 1635, he founded the Académie Française, the board responsible for conserving the purity of the French language. And according to legend at least, he used his sway within the French court to champion – if not to invent – the modern table knife.

At the time, dinner knives were typically sharpened to dagger-like points and were used to skewer rather than cut food. But having razor-sharp cutlery on the table not only marred royal banquets with the near constant threat of assassination, but gave Richelieu's fellow diners the perfect tool with which to pick their teeth after their meal. Keen to have neither a murder nor *rag-manners* at the dinner table, on 13 May 1637 Richelieu requested that the dinner knives in Louis XIII's collection be ground down and blunted at the tip – a design that, no doubt thanks to his high status at the time, soon caught on across France and beyond.

periegesis *(n.)* a geographical survey; a description of a place or account of a journey

A year after the United States completed the Louisiana Purchase with France – doubling the American territory with the purchase of land now covering fifteen US states – President Thomas Jefferson commissioned an expedition to explore this newly acquired land and find a practical route overland to the Pacific Ocean.

The expedition left St Louis, Missouri, on 14 May 1804 and sailed up the Missouri river through modern-day Kansas, Nebraska and South Dakota to reach North Dakota, where they stopped for the winter. The following year, they headed west through what is now Montana and Idaho, over the Rocky Mountains, and into Washington and Oregon, reaching the Pacific Ocean at the mouth of the Columbia river in November 1805.

Known originally as the Corps of Discovery Expedition, the exploration eventually came to be known by the names of the two friends and governors who commanded it: Captain Meriwether Lewis, Jefferson's former private secretary, and William Clark.

A geographical survey or an account of a trip or journey like the Lewis and Clark Expedition can be called a *periegesis* (pronounced 'perry-uh-*jee*-sis'). Built from Greek roots meaning 'around', *peri* (as in *perimeter* or *periphery*), and 'leading' or 'commanding', *hegesis* (an etymological cousin of *hegemony*), in its native Greek *periegesis* was used to refer to a guide or guide's description or account of a journey, and in that sense the word was first borrowed into English in the late 1500s.

deliquium *(n.)* a fainting, a swooning; a total eclipse

On 15 May 1836, the English astronomer Francis Baily travelled to the Scottish borders to observe a solar eclipse – during which he happened to glimpse a peculiar phenomenon that lasted only a few seconds, but was enough to pique his interest:

> A row of lucid points, like a string of bright beads irregular in size and distance from each other . . . suddenly formed round that part of the circumference of the moon that was about to enter on the sun's disc.

What he had observed became known as 'Baily's Beads', an extraordinary phenomenon caused by light from the sun shining through the rough craters and valleys on the lunar surface during an eclipse to create an irregular circle of glowing 'beads' around the moon. The phenomenon is now a well-documented and much anticipated aspect of solar eclipses worldwide.

The word *eclipse* was borrowed into English from French in the fourteenth century, but its roots lie in a Greek word meaning 'to fail to appear', or 'to leave one's usual place'. And it is the notion that an eclipse represents a 'failure' of the sun to shine that is mirrored by the word *deliquium*.

Literally meaning 'want' or 'failure' in Latin, the word *deliquium* was originally used to refer to a swoon or a loss of consciousness when it first appeared in English around the turn of the seventeenth century, but by the mid 1600s it was being used to refer to solar eclipses, with the English clergyman and Cambridge scholar John Spenser writing about a 'strange deliquium of light in the sun' as early as 1663. The word remained in use in this sense for another century, before largely falling out of use in English in all contexts towards the end of the nineteenth century.

premiation *(n.)* a prize-giving, the act of bestowing a reward

Premiation is a sixteenth-century word for a prize-giving or rewarding. To *premiate*, likewise, is to bestow or award a prize, while something that is *premiable* is deserving of just such a reward.

All of these derive ultimately from the same Latin root as *premium*, a word that literally meant 'prize', 'payment' or 'booty' and has at its root the Latin verb *emere*, meaning 'to buy' or 'to take'.

A word relating to the awarding of prizes is an appropriate one for today, as the first ever Academy Awards took place on 16 May 1929 in a ceremony presented by actor and film director Douglas Fairbanks at the Hollywood Roosevelt Hotel in Los Angeles. Understandably, there were a number of differences between these inaugural Academy Awards and the glitzy, worldwide spectacle that takes place today. For one, the 1929 ceremony was not broadcast in any way, and there were just 270 invited guests. The winners had already been announced in the press some three months earlier alongside the nominees. The awards honoured the best films of the previous two years, not just the past twelve months (*Wings*, a silent First World War drama and the first Best Picture winner, had been released in August 1927). And the prize-giving ceremony itself lasted a mere fifteen minutes, during which time a total of fourteen statuettes, including two honorary awards for Charlie Chaplin and Warner Brothers, were handed out.

It would, incidentally, be another five years before the Academy Awards themselves became known as the Oscars.

Slurvian *(n.)*   nonsense, incoherent speech

On 17 May 1965, a curious incident in the history of pop music finally came to a head when the FBI was forced to declare that the lyrics of The Kingsmen's 1963 hit single 'Louie Louie' were officially unintelligible.

'Louie Louie' was written in 1955 by an American singer-songwriter named Richard Berry, who recorded his own version of the song two years later. The song's lyrics (as they were on Berry's original version, at least) told of a sailor drowning his sorrows and professing to a barman named Louie his love for his sweetheart, who now lived far away. But in The Kingsmen's version – recorded in a single take barely a month before its release in a cramped studio in Portland, Oregon – the lyrics are so slurred that little of Berry's original storyline is decipherable. As a result, many listeners began to concoct their own notions of what the song was about, quickly leading to an urban myth that lead singer Jack Ely was singing about some very risqué subjects indeed.

Eventually, one concerned parent wrote to Robert Kennedy, Attorney General of the United States, claiming that the lyrics to the song were obscene, and the FBI was swiftly called in to investigate. Berry was interviewed, as well as The Kingsmen and their record company representatives, but after a full two years' investigation, the conclusion was made that the record was 'unintelligible at any speed'.

Unintelligible language, such as it is, can be known as *Slurvian*, a term originally coined in the 1940s to describe the characteristic slurring speech – '*tsamatta?*' '*fuggedaboudit!*' – of native New Yorkers.

volcanoism *(n.)*   volcanic activity or nature,
volcanicity; a seething or erupting
anger

The word *volcano* derives from the name of the Roman god of fire, flames and blacksmiths' furnaces, *Vulcan*, and in fact volcanoes were originally known as *Vulcans* before the word *volcano* was borrowed into English from Italian in the early seventeenth century. Volcanic activity, likewise, is often referred to as *vulcanicity* – but it can also be called *volcanoism*, a term coined in the mid nineteenth century that, on its first appearance in the language, was also used in a figurative sense to refer to a seething or erupting anger.

Those two meanings – volcanic activity and a slow-building rage – collide on this date: 18 May 1980 saw the devastating eruption of Mount St Helens in Washington State, USA, which claimed the lives of fifty-seven people and threw a cloud of volcanic ash as far afield as Minneapolis.

Seismic activity in the region had been building for two months prior to the eruption, creating an enormous swollen bulge on the northern side of the mountain that burst apart at 8.32 a.m. in a colossal 24-megaton blast. The resultant landslide sent almost a cubic mile of debris crashing down the mountainside, displacing all the water in the nearby Spirit Lake, while a gigantic ash cloud was sent high into the air, eventually growing large enough to be visible from space. More than 1,000 feet was blown from the top of the mountain (which went from 9,677 feet to 8,363 feet high), while hundreds of homes, miles of highway and railroad, thousands of animals and more than a million trees were destroyed. The disaster remains one of the largest, deadliest and costliest in modern American history.

spousebreach *(n.)* adultery

Despite first impressions (or what linguistic folklore might have you believe) *adultery* has nothing to do with being an *adult*. Instead, it has at its root the Latin word *alterere*, merely meaning 'to change' or 'to alter'. Being an *adult*, meanwhile, is related to being an *adolescent*: both derive from the Latin verb *adolescere*, 'to grow up', which in turn comes from the Latin *alescere*, meaning 'to nourish'.

But before the word *adultery* was borrowed into English from French in the fourteenth century, the voluntary violation of a marriage vow was known by the decidedly English name of *spousebreach*, a term first recorded in the late 1200s.

On 19 May 1536, Anne Boleyn – second wife of Henry VIII – was executed on a likely fabricated charge of adultery, added to which were equally groundless accusations of incest and conspiracy. Anne had suffered a miscarriage the previous January and Henry, already busy wooing his third wife, Jane Seymour, had thereby lost the male heir he so desperately craved. The royal marriage, by this point, was doomed.

With Henry declaring that he had been unfairly coerced into the marriage, Anne was arrested along with five men with whom she was supposed to have committed adultery, among them her own brother, George Boleyn. As unconvincing as the evidence against them was, all six were found guilty and sentenced to death on 15 May. Four days later, Anne was beheaded before a crowd of spectators in the Tower of London.

quatorzain *(n.)*　a poem of fourteen lines

On 20 May 1609, a publisher named Thomas Thorpe entered a new book on to the Stationers' Register, a record of all publishing activities in London:

> Tho. Thorpe. Entered for his copy under the hands of master Wilson and master Lownes Wardenes, a booke called Shakespeares sonnettes.

William Shakespeare's sonnets had been published for the first time. Scholars are divided over just how reputable a publisher Thomas Thorpe was. Some claim that Shakespeare sold the manuscripts to Thorpe, who published them entirely lawfully. Others claim Thorpe merely procured a copy of the text, and published the entire collection without Shakespeare's permission. Either way, it's likely that he is responsible for the order in which the sonnets still continue to be printed today.

A *sonnet* is literally a 'little song', a meaning that was originally adopted into English from French, along with the word itself, in the early fifteenth century. But by the mid sixteenth century, *sonnet* had also come to refer to a type of fourteen-line poem following a strictly defined rhyme scheme, a style that had originally developed in Italy during the Renaissance but flourished again in Elizabethan England.

A *quatorzain* is also a fourteen-line poem. Derived from *quatorze*, the French word for 'fourteen', it too first emerged in the sixteenth century and was originally used to refer to any poem of fourteen lines. But as the strict sonnet form (following the rhyme scheme *abab-cdcd-efef-gg*) grew in popularity, the word *quatorzain* came to be used of any poem that does not follow the sonnet's firmly established structure.

transmarine *(adj.)* crossing or located on
the opposite side of the sea

On 21 May 1927, the aviator Charles Lindbergh landed his *Spirit of St Louis* on an airfield outside Paris to complete the first solo, non-stop transatlantic flight in history. Having departed from New York the previous day, the 3,500-mile trip had taken him an exhausting thirty-three-and-a-half hours.

Five years later to the day, on 21 May 1932, Amelia Earhart replicated Lindbergh's transatlantic flight. Setting off from Newfoundland on the afternoon of 20 May, Earhart had to deal with bad weather and exhaust problems on her crossing, but nevertheless managed to land safely in a field outside Culmore, Northern Ireland, fourteen hours and fifty-six minutes later – successfully halving Lindbergh's time, and becoming the first woman to fly solo across the Atlantic Ocean.

Both Lindbergh's and Earhart's flights could be described as *transmarine*, a sixteenth-century adjective describing anything that crosses or extends over the sea, or that is located or dwells on the opposite side of a sea or ocean. Derived from Latin roots, it is one of a number of similar adjectives describing a location 'beyond' or 'opposite' – see 24 January for *transmural* and 30 June for *transpontine*, but in the meantime, here are five more:

- *tramontane* (adj.) located on the other side of a mountain
- *transequatorial* (adj.) located on the opposite side of the equator
- *transfluvial* (adj.) located on the other side of a river
- *transmundane* (adj.) lying beyond or outside of the world
- *trans-Stygian* (adj.) located in Hell – literally 'on the other side of the Styx', referring to the river dividing earth from the Underworld in Greek myth

three-pipe *(adj.)*   extremely complex, requiring much thought

Arthur Conan Doyle was born in Edinburgh on 22 May 1859. Before embarking on a career in detective fiction, Doyle studied medicine at the University of Edinburgh and is known to have based Sherlock Holmes at least partly on one of his university lecturers, Dr Joseph Bell, president of the Royal College of Surgeons. Even fellow writer and Edinburgh alumnus Robert Louis Stevenson recognised the connection: writing to congratulate Doyle on his 'very interesting adventures of Sherlock Holmes', Stevenson wrote that, 'Only one thing troubles me: can this be my old friend Joe Bell?'

After moving to England in 1882, Doyle set up a medical practice in Southsea, Portsmouth, and began writing fiction between patients. The first Sherlock Holmes story, *A Study in Scarlet*, was published in 1887, and by 1891 Doyle was writing regular Holmes stories for *The Strand*, quitting his practice to dedicate himself to his writing.

It was in one of Doyle's *Strand* stories that Sherlock Holmes first used the expression 'three-pipe problem' to describe a perplexing conundrum requiring a lengthy amount of consideration – namely, the amount of time it takes to smoke three pipes. In 'The Red-Headed League' (1891), a London pawnbroker comes to Holmes to ask him to investigate why he has been hired by a gentleman looking exclusively for someone with red hair to sit in an office and copy out pages from the *Encyclopaedia Britannica*. Naturally, Holmes solves the case – but requires some time to think first. 'It is quite a three-pipe problem,' he says to Dr Watson. 'I beg that you won't speak to me for fifty minutes.'

dimber-damber *(n.)* the leader of a gang of criminals

Before it came to mean 'attractive' or 'sweet', *pretty* originally meant 'skilful' or 'crafty', a meaning derived from an Old English word, *prætt*, for a trick or scam. But over time that meaning developed, so that before long *pretty* was being used to describe anything particularly skilfully or artfully made or done – and it's from there that the modern sense of the word developed in the mid fifteenth century.

Although less familiar today, the original, less complimentary meaning of *pretty* nevertheless survived for a time in English – so that when the lexicographer Francis Grose defined a *dimber-cove* as 'a pretty fellow' in his *Dictionary of the Vulgar Tongue* (1785), we can be fairly sure he wasn't describing their appearance.

Dimber has been used to mean 'cunning' or 'wily' in criminal slang since the mid seventeenth century at least, although precisely where the word comes from is a mystery. Nevertheless, add to that the word *damber* – an equally old-fashioned word for what Grose calls 'a rascal' – and you'll have a *dimber-damber*:

DIMBER-DAMBER. A top man, or prince among the canting crew, also the chief rogue of the gang, or the compleatest cheat.
A Classical Dictionary of the Vulgar Tongue (1785)

Speaking of which, it was on this date that one of the most notorious criminal gangs of the twentieth century met a bloody end: on 23 May 1934, outlaws Clyde Barrow and Bonnie Parker were shot and killed by a hail of police bullets while making a getaway in a stolen car outside Bienville, Louisiana. Their deaths brought to an end a two-year crime spree that had captivated America.

iddy-umpty *(n.)* Morse code

On 24 May 1844, Samuel Morse exhibited his new system for telegraphing coded messages in a demonstration in Washington, eagerly watched by a crowd of dignitaries and congressmen (who had funded Morse's experimental telegraph system to the tune of $30,000, equivalent to several million dollars today). Morse relayed a message down a 38-mile telegraph line connecting the Supreme Court Chamber of the US Capitol to a railroad station in Baltimore. Given the impact his invention would have on turn-of-the-century America, the message he sent – 'What hath God wrought?' – was an apt quotation from the Old Testament.

The demonstration was a resounding success: within a decade, more than 20,000 miles of telegraph wire would criss-cross the United States.

Morse spent twelve years developing his telegraph system, during which time he developed his ingenious code that used combinations of dots and dashes to represent letters: having counted the number of movable-type letters in a local printworks, Morse cleverly used simpler combinations for more frequent letters (E · , A · –) and vice versa (Q ––·–, Z ––··). The system revolutionised turn-of-the-century communication, especially among the military – and by the early 1900s had become affectionately known as *iddy-umpty*.

Umpty had been in use since the mid nineteenth century as a slang term for an unspecified or seemingly impossibly large number (which eventually gave us the word *umpteen* in the early 1900s). To that was attached the apparently random prefix *iddy* to form *iddy-umpty*, a word intended perhaps to imitate the stuttering sound of a Morse code transmission, and to allude to its seemingly countless stream of 'dits' and 'dahs'.

raccommode *(v.)*   to restore, to put back into place

On 25 May 1660, Charles II arrived back in England to reclaim the throne: the restoration of the English monarchy had finally come after more than a decade of Commonwealth rule.

The eldest son of Charles I, Charles had fled to France in 1646 when it became clear that his father was losing the English Civil War. After the king was captured and executed in 1649, the leader of the Parliamentarian cause, Oliver Cromwell, installed himself as Lord Protector and transformed England into a republic. The exiled Prince of Wales – now Charles II by default – invaded England in 1651 in an attempt to retake the throne by force, but he was defeated at the Battle of Worcester and fled once more to the Continent. Eventually, however, the Commonwealth would fail of its own accord: as the Parliamentarians imposed ever more puritanical laws on the country, the system grew less popular with the population at large, and after Cromwell's death in 1658 his son Richard proved an inadequate replacement. In 1660, Charles was invited to retake the throne, and he landed at Dover on 25 May. Four days later – his thirtieth birthday – he arrived in London to a rapturous reception.

To restore something to its rightful place is to *raccommode* it, a word borrowed into English from French in the fifteenth century. Also used to mean 'to atone' or 'to reconcile with', *raccommode* literally means 'to re-accommodate'.

sanguisugent *(adj.)*   blood-sucking

A *sanguisugent* creature is one that sucks or drinks blood. The word derives from the Latin verb *sugere*, 'to suck', which also crops up in the likes of *exsuction* ('the act of drawing the air out of something'), *florisuge* ('a creature that drinks nectar') and *potisuge* (a seventeenth-century word for a drunkard; literally a 'drink-sucker'). Added to that is the Latin word for blood, *sanguis*, which is found at the root of words like *sanguiduct* ('a vein or blood vessel'), *consanguineous* ('related by blood') and *exsanguinated* ('drained of blood'). *Sanguis* is also the origin of the adjective *sanguine*, which originally meant 'blood-red' but came to mean 'upbeat' or 'confident' in the sixteenth century as these were qualities once associated with an excess of bodily blood.

All of these bloodthirsty words are wholly appropriate for today – as it was on 26 May 1897 that Bram Stoker's *Dracula* first went on sale.

Originally a drama critic (and later an assistant to the renowned nineteenth-century actor Sir Henry Irving), Stoker began writing horror stories in the 1880s and published the first of his seventeen novels, *The Snake's Pass*, in 1890. But it is for his story of a Transylvanian vampire, Count Dracula, that he is best remembered today – although at the time the novel enjoyed only negligible success and made little money for its author.

It was only after Stoker's death in 1912 that the *Dracula* craze began to grow, partly due to a bitter lawsuit between Stoker's widow and the German film director F. W. Murnau, whose 1922 film *Nosferatu* borrowed much, without acknowledgement, from Stoker's story. But at last, the 1931 film adaptation starring Bela Lugosi firmly established the story's cult status and it has remained enduringly popular ever since.

shivviness *(adj.)*   the uncomfortable feeling of
wearing new undergarments

As well as being the name of the thin, wedge-shaped plug used
to stop a barrel, a *shive* is a thin sliver or splinter. Etymologically,
it derives from the same ancient Germanic roots as words like
sheave and *shiver* (which, in contexts like *shiver my timbers!*
means 'splinter to pieces', not 'shake with cold'), and is found
at the root of the word *shivelight*, a word coined by the poet
and writer Gerard Manley Hopkins to refer to a single shaft of
sunlight shining through the leaves of a tree. And according to
the *English Dialect Dictionary* (Vol. V, 1904), *shive* is also the
root of an old Yorkshire word, *shivviness*, defined as 'the feeling
of roughness caused by a new undergarment'.

Oddly, today's date is an important one in the history of
undergarments: Amelia Bloomer, namesake of women's *bloomers*,
was born in New York on 27 May 1818.

A writer and women's rights activist, Bloomer did not invent
the billowing underwear that bears her name today herself, but
rather promoted the wearing of 'pantalettes' (a combination of
a skirt worn over loose trousers, gathered at the ankles) in her
writing, as a less restrictive outfit than was fashionable at the
time. Her advocacy of the style quickly led to her name becoming
attached to it, and before long 'bloomer suits' had become
a popular – if often ridiculed – fashion in 1850s America. The
name *bloomer* remained in place even after the style fell out of
fashion, in reference to any loose-fitting trousers or knicker-
bockers, and eventually came to refer to women's knee-length
underwear.

nauscopy *(n.)*   the supposed ability to spot a ship before it crosses the horizon

In 1782, the French governor of Mauritius, François de Souillac, heard word that a flotilla of British ships was approaching the island. De Souillac quickly put the island on high alert, but before long word arrived that the flotilla had changed its course and the threat had passed.

In the days before radar, information like this typically had to come from lookouts or signal ships posted offshore, but in this case the threat was reported by one man, Étienne Bottineau, who claimed to have devised a 'science' that he called *nauscopy*: the ability to see ships at a great distance.

Employed in the local engineering corps, Bottineau made a name for himself on Mauritius by betting on when, where and how far apart the next ships to cross the horizon would be. His uncanny and often entirely accurate abilities allowed him to predict the appearance of ships from as far away as 700 miles from the island – and before long had brought him to the attention of the French navy. In 1784, de Souillac approved Bottineau's return to France to explain his abilities to the French Marine Ministry, but unfortunately few there were willing to hear the testimony of a man with a seemingly preternatural gift, and Bottineau and his talent drifted into obscurity.

Nevertheless, the name of the science he invented, *nauscopy* – a combination of the Greek words for 'ship' and 'observation' – remains in place in the dictionary to refer to the spotting of faraway ships from on land, or of land from ships far out at sea. It is also a word nicely suited to today: on 28 May 1588, the Spanish Armada set sail for England from Lisbon.

transnivean *(adj.)*　　located beyond the snows,
　　　　　　　　　　　　beyond snow-capped mountains

In his *Himalayan Journals* (1854), the British botanist and explorer (and best friend of Charles Darwin) Sir Joseph Dalton Hooker described an encounter with the Lepcha people of eastern India in 1848. The Lepcha, he noted, looked 'so Tibetan in [*their*] character' that he presumed their culture and history must be intertwined with that of 'the trans-nivean races'.

Hooker's word *transnivean* – built around the Latin word for 'snowy', *niveus* – literally describes anything or anyone located beyond snow-covered mountains, in this case, all those who live on the other side of the Himalayas. And, appropriately, it was on this date that the Himalayan mountains were finally conquered.

On 29 May 1953, New Zealander Edmund Hillary and his Nepalese Sherpa partner Tenzing Norgay became the first people in history to reach the summit of Mount Everest, 29,035 feet above sea level. The pair were part of a larger Commonwealth expedition launched by British Colonel John Hunt that began their ascent in April, climbing a mostly untested route up the south-east ridge of the mountain, to reach a height of 26,000 feet. On 26 May, two climbers from the expedition – Charles Evans and Tom Bourdillon – made an attempt at the summit, coming within 300 feet of it before Evans' oxygen supply failed and they were forced to turn back. Two days later, Hillary and Norgay made their attempt: after establishing a camp at 27,900 feet, they spent a hellish, sleepless night within sight of the summit, before waking the following morning for the final climb. Inching their way up a near vertical crack in the mountain face, they finally reached the summit at 11.30 a.m.

holmgang *(n.)*   a duel to the death

On 30 May 1806, the thirty-nine-year-old future president of the United States Andrew Jackson fought a duel with a lawyer and horse-breeder from Tennessee named Charles Dickinson.

The pair had initially disagreed over an apparent gambling debt, but the argument quickly spiralled out of control and led to Dickinson publishing a statement in the local newspaper that labelled Jackson a 'scoundrel' and a 'poltroon'. That might have been the end of it, except that Dickinson's next move was to take aim at Jackson's wife, Rachel, whom he called a bigamist for having married Jackson before her divorce from her first husband had been finalised. Not one to stand by and see his wife insulted, Jackson challenged Dickinson to a duel, and the pair met at an isolated spot on the Red River in southern Kentucky.

Dickinson shot first and struck Jackson in the chest. Jackson recoiled but somehow managed to compose himself, take aim and fire. Initially his gun misfired but (in a breach of duelling etiquette) he took aim once more and fired again, this time striking his opponent in the abdomen. Dickinson died several hours later. The bullet that struck Jackson, meanwhile, remained lodged in his chest for the rest of his life.

A duel to the death of any kind can be known as a *holmgang*. Although dating from the mid nineteenth century in English, *holmgang* has its origins in an ancient Old Norse term, *holmganga*, that literally means 'a going to the island' – a reference to the kind of isolated site where many ancient Scandinavian duels would once have been fought.

tell-clock *(n.)*   something or someone who marks or
tells the time; an idler

Dating back to the early 1600s in English, a *tell-clock* is literally someone who tells or marks the time. But, more often than not, the word is used in a figurative sense to refer to a clock-watching idler or layabout, or else someone who contributes little to an enterprise. In that sense, *Baron Tell-Clock* is an old seventeenth-century nickname for a cockerel (referring to the bird's habit of crowing at dawn), while *tell-clock* itself was once a nickname for an uninterested or inattentive judge:

> The puisne [superior court] judge was formerly called the Tell-clock; as supposed to be not much employed with business in the courts he sat in, but listening how the time went.
>
> Treadway Russell Nash (1793), footnote to
> Samuel Butler's *Hudibras* (1684)

Of all these meanings, it is the literal *tell-clock* that concerns us today: it was on 31 May 1859 that 'Big Ben' rang out across London for the very first time.

After a fire destroyed much of the former Palace of Westminster in 1834, a new design was drawn up that included an enormous four-face chiming clock atop a 315-foot tower, intended to be the largest and most accurate clock of its kind in the world. Its mechanism was developed by the Astronomer Royal, Sir George Airy, and Sir Edmund Beckett Denison, a lawyer and amateur horologist, who took three years to complete it. Installed in 1854, the gigantic bell followed in 1858 (after an earlier model cast two years earlier broke in testing), and the full clock finally entered service the following year.

tanglefoot *(n.)*   Scotch whisky

On 1 June 1495, an entry was written into the Scottish Exchequer Rolls:

> To Friar John Cor, by order of the King, to make aqua vitae, VIII bolls of malt

The king in question was James IV of Scotland. Friar John Cor was a monk (and presumed apothecary) based at Lindores Abbey in Newburgh, Fife. And the eight 'bolls' of malt he had received from the king were equivalent in modern terms to forty-eight bushels, or just under 400 gallons. Put all of those together, and this receipt represents the earliest known reference to Scottish whisky.

The word *whisky* is an anglicised corruption of a Gaelic word, *uisgebeatha*, that literally means 'water of life' (as does the *aqua vitae* mentioned in the order above). When the word first appeared in English in the late 1500s it was still spelled *usquebaugh*, but as time went by that form grew steadily more old-fashioned and the decidedly simpler spelling we use today eventually became standard.

As well as *whisky*, you can call it *spunkie* (an eighteenth-century term, originally a Scots nickname for a burning will-o'-the-wisp); *smile* (early-1800s slang); *snake juice* or *snake poison* (mid 1800s); *pine-top* or *wild-cat* (nineteenth-century American words for illicit whisky); *bluestone* (Victorian slang, originally a nickname for copper sulphate); *pinch-bottle* (early 1900s); and *smoke* (early 1900s). The nickname *tanglefoot*, meanwhile, emerged in the United States in the mid 1800s and alludes to whisky's befuddling, intoxicating potency.

vespering *(adj.)* flying westwards, heading towards sunset

Vesper is the Latin name for the Evening Star (which is, in fact, no star at all but the planet Venus). The name of the sixth of the seven canonical hours of the Christian church, *vespers*, derives from the same root, as do a host of less familiar words like *vespertilio* (a seventeenth-century word for a bat), *vesperate* ('to darken, to become night'), and *vespering*, an adjective describing anything heading west or flying towards the sunset.

Vespering was coined by the poet and author Thomas Hardy in his 1910 poem 'The Year's Awakening':

> How do you know that the pilgrim track
> Along the belting zodiac
> Swept by the sun in his seeming rounds
> Is traced by now to the Fishes' bounds . . .
> O vespering bird, how do you know?

Born on 2 June 1840, Hardy gained fame as the author of novels like *Far from the Madding Crowd* (1874) and *Tess of the d'Urbervilles* (1891), but considered himself primarily a poet; the backlash that met his final novel, *Jude the Obscure* (1895), is often considered one of the reasons why he never wrote another, and dedicated the final three decades of his life purely to poetry.

By the time of his death in 1928, Hardy had achieved such status that his ashes were buried in Westminster Abbey, with Rudyard Kipling, J. M. Barrie and even Prime Minister Stanley Baldwin among the mourners. Hardy's wish, however, had been to be buried with little ceremony in his local village of Stinsford in Dorset – so, by way of a compromise, his heart was buried in Dorset, while the rest of his remains were interred in London.

morganatic *(adj.)* designating a marriage between two people of unequal social rank

When Edward VIII made clear his intentions to marry Wallis Simpson in 1936, he faced stiff opposition from all those who did not believe a twice-divorced American socialite was a suitable prospective queen. The Church of England and many of Britain's highest-ranking politicians stood in his way, but the king could not be deterred. So, by means of a compromise, he suggested a little-known loophole that would allow him to maintain the throne: a *morganatic* marriage.

A *morganatic* union is one between an ennobled or high-ranking man and a low-ranking woman (seldom the other way around), in which the wife and any future children the new couple have are prohibited from inheriting the husband's properties, titles or rank. Etymological folklore will have you believe that *morganatic* derives from Morgan le Fey, a sorceress in Arthurian legend who was unhappily married to the fabled King Urien, but in fact the true story is much more straightforward.

Morganatic comes from *morganaticum*, a Latin word for a 'morning gift', which tradition once dictated husbands would present to their new wives the morning after their wedding – the implication being that in a *morganatic* marriage, this gift was all the bride got to keep. In relation to these kinds of gifts, the adjective *morganatic* first appeared in English in the late 1500s, before the first *morganatic* marriage was described in the early eighteenth century.

As for Edward VIII, his offer of a morganatic marriage was rejected by Prime Minister Stanley Baldwin's government, and in December 1936 he abdicated the throne. His younger brother Prince Albert, Duke of York, became King George VI in his place – leaving Edward free to marry Mrs Simpson on 3 June 1937.

anaphora *(n.)* a figure of speech that repeats a sequence of words at the start of successive clauses

On this day in 1940 – just nine months into the start of the Second World War – the evacuation of more than 330,000 Allied troops from the French port of Dunkirk came to an end. The men had become stranded there following the successful Nazi invasion of France, which had forced a huge Allied force to retreat to the English Channel. Faced with having to admit that the Allies had lost the Battle of France, on 4 June 1940, Prime Minister Winston Churchill stood to address the House of Commons and delivered one of his – and one of modern history's – most stirring speeches:

> We shall go on to the end. We shall fight in France, we shall fight on the seas and oceans, we shall fight with growing confidence and growing strength in the air, we shall defend our island, whatever the cost may be. We shall fight on the beaches, we shall fight on the landing grounds, we shall fight in the fields and in the streets, we shall fight in the hills; we shall never surrender.

Through this address and countless others like it, Churchill earned a reputation as an exceptionally skilled orator, who employed classical rhetorical techniques to produce speeches of extraordinary effectiveness. His 'We shall fight on the beaches' speech is an example of *anaphora*, a rhetorical device in which a phrase or sequence of words ('we shall fight') is repeated at the start of successive sentences or clauses to produce a rousing, driving emphasis. In that sense, *anaphora* literally means a 'carrying back' in Greek.

orthophony *(n.)* perfectly correct speaking or enunciation

If you have a sweet-sounding or pleasant voice, you could be described as *dulciloquent*, or else *chrysostomatical*, a seventeenth-century word literally meaning 'golden-mouthed'. If you're *altiloquent* you have a loud, pompous-sounding voice, or like to talk in a haughty, overbearing manner. *Coelostomy* is hollowness or indistinctness of voice, while *trachyphonia* is the hoarse or rough-sounding quality of a person's voice. And *orthophony*, a term derived from the Greek word *orthos*, meaning 'straight' or 'true', is perfect diction or enunciation.

Which of these best suits today's date is hard to say: on 5 June 1938, scientists working at the Bell Telephone Laboratory in New Jersey successfully demonstrated the first electronic device in history that could accurately reproduce human speech. The *Voder* – an abbreviation of 'voice operating demonstrator' – worked by imitating the actions of the human vocal tract to produce one of two basic sounds, either a hiss or a buzz, that could then be manipulated by an operator working two small, piano-like keyboards to produce more than twenty separate sounds. These were then fed into a bank of filters that could shape the tone and timbre of the sound, giving it remarkably human-like inflections and stresses, before being sent to a loudspeaker for broadcast; a skilled operator could use the *Voder* to speak different languages, and even recreate animal noises should they so desire.

Although the voice that the *Voder* produced was still fairly robotic, it was nevertheless perfectly clear and understandable – if not entirely *orthophonic*.

extra-foraneous *(adj.)*   outdoor

Something that is *extra-foraneous* is located, quite literally, out of doors: at the root of this word – an adjective dating back to the late 1700s in English – is the Latin word *foris*, meaning 'entrance' or 'doorway'. That etymological heritage makes *extra-foraneous* an etymological cousin of words like *forest*, *foreign* and *forfeit* (literally something 'done outside' ordinary conduct), as well as the French preposition *hors*, familiar to English speakers thanks to terms like *hors d'oeuvre* (an appetiser eaten 'outside' of a main meal) and *hors de combat* (literally 'out of the fight', and so unable to continue).

On the subject of all things *extra-foraneous*, the world's first drive-in movie theatre opened on 6 June 1933 in Camden, New Jersey. The enterprise was the brainchild of a local autoparts dealer named Richard Hollingshead Jr, who was inspired to open the business after seeing his mother struggle to sit comfortably in the cramped seats of their local cinema. Hollingshead originally called his business a 'Park-In' theatre (it would be another eight years before the first 'Drive-In' theatre was so called) and charged patrons 25 cents per car, and 25 cents per person.

By the 1960s, there were more than 5,000 drive-in theatres across the United States.

Wunderkammer *(n.)* a collection of oddities; a room set aside for just such a collection

Perhaps without knowing it, you're holding a linguistic *Wunderkammer* in your hands. Borrowed into English from German, a *Wunderkammer* is a collection – or else a room set aside for just such a collection – of often fairly miscellaneous oddities, antiquities and curiosities. Its literal translation is 'wonder-chamber', but these kinds of collections have over time also gone by a variety of names like *Kunstkabinett* (literally an 'art cabinet'), *wonder-room* – and of course, a *cabinet of curiosities*.

One of the most notable owners of one of these cabinets was Sir Hans Sloane, an English physician and naturalist born in Ireland in 1660. Throughout his life, Sloane amassed a vast and highly valuable collection of artefacts and antiquities, including maps and manuscripts, books, paintings, specimens of various flora and fauna, seals, medals and coins. Many of these he collected himself, but a great many more he accrued from other collectors, who, knowing his enthusiasm, bequeathed their curiosity cabinets to Sloane.

Not wanting to see his collection broken up, on Sloane's own death in 1753 he chose to bequeath all 70,000 items he had assembled in his lifetime to King George II, and on 7 June 1753 the king gave formal assent to an act of parliament that established the British Museum using Sloane's collection as its basis. Today, the British Museum houses some 8 million items – but it was the contents of Sloane's *Wunderkammer* that started it all.

boot-hale *(v.)*   to pillage, to plunder

Booty has been used to refer to the stolen items taken by robbers or invaders since the fifteenth century, and is likely derived from the older use of *boot* to mean 'profit' or 'advantage'. *Hale*, meanwhile, can be used as a verb to mean 'to haul', or 'to draw or pull along'. And if what you're pulling along is the loot you have just stolen, then you're *boot-haling*: a late sixteenth-century word meaning 'to pillage', 'to plunder' or 'to carry off the spoils'.

According to the writers of the Anglo-Saxon Chronicle – a vast record of more than three centuries of history dating from the reign of Alfred the Great – one of the most notorious instances of *boot-haling* happened on 8 June 793 AD:

> On June 8th, the ravages of heathen men miserably destroyed God's church on Lindisfarne with plunder and slaughter.

The 'heathen men' were Viking invaders and this is the earliest known account of an unprovoked Viking attack on Western Europe. They had been raiding the east coast of Great Britain for several years, but this assault on Lindisfarne, on the monastery and Church of St Cuthbert, was unprecedented in its violence. Buildings were burned, treasures stolen, monks and priests slaughtered: 'The church of St Cuthbert is spattered with the blood of the priests of God,' wrote Alcuin, a Northumbrian scholar, when he heard of the atrocity. 'Stripped of all its furnishing [and] exposed to the plundering of pagans.'

Over the years to come, Viking raids on the British Isles intensified, and by the ninth century vast swathes of the country had fallen under Viking control. The *boot-haling* of Lindisfarne, it seems, was just the beginning.

curfuggle *(n.)*   a confused mess; disorder, disarray

The Roman Emperor Nero committed suicide on 9 June 68 AD, bringing to an end a tumultuous and tyrannical thirteen-year reign. Unfortunately for Rome, his death threw the Empire into an even more tumultuous twelve months, known as the Year of Four Emperors.

Nero's successor, Galba, quickly proved just as unstable and unpopular as his predecessor, and was assassinated early the following year by troops loyal to the next emperor, Otho. During Galba's reign, however, the northern province of Germania had turned its back on Rome and appointed its own ruler, Aulus Vitellius, who marched on Rome in April and ousted Otho from the throne. But Vitellius' reign in turn lasted only a matter of months: unrest in the east saw the eastern provinces appoint their own rival emperor, Vespasian, and while preparing to abdicate Vitellius was killed and his body thrown in the Tiber. Thankfully, Vespasian soon set about restoring some much needed stability to the Empire.

Confusion or disorder like that into which Rome was thrown in 68 AD can be called a *curfuggle*, an old Scots dialect word based on the earlier word *fuggle*, or *fugle*, variously meaning 'a rough heap', 'a tangled bundle of sticks or straw', or by extension, 'a useless plug of unburned tobacco in a pipe'. Added to that, the prefix *cur–* is used to apply emphasis to whatever base word it is attached to – so a *curfuggle* could ultimately be defined as a total mess or complete state of disarray.

sheep-biting *(n.)*   treacherous, underhand behaviour

On 10 June 1940, President Franklin D. Roosevelt was invited to give a commencement address at the University of Virginia, where his son Franklin Jr was graduating with a degree in Law. On the morning of the ceremony, however, the president was informed that Mussolini's Italy had chosen to ally itself with Adolf Hitler's Germany, and in doing so had declared war on Great Britain and France. Instead of delivering the commencement he had prepared, Roosevelt instead delivered an angry and highly politicised address that became known as his 'Stab in the Back' speech:

> The government of Italy has now chosen to preserve what it terms its freedom of action and to fulfil what it states are its promises to Germany. In so doing, it has manifested disregard for the rights and security of other nations, disregard for the lives of the peoples of those nations which are directly threatened by this spread of the war . . . On this, tenth day of June, 1940, the hand that held the dagger has struck it into the back of its neighbour.

Treacherous, double-crossing behaviour has been known as *backstabbing* since the early 1800s, with derivatives like *backstab* and *backstabber* first emerging around the turn of the century. *Sheep-biting* is a much earlier equivalent: back in sixteenth century English, a *sheep-biter* was literally a dog that bit or harassed sheep, but by the early 1600s it was being used figuratively of any malicious or shifty character. *Sheep-biting* likewise had come to refer to knavish behaviour or thievery, and eventually any underhand act of treachery or duplicitousness.

abscotchalater *(n.)*   someone hiding from the police

In their 1889 *Dictionary of Slang, Jargon and Cant*, the lexicographers Albert Barrère and Charles G. Leland defined the curious word *abscotchalater* as 'one who is hiding away from the police'. The pair tentatively suggested the word derived from the earlier slang word *absquatulate*, meaning 'to run away', which is itself thought to be a fairly random mishmash of *abscond, squat* and *perambulate* coined in the early nineteenth century.

On 11 June 1962, three *absquatulating abscotchalaters* – Frank Morris and brothers Clarence and John Anglin – became perhaps the only inmates of Alcatraz Prison in San Francisco, California, ever to successfully escape the facility.

According to accounts of the trio's escape, late on the evening of 11 June the men carefully tucked papier-mâché likenesses of their own heads into their beds and made their escape via a ventilation duct that led to an unguarded utility corridor. From there, they fled the island on a makeshift raft made from dozens of raincoats sewn and melted together using steam from a radiator. What happened to them after that is a mystery: a fellow inmate, Allen West, later claimed the men's plan had been to steal a car once they reached the mainland, but as no car thefts were reported in the area around the time of the escape, the FBI investigation of the escape concluded that the men drowned or died of exposure attempting to paddle across San Francisco Bay. Popular history, however, claims the escape was successful; a US Marshals Service warrant remains in force for the men's arrest.

gifture *(n.)*   a gift or present; the act of giving

People have been giving each other *gifts* since the twelfth century, when the word *gift* was likely borrowed into English from Scandinavia. Derived from that, the word *gifture* first emerged in the early 1500s to refer either to the act of giving a gift, or else the actual gift or present itself; to do something *upon gifture*, meanwhile, once meant to do it freely or gratuitously. *Gifture* largely fell out of use in the late seventeenth century, and has remained in neglected obscurity ever since.

On 12 June 1942, a young German-born girl living in Amsterdam was given a red-and-white backed notebook as a *gifture* for her thirteenth birthday. Although the book itself was sold as an autograph book, she decided to use it as a diary and two days later wrote her first entry, addressing the diary itself:

> I'll begin from the moment I got you, the moment I saw you lying on the table among my other birthday presents. (I went along when you were bought, but that doesn't count.)

The girl in question was Anne Frank, and her diary – later published in English as *The Diary of a Young Girl* (1952) – recorded her and her family's two-year ordeal hiding from the Nazis in a secret annex, hidden behind a bookcase, in the building where her father Otto worked.

In August 1944, the family were captured by the Gestapo and transported to concentration camps. Anne, aged just fifteen, died in the Bergen-Belsen camp the following year.

singultus *(n.)*   a hiccup

On 13 June 1922, a gentleman named Charles Osborne in Anthon, Iowa, started hiccupping while straining himself attempting to weigh a hog. He didn't stop hiccupping for the next sixty-eight years. According to the *Guinness Book of Records*, Osborne's bout of hiccups – which totalled an estimated 430 million hiccups, at anywhere from twenty to forty a minute – is the longest in recorded history.

The word *hiccup* itself is imitative: first used in English in the late 1500s, it was coined onomatopoeically merely to resemble the sound it describes. But a single hiccup or single bout of hiccups can also be known as a *singultus*, a word borrowed directly into English from Latin.

Although it could also be applied to the croaking of ravens, the hackling heard in the back of the throat, or even the rasping 'death rattle' of a dying person, back in its native Latin a *singultus* was literally a sob or a speech disrupted by sobbing, and that meaning remained in place when the word first appeared in English in the late sixteenth century. By the mid 1600s, however, *singultus* or *singult* had come to be used as the medical name for what one seventeenth-century naturalist described as 'a convulsive motion of the stomach', and it has remained in infrequent use – chiefly in medical contexts – ever since.

enstaff *(v.)*   to hoist a flag

On 14 June 1777, the Second Continental Congress, the ruling body of the United States during the American Revolution, passed the so-called 'Flag Resolution', which stated that 'the flag of the thirteen United States be thirteen stripes, alternate red and white', and that 'the union be thirteen stars, white in a blue field, representing a new constellation'. The Stars and Stripes, as it is now known, was officially adopted as the flag of the United States of America.

A few days later, it is thought to have been flown – or rather *enstaffed*, to use a seventeenth-century word for hoisting a flag – for the very first time at Middlebrook, an encampment of the Continental Army in rural New Jersey.

There have since been twenty-seven different versions of the US flag, with a new star added to the design every time a new state has joined the Union. When Vermont and Kentucky were added to the Union as the fourteenth and fifteenth states, in 1791 and 1792 respectively, an extra stripe was also added, but when it became clear that this would be unwieldy as the number of states continued to grow, the original thirteen stripes were restored and only the stars have been updated since.

When Alaska and Hawaii joined the Union in 1959, President Eisenhower received thousands of submissions for an updated flag – including one from Robert G. Heft, a seventeen-year-old high school student from Ohio, whose design was created for a school project. From all those submitted, Heft's design – which added two new stars, rearranging all fifty into alternating rows of six and five stars each – was chosen and remains in use nationwide to this day. He received a B– for his work.

sign-manual *(n.)*   a signature

The word *manual* derives from the Latin word for 'hand', *manus*, which is the same root that appears in words like *manuscript, manicure, manipulation* and *amanuensis* (literally a 'hand-servant'). That makes a *sign manual* literally a 'hand-written sign' – or, more specifically, a person's signature or autograph – and it's in that sense that the word has remained in infrequent use since the early fifteenth century. The signature of the king or queen, meanwhile, is still properly known as the *royal sign-manual.*

Speaking of which, Magna Carta was signed by King John 'in the meadow which is called Runnymede between Windsor and Staines' on 15 June 1215. Magna Carta is believed to have been drawn up by the Archbishop of Canterbury, Stephen Langton, and essentially acted as a peace treaty between the failing King John and his rebellious barons. Neither side stuck too closely to its terms, however, and the original document was nullified by Pope Innocent III, throwing England into a brief civil war. After John's death in 1216, later versions of the document that excised some of its more radical or controversial content were drawn up, including one signed by John's successor, Henry III, in 1217. It was then that the name Magna Carta – literally the 'great charter' – was used for the first time.

mrkgnao *(n.)*   the meow of a cat

In the literary world, today is commemorated as 'Bloomsday', a celebration of James Joyce's novel *Ulysses* (1922), which famously relates the events in the life of one man, Leopold Bloom, on one day, 16 June 1904.

Ulysses is based in part on (and is the Latin translation of) Homer's *Odyssey*, with Joyce drawing parallels between the characters in his story and Homer's tale of the great hero Odysseus' journey home from the Trojan War. As with much of his writing, the language and style of *Ulysses* is highly idiosyncratic, with Joyce drawing heavily on Irish dialect and slang as well as inventing many of his own words:

- *pornosophical* (adj.) a nonsense word that has puzzled Joyce fans and scholars since he first used it in *Ulysses*; the *Oxford English Dictionary* suggests *pornosophical* might be intended to mean 'of or relating to the philosophy of the brothel'
- *smilesmerk* (v.) to smile in a smirking, supercilious way
- *ripripple* (v.) to wash or pour over repeatedly, like water over rippling over stones ·
- *poppysmic* (adj.) produced with a smacking of the lips
- *yogibogeybox* (n.) the paraphernalia carried by a spiritualist

But perhaps one of Joyce's most peculiar inventions, however, is *mrkgnao*, a word he uses several times (with several different spellings) in *Ulysses* to describe the meow of a cat.

gaping-stock *(n.)* someone or something being stared at by a crowd

In words like *laughing-stock* ('someone who is the butt of a joke or the object of humiliation') and *whipping-stock* ('one who is the subject of a brutal punishment'), *stock* is an old English word for a tree trunk or a stake, with the allusion here likely being to someone being tied or held against a 'stock' while they are punished or mocked.

This same root survives in other compound words that have, regrettably, not stood the test of time. *Jesting-stock*, for instance, is an early sixteenth-century version of a *laughing-stock*, and a *loathing-stock* is someone who is held in general contempt or dislike. A *gaping-stock*, meanwhile, is someone or something that is being stared at by a crowd of ogling bystanders.

As public displays go, one of the darkest and bloodiest took place on this date in 1939, when a German-born criminal named Eugen Weidmann became the last person publicly executed by guillotine in France. Weidmann began his life of crime as a small-time thief but while serving a five-year prison sentence for robbery he met two accomplices, Roger Million and Jean Blanc, with whom he launched a murderous spree of violent robberies in the mid 1930s. Eventually apprehended and arrested, Weidmann confessed to the murders of six people and after a much publicised trial was sentenced to death.

On 17 June 1939, before a small crowd outside the Prison Saint-Pierre in Paris, Weidmann was placed in the guillotine and promptly executed. The behaviour of the crowd – later described by the *Soir* newspaper as 'disgusting' – was so unruly that the French president immediately banned all future public executions. Nevertheless, the guillotine was still used as a method of capital punishment in France right through to 1977.

noctilucy *(n.)*   the shining of the moon

The word *noctilucy* first appeared in English in the early 1600s to describe the shining of the moon. It derives from *noctiluca*, a Latin word for a lantern (or a glow-worm), which in turn combines the Latin word for 'night', *nox*, with the Latin for 'shine', *lucere*. Those roots make *noctilucy* an etymological cousin of words like *nocturnal*, *equinox* and *noctambulator* ('a sleepwalker, one who walks around at night'), as well as *translucent*, *elucidate* and *lucidity*. The *noctilucent* shining of the moon, however, was not the brightest thing in the night sky on 18 June 1178.

According to an English chronicler and monk known as Gervase of Canterbury, around an hour after sunset on this date the upper part of the east-facing crescent moon appeared to 'suddenly split in two'. From this opening, 'a flaming torch sprang up, spewing out . . . fire, hot coals and sparks' while the moon below it 'writhed [and] throbbed like a wounded snake'. The moon continued to appear to writhe in its orbit, 'assuming various twisting shapes at random' before returning almost to normal, except that 'from horn to horn, that is along its whole length [the moon] took on a blackish appearance'.

What had the monks who witnessed this occurrence actually seen? One theory claims that they saw a meteor shower – or else the explosion of a larger single meteor – passing directly in front of the moon, but another gives a more precise explanation. Going by the date and location of Gervase's account, it's possible that they had witnessed the asteroid impact responsible for a vast lunar crater on the far side of the moon, now known as *Giordano Bruno* (in honour of a famed Italian philosopher of the late Middle Ages).

Either way, Gervase and his companions had seen quite the *noctilucent* display.

esclop *(n.)*   a police officer

Esclop is a Victorian-era nickname for a police officer, first recorded in 1851 and coined during a craze for so-called 'back slang', in which new words were created by reversing existing ones (which also saw the word *yob* coined by reversing the word 'boy').

There are countless slang nicknames for police officers in the dictionary, of which *esclop* is just one. Because of their dark-blue uniforms, policemen were also known as *raw* or *unboiled lobsters* in the early 1800s, as well as *blue boys*, *bluebottles* and *grey-coats*. *Truncheoner* and *truncheonist* both refer to the trad-itional policeman's bludgeon, and both likewise originate in the nineteenth century. *Nabber* and *nabman* are eighteenth-century nicknames alluding to policemen 'nabbing' criminals. *Johnny Hop* and *ginger-pop* are both old rhyming slang terms for 'cop', while *grasshopper* is a rhyming play on *copper*; as for *copper* itself, no one is entirely sure of its origin but it's likely to be nothing more than an extension of the verb *cop*, which has been used to mean 'to capture' since the early eighteenth century. And both *bobby* and *peeler* refer to the then British Home Secretary Sir Robert Peel, who is credited with establishing the first pro-fessional police force in modern times.

It was on 19 June 1829 that Peel's Metropolitan Police Act received its royal assent from George IV, paving the way for the foundation of London's Metropolitan Police Force; the first Met policemen began patrolling the streets of London the following September.

polymicrian *(adj.)* extremely cramped, containing a great deal in a small space

On 20 June 1756, a British Indian garrison named Fort William in the centre of modern-day Kolkata fell to invading Bengali troops loyal to Siraj ud-Daulah, nawab of Bengal. The fort had been built to protect the British East India Company's trade in the city, but when the company began to interfere in local affairs the nawab ordered the tower be attacked. Many of the British troops inside fled, but reportedly 146 remained behind under the command of one of the company's civilian employees, John Zephaniah Holwell. As the defences fell, Holwell and the remaining men became prisoners of war – and were all forced into a single holding cell for the night.

The cell – nicknamed 'the Black Hole' – was just 14 by 18 feet wide, and many of the men inside succumbed to the stifling conditions. Although accounts of the incident vary, Holwell's own version of events claims that by the time the cell was unlocked the following morning, only twenty-three men had survived the night. The grim incident soon became notorious, and the phrase 'Black Hole of Calcutta' soon became a common allusion for anywhere with a filthy, stifling or cramped environment.

Somewhere or something that is impossibly cramped can be described as *polymicrian*, an adjective that first appeared in the language in the early nineteenth century in reference to books or pages of handwriting that cram as many words as possible on to a single page. Combining Greek roots meaning 'many' or 'much', *polys*, and 'small', *mikros*, the word literally implies 'much in a small space'.

malison *(n.)*   a curse, an accursed person or thing

Dating from as far back as the fourteenth century in English, a *malison* is either a curse, or else something or someone who has had a curse put upon them; as a verb, it can be used to mean 'to pronounce or set a curse on someone'. In either case, the word comes from its French equivalent *maleison*, which in turn is taken from the Latin words for 'evil', *male*, and 'speech', *dictio* – the same roots from which the more familiar *malediction* is taken.

As accursed days go, 21 June is likely no more infamous than any other – unless you happen to believe in the curse of Timur, a Mongol leader known for the barbarity of his conquests across fourteenth-century Asia.

In June 1941, the Soviet leader Stalin sent a team of archaeologists, headed by a renowned Russian anthropologist named Mikhail Gerasimov, to Uzbekistan to open Timur's tomb. Gerasimov was a pioneer of so-called forensic sculpture, a technique by which the faces of the deceased can be reproduced by analysing their skeletal remains, and Stalin wanted him to apply the same technique to Timur to have an idea of how he may have looked. The tomb was opened later that month, and on 21 June 1941 Gerasimov took Timur's skull. The following day, the Soviet Union was invaded by Nazi Germany.

According to legend, the inscription on Timur's gravestone read: 'When I rise from the dead, the world shall tremble.'

hiemate *(v.)*   to spend the winter

Derived from *hiems*, a Latin word for 'winter', *hiemate* is a seventeenth-century word meaning to spend or see out the winter. What does seeing out the coldest season of the year have to do with a date at the height of summer? Well, despite the fact that the summer solstice typically takes place around 20–22 June – so that from now until the end of the year the nights are drawing in – today's date is linked to an unfortunate incident in global exploration that led to the mutiny and death of one of England's greatest explorers.

In April 1610, Henry Hudson set sail on his fourth transatlantic voyage, hoping to locate a long-sought-after easterly route through the Arctic and on to Asia. Sailing north to Iceland and Greenland, Hudson's ship *Discovery* reached the Labrador Peninsula on the far east coast of Canada in June, and from there sailed into a vast, open bay. Believing they had found the fabled Northwest Passage, Hudson spent the following months carefully mapping the bay's shoreline – but as winter set in, no passage to Asia ever materialised. Before long the *Discovery* had become trapped in the ice and her crew was forced to head to the shoreline to see out the winter on land.

During the long Canadian winter, discontent began to grow among Hudson's crew and the following year they mutinied. When the ice retreated and the *Discovery* was freed, on 22 June 1611, Hudson, his teenage son John and a handful of loyal crewmembers were set adrift in a small, open-topped boat. They were never seen again.

Hudson's fate remains unknown – but the vast bay he discovered, and into which he was eventually cast adrift, still bears his name to this day.

qwertyuiop *(n.)*   the standard QWERTY keyboard layout; a nonsense piece of filler text

On 23 June 1868, American inventors Christopher L. Sholes, Samuel Soule and Carlos Glidden patented one of the earliest modern typewriters.

Although they called their invention the 'type writing machine', the layout and mechanism of the Sholes, Glidden and Soule model was vastly different from the keyboards we use today: instead of individual push buttons, it had two tiers of letters that were arranged like a musical keyboard. The top tier – 3 5 7 9 N O P Q R S T U V W X Y Z – was even made of ivory and the bottom tier – 2 4 6 8. A B C D E F G H I J K L M – from ebony, leading the *Scientific American* magazine to nickname it the 'literary piano'.

Over the years that followed, Sholes, Glidden and Soule continued to make refinements to their design, but one problem continued to plague them: the mechanism was slow, and when typing at speed, the keys of frequently used letters positioned next to one another on the alphabetical keyboard – like D and E, or R, S and T – would often jam. As a result, in 1878 Sholes patented a renewed design for their keyboard that separated the most frequently used letters evenly across three rows: Q W E R T Y U I O P, A S D F G H J K L and Z X C V B N M. The modern *qwerty* keyboard was born.

Keyboards using Sholes' design have been known as *qwerty* keyboards since the late 1920s, but before then oddly the more usual term was *qwertyuiop* (pronounced 'qwerty-*you*-ee-op'), which called upon the entire top row for its name.

choreomania *(n.)*   a mania for dancing

Thanks to one single root, *khoros*, that could be variously used in Greek to refer to a band of singers or dancers, a dance accompanied by a song or else a place for singing, dancing or performing, a great many English words relating to singing have etymological cousins in words relating to dancing. Hence *chorus*, *choir*, *carol* and *chorister* are all distantly related to words like *choreography* (the arrangement of the moves of a dance), *Terpsichore* (the Greek muse of dancing) and *choreomania* – a mania or madness for dancing.

Nowadays, the word *choreomania* tends to be used fairly loosely, referring merely to a fondness or enthusiasm for dancing. But when it first appeared in English in the mid 1800s, use of the word wasn't quite so frivolous: originally, *choreomania* referred to a literal and sometimes even fatal 'dancing madness', an epidemic of which broke out in Aachen, Germany, on 24 June 1374.

On this date, hundreds of townspeople in Aachen and the surrounding villages began inexplicably to dance around the streets, gyrating and leaping into the air for hours – and eventually days and weeks – on end. The maniacal 'dancers' would not eat or sleep, but merely dance continuously until they collapsed from total exhaustion.

Precisely what caused this outbreak of *choreomania* – which is also known simply as *chorea*, or *St Vitus' dance* in honour of the patron saint of dancing – is unknown. One theory claims that it was the work of some radical brainwashing sect or cult, while another suggests that it could have been caused by consuming tainted bread. Whatever the cause, curiously, the epidemic vanished just as quickly as it had started.

decapulate *(v.)*   to pour a liquid from one vessel into another

Derived from a Latin word, *capulare*, meaning 'to decant', *decapulate* is a seventeenth-century word meaning 'to pour something from one container into another', while the act of doing precisely that can be known as *decapulation*. That's also the literal and original meaning of the word *transfusion*, which first appeared in the language in the mid 1500s and, long before its associations with donating blood, merely referred to the act of transferring a fluid from one vessel to another. In that sense, *transfusion* and *transfuse* derive from *fundere*, a Latin word meaning 'to pour', which is also found at the root of words like *diffuse*, *perfusion* and *futile* (the Latin ancestor of which originally referred to untrustworthy boats or leaky containers).

On the subject of *transfusing*, the first successful human blood transfusion is believed to have taken place on 25 June 1667. The patient receiving the transfusion was a fifteen-year-old boy who had been bled so profusely by the doctors of the day that only a blood transfusion could save him. The physician performing the operation was Jean-Baptiste Denys, personal physician to Louis XIV. And the blood being transfused, oddly, was that of a sheep.

The precise details of medicine's first blood transfusion are hazy: some accounts claim British physician Richard Lower, who had earlier performed blood-swapping experiments with dogs, was the first, while others place the date of the operation somewhat earlier. Whatever the truth however, one thing is known for certain: miraculously, the boy survived.

muggle *(n.)*   a fish's tail

The very first book in J. K. Rowling's *Harry Potter* series, *Harry Potter and the Philosopher's Stone*, was published in the UK on 26 June 1997. Initially, only 500 copies of the book were printed; within two years, it had sold more than 300,000, while the entire *Harry Potter* series has gone on to sell more than half a billion copies worldwide.

The enormous popularity of J. K. Rowling's work has led to several of her invented words slipping into more widespread use in the language. In 2017, for instance, *quidditch* was added to the online arm of *Oxford Dictionaries*, defined as 'a team sport played while straddling broomsticks, in which goals are scored by throwing a ball through any of three hoops fixed at either end of the field'. And while a *muggle* in the world of *Harry Potter* is a person possessing no magical powers, according to the *Oxford English Dictionary* it can be used allusively to describe 'a person who lacks a particular skill or skills, or who is regarded as inferior in some way'.

Or at least, that's one definition of it. In fact, the word *muggle* has been in use in English since the thirteenth century – not, alas, in relation to those lacking magical powers, but rather as another name for a fish's tail. In that sense, the word probably derives from *mugil*, the Latin name for the grey mullet.

Mavortian *(adj.)* warlike, martial

Derived from the Roman god of war, Mars, someone described as *Mavortian* would be belligerent or battle-hardened. The word first appeared in English in the sixteenth century – and thanks to a battle fought a century later, is a fitting word for today.

The Battle of Dettingen was fought in Dettingen, Germany, on 27 June 1743. The conflict was an early encounter in the War of the Austrian Succession, a series of conflicts sparked by Europe-wide infighting over the succession of a female monarch, Maria Theresa, to the throne of the Habsburg Empire. Thirty years earlier, Maria's father, Charles VI, had foreseen the problems that having no male heir could cause and had issued an edict making arrangements for his daughter to succeed him, signed by most of Germany's constituent dominions. After Charles's death, however, the edict was quickly challenged, and as rival claimants to the throne began to put themselves forward, war broke out.

Britain became embroiled in the conflict as one of the supporters of Maria Theresa's rule. Allying his British forces with troops from across Europe, George II entered the fray – becoming the last British monarch in history to lead his troops into battle.

As if that were not enough to ensure the Battle of Dettingen's place in history, just as the British took up their places on the battlefield, a formidable Scottish lieutenant named Sir Andrew Agnew commanded his men not to fire at their enemies until they could 'see the whites of their e'en'. His order – later reiterated by American officer William Prescott at the Battle of Bunker Hill – has since become a proverbial warning not to act too quickly.

Carthaginian peace *(n.)* a peace settlement imposing severe penalties on the defeated party

The Second Punic War, fought between Rome and Carthage from 218 to 201 BC, ended with Rome securing a decisive victory over the Carthaginian general Hannibal. In the conflict's aftermath Rome took control of much of Carthage's Mediterranean territory, but to ensure that the Carthaginians would never again pose a threat, the Romans drew up a peace treaty imposing harsh penalties on Carthage. The city was forced to pay hefty financial tributes to Rome, was made to demilitarise (limiting its navy to just ten ships) and was expressly forbidden to raise an army without Roman permission. When Carthage broke the terms of this agreement and sparked the Third Punic War in 149 BC, the Romans destroyed the city.

The harshness of the terms Rome imposed on Carthage in 241 BC is the origin of the expression *Carthaginian peace*, a treaty or conclusion to a disagreement that is fiercely and punitively one-sided and imposes harsh penalties on the losing side. In that context, the term was popularised by the English economist John Maynard Keynes in the aftermath of the First World War, when, on 28 June 1919, Germany signed the Treaty of Versailles.

The terms of the treaty were controversial: Britain and France were keen to make Germany pay reparations for the damage the war had caused, but Keynes – who was in Paris as a representative of the Treasury – warned that it was too punitive and would cripple the German economy, leading to continued resentment against the Allies. In *The Economic Consequences of Peace* (1919), Keynes grimly prophesied that, 'If we aim at the impoverishment of Central Europe, vengeance, I dare say, will not limp.'

scathefire *(n.)* a vast, destructive conflagration

The original Globe Theatre burned to the ground on 29 June 1613, midway through a performance of William Shakespeare's play *Henry VIII*. The fire was started by a theatrical cannon, kept just inside the open roof of the theatre, that was set off to announce the arrival of an important character on stage. In this instance, however, just as Henry VIII was about to make his appearance, the cannon set light to a wooden beam, and the resulting fire soon spread to the Globe's thatched roof. Within an hour, the entire theatre had been destroyed.

Miraculously, no one was injured – although one man had a narrow escape:

> Yet nothing did perish but wood and straw, and a few forsaken cloaks; one man had his breeches set on fire, that would perhaps have broyled him, if he had not by the benefit of a provident wit, put it out with a bottle of ale.
>
> Sir Henry Wotton, a letter dated 2 July 1613

A great destructive fire like that which destroyed the Globe can be known as a *scathefire*, a word dating back to the early seventeenth century. *Scathe* is an Old English word for damage or injury that is seldom encountered in English today outside of 'scathing reviews', or descriptions of a 'scathing wit', but over the centuries it was used in a number of different phrases and expressions. *To think no scathe* of something once meant not to regret it, for instance, while *to wait scathe* was to cause harm, and *it is scathe!* was an early Middle Ages equivalent of 'what a pity!'

transpontine *(adj.)* located on the opposite side of a bridge

On 30 June 1894, after eight years of work, London's monumental Tower Bridge was officially opened, providing the city's growing population with another route across the river.

Something located on the opposite side of a bridge can be described as *transpontine*, derived from *pons*, a Latin word for 'bridge'. In the mid nineteenth century, however, that word gained an entirely new meaning, thanks to the varying types of show available to theatregoers in Victorian London. Back then, the upmarket theatres around the West End were well known for their sophisticated productions of classical dramas and tragedies, while those south of the Thames, in Surrey and Lambeth, played to a different audience. Here, the order of the day was for sensational, scandalous or salacious stories and performances. As the English writer and publisher Charles Knight commented:

> Look at our theatres; look at the houses all around them. Have they not given a taint to the very districts they belong to? . . . At Christmas time, at each of these minor theatres, may be seen . . . an appalling amount of loathsome vice.
>
> *Penny Magazine*, 1846

The shows performed in these 'transpontine theatres', as they became known, may not have been to Knight's taste, but they remained enduringly popular throughout the nineteenth and early twentieth centuries. As a result, alongside its literal meaning *transpontine* came to be used to mean 'sensational' or 'melodramatic' – a reference not only to the location of the theatres, but to the type of shows they staged.

backronym *(n.)* an acronymic explanation invented for a word that is not an acronym

In 1983, a competition appeared in the *Washington Post* asking readers to invent their own words. Among the submissions was the word *backronym*, defined as 'the same as an acronym, except that the words were chosen to fit the letters'.

Despite the competition being understandably light-hearted (*rainbrella*, *administrivia* and *troublem*, 'a cross between a trouble and a problem', were also shortlisted), *backronym* somehow managed to shake off its fairly flippant origins and is now listed in the *Oxford English Dictionary* – though not with its original definition.

According to the *OED*, a *backronym* is 'a contrived explanation of an existing word's origin, positing it as an acronym'. So the idea that *golf* is an acronym of 'gentlemen only, ladies forbidden', or that *posh* stands for 'port out, starboard home' (a reference to wealthy cruise-ship passengers paying for the best views on both legs of a journey), would both qualify. And so too would *SOS*.

Following an International Radiotelegraphic Convention in 1906, SOS (· · · – – – · · ·) was adopted worldwide as the standard Morse code distress signal on 1 July 1908. Although linguistic folklore will have you believe the letters were chosen to stand for 'save our souls', the truth is that SOS was picked simply because that particular combination of dots and dashes is so instantly recognisable. Before SOS, the letters CQD were the standard distress signal worldwide: CQ because it sounds like *sécu*, an abbreviation of a French word *securité*, meaning 'safety', with D added to stand for 'distress'. But despite that straightforward explanation, even CQD fell foul of the *backronym* treatment – so don't believe anyone who tells you that it stood for 'come quickly: danger!'

meditullium *(n.)* the absolute middle or core of something

Tellus, or *Tellus Mater* ('Mother Earth'), was the name of a goddess personifying the earth in Roman mythology. Considered one of twenty principal gods and goddesses of Rome, alongside the likes of Jupiter, Apollo and Venus, Tellus was an important agricultural deity who was celebrated at festivals throughout the year to coincide with crops being sown or harvested and livestock producing their young.

Tellus' name crops up in a handful of English words, including the chemical element *tellurium*, named by the German chemist Martin Heinrich Klaproth in 1798. A *tellurometer*, likewise, is a device for measuring the movement of the earth, while a *tellurion* is a clockwork mechanism used to demonstrate the earth's rotation and revolution and its effect on the days and seasons.

A *telligraph* is a written description of an area of land, particularly one used as the basis of a legal document or to establish a common boundary. Something that is *intratelluric* is found or formed inside the earth. And, back in its original Latin, the word *meditullium* – which combines Tellus' name with the adjective *medius*, meaning 'middle' or 'centre' – was used to refer to the interior or absolute centre of a region or territory.

That original meaning had broadened by the time *meditullium* was first borrowed into English in the early 1600s, and since then the word has merely been used to refer to the absolute centre or core part of something. And in that sense, it is a fitting word for today: 2 July is the 183rd day of a normal calendar year, and as 182 days have already gone and are there 182 days remaining, today is the exact midpoint of the year.

cosmognosis *(n.)*   the natural instinct that tells a
creature when to migrate

Derived from Greek roots literally meaning 'earth-knowledge',
cosmognosis is the curious instinct that tells a creature when to
begin its annual migration – or, as the 1882 *New Sydenham
Society's Lexicon of Medicine and the Allied Sciences* defined it,
'the instinct which teaches animals the right time for migration,
and the fitting place to which to go'.

The seasonal arrival and disappearance of birds long puzzled
scientists, and the theories put forward to account for it were not
always well informed. Aristotle, for instance, famously theorised
that swallows must hibernate at the bottom of ponds each winter,
and oddly that belief continued right through to the late eighteenth century, when the English naturalist Thomas Bewick wrote
of a sea captain 'between the islands of Minorca and Majorca,
[who] saw great numbers of swallows flying northward'. Based
on that anecdotal evidence, Bewick concluded that:

> Swallows do not in any material instance differ from
> other birds in their nature and propensities . . . they
> leave us when this country can no longer furnish them
> with a supply of their proper and natural food.
> Thomas Bewick, *A History of British Birds* (1797)

By the late nineteenth century the theory of the seasonal
migration of birds was almost universally acknowledged – and
eventually acquired some extraordinary proof to support it. On
3 July 1913, an Arctic tern was captured and tagged in Maine
in the eastern United States. In August 1917, the same bird was
found dead at the delta of the Niger River in Africa. It was the
first bird in history proved to have crossed the Atlantic Ocean.

monadnock *(n.)*   an isolated hill or mountain

Also known as an *inselberg* (literally an 'island-mountain'), a *monadnock* is an isolated hill or ridge. Specifically, this kind of landmark is made from a harder, more resistant rock than its surrounding environment, so while the rock around it is eroded away the *monadnock* remains in place to create a single, mountainous land mass jutting up from an otherwise largely flattened landscape. Mount Monadnock in New Hampshire, USA, is a particularly fine example of this kind of feature – and hence gave its name to all similar landforms in the late nineteenth century.

Fittingly for 4 July, American Independence Day, *monadnock* isn't the only American place name to have ended up in the dictionary. *Tuxedos*, for instance, take their name from the Tuxedo Club, a country club in Tuxedo Park in New York, where they first became popular (flip through to 10 October for more on that). Chautauqua in New York was once home to a summer school organisation that gave its name to a type of outdoor educational symposium that has been known as a *chautauqua* since the late nineteenth century. And the state of Texas gave its name to the largest or uppermost deck of a riverboat steamer, where the officers' quarters are located, in the mid 1800s. No one is entirely sure why these *texas decks* are so called, but perhaps the name somehow alludes to the fact that Texas was the largest state in the Union at the time. (And turn back to 25 February to find out how Buncombe, North Carolina, came to give its name to tedious or nonsensical talk.)

paw-paw *(adj.)*   immoral, obscene

Spelled without a hyphen, *pawpaw* is a seventeenth-century word for the papaya fruit. Spelled with a hyphen, *paw-paw* is something quite different:

> *Paw-paw Tricks.* Naughty tricks: an expression used by nurses, &c. to children.
>
> Francis Grose, *A Classical Dictionary of the Vulgar Tongue* (3rd ed., 1796)

Seldom used since the late 1800s, *paw-paw* first emerged in the English language in the unpredictable slang of the early eighteenth century, when it was originally used to mean 'nasty', 'improper' or, stronger still, 'obscene'; a derivative term, *paw-pawness*, meaning 'obscenity' or 'immorality', emerged in the 1820s.

Etymologically, the word is thought to derive from a reduplication of *pah!* or *paw!*, which has been recorded as an expression of scorn or disgust since the late sixteenth century. Something that is *paw-paw*, ultimately, is enough to make someone shout out in contempt.

Shouts of obscenity abounded on 5 July 1946, when the world's first bikini swimsuit was introduced by the French designer Louis Réard. Made from a scant 30 square inches of fabric, Réard's bikini – famously named after the Bikini Atoll nuclear weapons test site in the Pacific Ocean – was marketed as 'smaller than the world's smallest bathing suit', and was so revealing that Réard had to hire a nude dancer from the Casino de Paris, Micheline Bernardini, to model it. Despite the controversy, however, Réard's bikini was a hit and the style has remained popular ever since.

immemorialness *(n.)*   the quality of something that makes it unrememberable or beyond memory

Immemorialness is the quality of something that makes it utterly incapable of being remembered. The word derives from the earlier adjective *immemorial*, which has been in use in English since the late 1500s but today survives largely only in the stock expression *time immemorial*, meaning 'time beyond memory'.

Although used fairly loosely today, *time immemorial* was originally a legal term used to define a period beyond legal memory that could ultimately be used to settle disputes of ownership – in which context, it has a curious connection to today's date.

Drawn up in 1275, the First Statute of Westminster was the first of three such statutes that set out to codify and standardise all the laws of England for the very first time. (Ironically, they were all written in French.) Clause 39, the Limitation of Prescription Act, established a precise date against which all grievances over ownership of property could be determined:

> No one is to be given a hearing to claim seisin [feudal ownership of land] by an ancestor of his further back than the time of King Richard, uncle of King Henry, the father of the present king.

So, if your ownership of something was challenged, all you had to do was prove that your ancestors had maintained ownership of it since before Richard I had come to the throne. Ultimately, the First Statute of Westminster established the date of Richard I's ascendancy – 6 July 1189 – as the cut-off point for living memory, while anything that occurred before that date was thereby deemed *time immemorial*.

Augean *(adj.)* horrendously filthy

On 7 July 1855, an open letter by Michael Faraday about a recent trip he had taken down the River Thames was printed in *The Times*:

> Sir – I traversed this day by steamboat the space between London and Hungerford Bridges . . . The appearance and smell of the water forced themselves at once on my attention. The whole of the river was an opaque pale brown fluid. In order to test the degree of opacity, I tore up some white cards into pieces . . . and then dropped some of these pieces into the water . . . Before they had sunk an inch below the surface they were undistinguishable . . . If there be sufficient authority to remove a putrescent pond from the neighbourhood of a few simple dwellings, surely the river which flows for so many miles through London ought not to be allowed to become a fermenting sewer.

By the mid nineteenth century, gallons of raw sewage were being swilled into the River Thames every day, leaving it horrifically polluted. But Faraday's letter – written by one of the most respected scholars of his day – marked a turning point, and parliament was compelled to act. The building of a new sewerage system was ratified in 1858, and completed in 1875.

Anything horrifically filthy can be described as *Augean*, a late-sixteenth-century adjective derived from the name of the legendary King Augeas of Elis. Augeas owned the greatest collection of livestock in the land, but their stables were renowned for having never been cleaned. The fifth labour of the hero Heracles was to clean out the stables – a task he completed by rerouting the Alpheus and Peneus rivers to wash away the mess.

decult *(v.)*　to hide something, to keep something
secret

On 8 July 1947, the front page of the *Roswell Daily Record* read,
'RAAF Captures Flying Saucer on Ranch in Roswell Region'.

An RAAF, or Roswell Army Air Field officer, the newspaper
explained, had recovered a peculiar 'flying disc' that had crashed
in the New Mexico desert. The military soon claimed respon-
sibility, and a statement was released explaining that the crash
had involved nothing more than a military weather balloon. But
before long rumours about the precise identity of the Roswell
'disc' had begun to spread, and the military was compelled to
call a press conference to dispel them and to allay any fears.
Pieces of wood, foil and other debris consistent with a military weather-monitoring balloon were displayed, and, with the
public duly reassured, the story dropped out of the headlines.

Since then, however, Roswell has become the unwitting
subject of an infamous conspiracy theory claiming that it was
an alien spacecraft that had crashed that day – and that the US
government surreptitiously collected the craft, and still keep it
in a top-secret military base in the desert. In the 1990s, US military papers were released that revealed the balloon had actually
been a nuclear test surveillance craft, but even that revelation
wasn't enough to quash the rumours, and the Roswell incident
continues to entice conspiracy theorists all over the world.

To keep something hidden, or to hide something in secret,
is to *decult* it, a word first recorded in the lexicographer Henry
Cockeram's *English Dictionarie* in 1623. Derived directly from
Latin, to *decult* something, Cockeram explained, is simply 'to
hide [it] privily'.

Boy Jones *(n.)*   a secret informant

At around 7 o'clock in the morning on 9 July 1982, a thirty-three-year-old man named Michael Fagan scaled the wall around Buckingham Palace, crossed the grounds, shimmied up a drain-pipe and found his way into the queen's bedroom. The break-in had gone completely unnoticed, and the queen herself was left to alert palace security – but not, according to reports, until after Fagan had sat on the end of her bed and asked for some cigarettes.

Oddly, this was Fagan's second break-in of Buckingham Palace (a month earlier he had found his way into the palace's post room after sneaking in through an open window). Stranger still, almost precisely the same thing had happened to Queen Victoria.

A teenager named Edward Jones broke into Buckingham Palace on a number of occasions between 1838 and 1841. In the first of his escapades, Jones – aged just fourteen – snuck into the palace disguised as a chimney sweep, before being chased from the premises by a porter after he stuffed some of the queen's underwear down his trousers. He again found his way into the palace in November 1840, and then again the following month, where he was discovered hiding under a sofa in the queen's dressing room. Finally, in March 1841 he was caught eating a snack in one of the royal apartments, arrested and sentenced to three months' hard labour. He later joined the Navy and emigrated to Australia, where he died in 1893.

Jones's audacious activities quickly earned him notoriety across the capital, where he became affectionately known as 'the Boy Jones'. By the mid 1800s, his nickname had become so well known that *boy Jones* had fallen into slang use in London, first as an expression – 'it's that boy Jones again!' – used when something goes unexpectedly missing, and then as a byword for a secret or unnamed informant.

lawrence *(n.)* a shimmering heat haze

As well as being a boy's name, a *lawrence* is also a heat haze – the shimmering, undulating appearance of the air above a hot surface.

Precisely how that meaning came about takes us back to third-century Rome, and the rather macabre death of a papal archbishop. In 258 AD, the Emperor Valerian called for all Christian senators to be stripped of their titles and assets, and all Christian clergymen to be arrested. In accordance with his orders, Pope Sixtus II and seven of his highest-ranking ministers were detained and forced to profess their faith to the gods of Rome. All refused, and so were promptly put to death – all, that is, except one.

Lawrence of Rome, an archdeacon in charge of the pope's treasury, was given a three-day stay of execution in which to collect the church's wealth and hand it over to the Roman state. Instead, he spent the next three days giving as much of the money away as he could, and returned to the senate with a group of Rome's neediest citizens, boldly claiming that these were the real treasures of the Church. It was a noble act, but one that earned him an especially cruel punishment: Lawrence was sentenced to be roasted to death.

This grim tale is argued by some to be apocryphal, but whether true or not, it nevertheless inspired the use of *lawrence* to refer to the shimmering haze we see over the ground on scorching hot days. It's also a fitting word for today: on 10 July 1913, a temperature of 56.7°C (134°F) was reportedly measured at Death Valley, California, which if accurate remains the hottest temperature ever recorded on earth.

bluenose *(n.)*   a strict prude; a priggish, puritanical person

In the early nineteenth century, *bluenose* was a nickname for a strict follower of Presbyterianism. How that name came about is debatable, but it is likely to be connected to the earlier expression *true blue*, which has been used to refer to anyone especially loyal and unfaltering since the early 1600s.

But because these strictest of Presbyterians were known for their equally strict and puritanical lifestyles, by the turn of the century *bluenose* had come to refer to anyone with prudish, priggish tastes or morals – and it's in that sense that it is a particularly relevant word for today.

Thomas Bowdler was born on 11 July 1754. As a child, Bowdler's father would read him and his siblings extracts from Shakespeare – but as an adult he discovered that his father had been deliberately omitting lines or passages of text from the plays that he deemed unsuitable for his family to hear. Inspired by that careful censorship, in 1807 Bowdler published *The Family Shakespeare*, a four-volume collection of twenty-four of Shakespeare's plays in which Bowdler either edited or omitted altogether any vulgar jokes, profanity, questionable or risqué references and – in Bowdler's own words – all other 'defects which diminish their value'.

Lady Macbeth's 'damned spot', for instance, became a 'crimson' spot. Ophelia's implied suicide in *Hamlet* became little more than a tragic accident. And the character of Doll Tearsheet, the bawdy prostitute in *Henry IV: Part 2*, is removed altogether.

Bowdler wasn't the first *bluenose* to attempt an expurgation of Shakespeare's work, but he was certainly among the most successful. And for that reason, we still talk of strictly edited or *bowdlerised* language today.

insulet *(n.)* a small island

The Latin word for 'island' was *insula*. That makes a *peninsula*, literally, 'almost an island'. *Insulating* something involves 'making it an island'. And *insulin* is so called because it's produced by bodies in the pancreas known as the 'islets of Langerhans'. *Insula* is also the origin of the diminutive *insulet*, a word coined in the mid 1600s as another name for a small island.

Speaking of which, on 12 July 1630, the colonial governors of New Amsterdam (later New York) purchased a low-lying, 3½-acre tidal island off the coast of New Jersey from the local Mohegan natives. The natives knew it as *Kioshk*, or 'Gull Island', a reference to the fact that the seabirds who lived there were its only inhabitants. The local Dutch settlers knew it as Oyster Island, a reference to the rich oyster beds that lay offshore. And after the island came to be used as a site to hang convicted criminals, by the turn of the eighteenth century the island had become known as Gibbet Island.

Sometime around the American Revolution, however, the island was purchased by a New York merchant named Samuel Ellis, who opened a small tavern for passing sailors there in 1776. After Samuel's death, the island was sold first to the State of New York, and then to the US government in 1808, who used the island as a military barracks, and eventually as an immigration centre. Opened in 1892, it became the first port of call for a staggering 12 million immigrants to America over the sixty-two years it was in operation. Throughout all of these later changes, however, the name Ellis Island stuck.

decurt *(v.)*   to shorten, to abridge

The iconic sign that overlooks Hollywood, California, was officially dedicated on 13 July 1913.

The sign began life merely as an advertisement for a new residential complex in the Hollywood Hills, whose developers commissioned a local signage company to produce a row of white upper case letters, 50 feet by 30 feet, to stand on the hillside above Los Angeles. The sign was intended to stand only for a year, but as it became increasingly associated with the ever-expanding film industry nearby it soon became a permanent fixture.

Originally, there were thirteen letters – the name of the residential development, and the original wording of the sign, had been HOLLYWOODLAND – but in 1949 the local chamber of commerce decreed that the final four letters be removed to better reflect Hollywood as a whole, not merely the residences it was built to promote.

To trim or abridge something in this way is to *decurt* it, a seventeenth-century word derived from the Latin *curtare*, meaning 'to cut short' or 'abbreviate'. *Curtail* and *curt* both derive from the same root, as does a *cortado* coffee, and *accurtation*, a formal term for the act of shortening or curtailing. And this wasn't the only *accurtation* in the Hollywood sign's history.

Over the years that followed, the sign became ever more dilapidated as its wooden framework deteriorated. In the 1940s, the H was destroyed by the sign's caretaker, Albert Kothe, who crashed his car into it while drunk. The final O later collapsed, as did the top of the second O, so that by the late 1970s it better resembled a lower case U. Thankfully, a fundraising campaign in 1978 attracted investment from a number of celebrities, and the Hollywood sign was promptly restored to its former glory.

acharnement *(n.)*   bloodthirsty enthusiasm

In France, 14 July is Bastille Day, commemorating the Storming of the Bastille on this day in 1789.

The fall of the Bastille, a prison and armoury in Paris, at the hands of fewer than 1,000 insurgents provided a huge boost for the French republican cause and acted as the tipping point of the French Revolution. Despite its symbolic importance, however, the prison housed just seven inmates at the time.

On the national day of France, it's worth remembering that roughly one-third of the English language is of direct French origin. Thanks to the Norman Conquest of 1066, French became the official language of English law, politics and finance, and as William the Conqueror's French-speaking court and supporters were brought from Normandy to help him rule his newly acquired lands, countless French political, legal, military and cultural terms were brought with them. *Money, government, soldier, tax, justice* and *art* were all adopted into the language around this time and have become so naturalised that their Continental origins have long since evaporated. But century by century, French words have continued to be adopted into English – including a great many obscure terms that arguably deserve a wider audience.

The French word for 'nail', *clou*, for instance, is used in English to refer to a centre of attention. An *étourderie* is an act of thoughtlessness or a careless blunder. A *mauvais coucheur* – literally, a 'bad bedfellow' – is an unsociable or uncooperative person. And, fittingly for a day on which the first spark of the French Revolution was kindled, *acharnement* – a French word for the act of enlivening a pack of hounds by giving them a taste of meat – is bloodthirstiness or ferocious enthusiasm for a cause.

triglot *(n.)*   a book or text written in three languages

According to the story, it was on 15 July 1799 that Lieutenant Pierre-François Bouchard, a French Napoleonic soldier posted to Egypt, stumbled upon a large stone slab covered in inscriptions while working on the reconstruction of a military base near the city of Rosetta. Realising the find was significant, Bouchard informed his commanding officer, who in turn sent word to Napoleon's Commission des Sciences et des Arts, a body of scholars and experts who had accompanied him on his campaign to the Middle East. Their report noted one extraordinary feature of the stone: two of its three inscriptions were written in different Egyptian scripts, while the third was in Ancient Greek. One of the members of the Commission, Michel Ange Lancret, rightly postulated that the three were translations of the same text, and as Ancient Greek was already well known to scholars and classicists, the so-called Rosetta Stone eventually provided the key to translating all Egyptian hieroglyphics.

The three different inscriptions on the Rosetta Stone make it an example of a *triglot*, a text or book written in three languages. The word *triglot* – which can also be used of someone who speaks three languages – was coined in the late nineteenth century, and combines Greek words meaning 'three', *trias*, and 'tongue', *glotta* or *glossa*, from which the *epiglottis* (literally 'upon the tongue') also takes its name.

As for Napoleon, his Egyptian campaign was defeated by an alliance of British and Ottoman forces. As part of the subsequent Capitulation of Alexandria, a treaty signed in 1801, the Rosetta Stone and all other Egyptian artefacts collected by the Commission des Sciences et des Artes became British possessions, and to this day the stone remains one of the chief treasures of the British Museum.

basiate *(v.)* to kiss

Derived from a Latin word for a kiss on the hand, to *basiate* is to kiss. To *suaviate* is also to kiss, a term derived from *suavis*, a Latin word meaning 'sweet'. And to *osculate* or *deosculate* is also to kiss, both of which come from a Latin word for 'kiss', *osculum*, that literally means 'little mouth'.

No matter how you choose to put it, however, *basiating*, *suaviating* and *osculating* were all banned in England on 16 July 1439.

The kissing ban was brought in by the parliament of Henry VI in an attempt to counteract a sudden and virulent outbreak of the plague that had started the previous year. By this time, the Black Death had been ravaging Europe for decades (the first human victims had reportedly died as far back as the mid 1300s), but given the poor-to-non-existent standards of hygiene in medieval England, the disease continued to break out sporadically even after it had appeared to die away. A widespread failure of the crops in England in 1438 worsened the situation, as it led to a famine that weakened the population, making them suddenly much more susceptible to disease than in recent years.

To counteract the problem, parliament issued a ban on kissing – including the kisses that the king's knights and ministers were supposed to offer the king himself as homage. Parliament petitioned the king, 'may [we] omit the said kissing of you, and be excused thereof', hoping that way to stop the disease spreading to the royal family. The king happily agreed, and the ban remained in place until the 'plague season' was finally deemed to be over.

steganogram *(n.)*   a coded text or message

A *steganogram* is a coded message, while the act of writing encrypted or secret language is known as *steganography*, a term used since the late fifteenth century. Both terms derive from a Greek word, *steganos*, literally meaning 'covered' or 'concealed'.

On 17 July 1586, the imprisoned Mary, Queen of Scots wrote an encrypted letter to her former page, Anthony Babington. By this time Mary, a Catholic, had been held in prison for eighteen years by her Protestant cousin, the reigning Queen Elizabeth I, who was fearful that Mary and her Catholic supporters could rise up and oust her from power. Babington, meanwhile, had been plotting with a Jesuit priest named John Ballard to have Elizabeth I assassinated, and, with the help of the reigning Catholic dynasties of France and Spain, restore both Catholicism to England and Mary to the throne. Mary and Babington's correspondence, however, was intercepted.

Sir Francis Walsingham, Elizabeth's chief spymaster, discovered the plot and set to work securing Mary's downfall. He placed two double agents among the staff at Chartley Castle in Staffordshire, where Mary was imprisoned, and arranged a system whereby all the secret messages sent to and from Mary – secreted inside the corks of wine barrels – would first pass by his code breaker, Thomas Phelippes. When the coded letter Mary sent on this day was deciphered by Phelippes, Walsingham had all the evidence he needed. In February the following year, Mary was executed for treason.

yellowplush *(n.)* a footman

The author and writer William Makepeace Thackeray was born on 18 July 1811. Although best known for his novel *Vanity Fair* (1848), Thackeray's complete works include countless essays, art and literary reviews, works of journalism, satirical sketches, travel literature, letters, short stories and a great many more novels, including *The Luck of Barry Lyndon* (1844), *Pendennis* (1850) and *The Newcomes* (1855). And throughout this vast creative output, Thackeray coined and contributed a great many new words to the English language.

Used in the introduction to his penultimate novel, *The Virginians* (1859), *partykin*, 'a little party', is just one of a number of words Thackeray invented using the familiar –*kin* suffix that was adopted from Dutch in the Middle English period and has since come to be used to form diminutives in English. *Birdkin, notekin, essaykin, grudgekin, mousekin, princekin* and *lordkin* are all among Thackeray's other inventions, as well as *parklet* ('a little park') and *courtlet* ('a small or petty court').

In his *Book of Snobs* (1848), Thackeray also coined the words *snobling* ('a little or young snob') and *snobographer* ('someone who describes or writes about snobs'), as well as introducing the word *snobbishness* (although the word *snobbish* had been introduced five years earlier in Dickens's *The Old Curiosity Shop*).

And a *yellowplush* is a courtier or footman, so named by Thackeray in allusion to the yellow velvet used to make their uniforms – and used by him as a pseudonym, Charles James Yellowplush, at the start of his career.

lagan *(n.)*   goods or wreckage lying on the seabed

In maritime law, four terms are used to classify the contents and remains of shipwrecks: *flotsam*, *jetsam*, *lagan* and *derelict*.

Of the four, the first two are the most familiar: *flotsam* ('goods left floating on the surface after a ship sinks') and *jetsam* ('goods deliberately jettisoned as the ship goes down') are often paired up and used more generally in English to mean 'odds and ends' or 'bits and pieces'. *Derelict* too has a more general use in English, meaning 'abandoned' or 'neglected', but in maritime law refers specifically to goods willingly or deliberately abandoned by their owner, with no hope of being reclaimed.

Lagan – perhaps derived from the same ancient word root as *lie* and *lay* – refers to goods that are lost in a shipwreck, but which can be salvaged at a later date. *Lagan* is often tied to buoys, flags or other floating markers so that they can be located and collected in the future by their owners, and so while technically lost to the seabed, *lagan* can eventually be reclaimed.

One of British history's most famous shipwrecks took place on 19 July 1545, when the *Mary Rose*, flagship of Henry VIII, sank in the English Channel during an attack on an invading French fleet. Although precisely what happened to the ship is debatable, contemporary reports suggest she was turning in the Solent – the stretch of water between the Isle of Wight and mainland England – when a sudden gust of wind caused her to take in water through her open gunports, causing her to founder and eventually sink.

Four centuries later, the wreck of the *Mary Rose* was rediscovered in 1971, and was brought back to the surface in one of the most complex projects in the history of marine archaeology in 1982. The remains of the ship are now on display in Portsmouth.

ecopoiesis *(n.)*   the establishment of a functioning
ecosystem on a lifeless planet

The term *ecopoiesis* (pronounced 'eck-oh-poy-*ee*-sis') was coined
in the 1980s by the Canadian biophysicist Robert Haynes, who
defined it as 'the fabrication of a sustainable ecosystem on a currently lifeless, sterile planet'. Fittingly, it is comprised of Greek
roots meaning 'house', *oikos*, and 'construction', *poesis*.

In particular, *ecopoiesis* refers to the expansion of a human
ecosystem on the planet Mars, a prospect that for a long time
seemed an impossibility. On 20 July 1976, however, the colon-
isation of Mars took one step forward: the *Viking 1* spacecraft
became the first in history to land successfully on the surface of
Mars and carry out its mission.

On board *Viking 1* were two cameras, as well as a complex
array of scientific instruments including pressure gauges, therm-
ometers, radiation detectors and seismographs. On landing in
the planet's so-called Golden Plain, a vast flat basin in the lower
northern hemisphere, *Viking 1* took the first colour photograph
of the Martian surface, then began a series of ground-breaking
experiments in the search for life.

Viking 1 collected and analysed soil samples, in the hope
that some sign of organic life could be detected. Most of the
experiments came back as negative – but one, which mixed
the Martian soil with water and radioactive carbon atoms and
analysed the results, came back positive. In light of the other
results, at the time this experiment was dismissed, but later
research has postulated that this anomaly might suggest that
microbial life could exist deeper beneath the surface of Mars,
amid a layer of water ice.

Life on Mars may yet, it seems, be a possibility.

pelmatogram *(n.)* a footprint

A single footprint is a *pelmatogram*, a word coined in the nineteenth century from *pelma*, the Greek word for the sole of the foot.

And just before 3 o'clock in the morning on 21 July 1969 GMT (or just before 10 o'clock at night on 20 July, Eastern Standard Time) one of the most famous footprints in history was made – when *Apollo 11* mission commander Neil Armstrong set foot on the surface of the moon.

The *Eagle*, the lunar module of the *Apollo 11* spacecraft, had touched down on the lunar surface a little under seven hours earlier, in which time the two men on board, Armstrong and his *Apollo* co-pilot Buzz Aldrin, had rested, surveyed the surrounding landscape for the best spot to plant their US flag and to collect lunar material – and, in the case of Presbyterian elder Buzz Aldrin, taken Holy Communion. Armstrong and Aldrin then readied themselves to leave the lunar module, and Armstrong set foot on the moon with the words, 'one small step for man, one giant leap for mankind'.

As there is no wind on the lunar surface, so long as it remains undisturbed by impacts from asteroids or similar debris, NASA estimates that Armstrong's footprint will remain in place on the moon's surface for the next million years.

handfast *(adj.)*   manacled, shackled

When it first appeared in the language in the Old English period, the word *handfast* was a verb meaning 'to commit to marry', or 'to betroth'; that meaning still survives in some dialects of English, and indeed *handfasting* is still used in certain contexts to refer to a betrothal or engagement. By the fifteenth and sixteenth centuries, however, *handfast* had come to be used both as a noun, meaning 'a firm grip', and an adjective, meaning 'shackled', 'manacled' or 'handcuffed'. Extended and figurative meanings were quick to follow, so that by the early 1500s a *handfast* had become someone absolutely dedicated to a cause; *handfastness* was a synonym for tight-fistedness or miserliness; and to *handfast* something was to take tight hold of it.

Of all these meanings, however, just one concerns us today, thanks to a bizarre and terrifying series of stunts carried out by one daredevil acrobat in the late nineteenth century.

Maria Spelterini was a twenty-three-year-old Italian tightrope walker who, as part of the United States Centennial celebrations in 1876, became the first woman to cross Niagara Falls on a tightrope on 8 July. Not content with that, four days later, on 12 July, she returned to the Falls and crossed the same tightrope wearing wooden peach baskets strapped to her feet. Not content with *that*, she then returned on 19 July, and crossed the Falls blindfolded. And then, on 22 July 1876, she repeated the stunt one last time – and crossed Niagara Falls by tightrope with her feet shackled and her hands held *handfast* in manacles.

abjudicate *(v.)*   to ban, to prohibit by rule of law

As Benito Mussolini's Fascist government began to strengthen its hold on Italy in the mid 1920s, widespread censorship began to be imposed nationwide – beginning, oddly, with the Italian language.

As early as 1923, Mussolini levied a tax on the use of any 'foreign' words that appeared on shop signs or public notices, and as the decade wore on this trend for maintaining the purity of Italian culture became ever more rampant. Finally, on 23 July 1929, all foreign words were banned in the Italian language.

Words of French, English or otherwise outside origin were all prohibited, with pure Italian-origin words coined to replace them. All of Italy's regional dialects were likewise banned – giving Mussolini an uphill struggle in imposing his rule, as at the time just 12 per cent of the Italian population spoke what could be regarded as the 'Italian' language, while the remainder spoke a dizzying array of regional languages, like Tuscan, Ligurian and Venetian.

Perhaps for that reason, the censorship didn't last, and happily Italian today contains just as much outside influence as the rest of the major European languages.

To prohibit something by rule of law is to *abjudicate* it, a term from the early seventeenth century derived from a Latin word meaning 'to take away by judicial verdict'. That strict legal meaning remained in place when the word was first adopted into English, but before long use of *adjudicate* had broadened to mean simply 'to reject', 'to disallow' or 'to forbid'.

opiniatre *(n.)*   a person who holds an opinion

First used in English in the late seventeenth century, an *opiniatre* is someone who holds an opinion. The word is believed to be derived from its French equivalent, *opiniâtre*, which in turn comes from the Latin roots *opinio*, meaning 'belief' or 'personal view', and the suffix *–aster*, which was used in Latin to form deprecatory nouns expressing contempt, or an incomplete or questionable resemblance. So, while a *poetaster* is a poor-quality poet and an *criticaster* a petty or inferior critic, an *opiniatre* was originally someone who stubbornly or dogmatically stuck to their own view.

As a survey of public opinion, the word *poll* was originally an anatomical term for the top of the head (the same *poll*, incidentally, crops up in *poleaxe* and *tadpole*), which makes an opinion poll literally a 'head count'. And on 24 July 1824, the world's first opinion poll was conducted by an American newspaper, the *Harrisburg Pennsylvanian*, in the run-up to that year's presidential election.

The incumbent president, James Monroe, was retiring and the race to replace him was open. A group of several hundred local citizens was surveyed to find out their favourite successor – with military hero Andrew Jackson emerging as a clear favourite with 70 per cent of the votes. Although Jackson went on to win the popular vote in the subsequent election, John Quincy Adams became Monroe's replacement when the result was handed over to the House of Representatives. Jackson remained enormously popular with the public, however, and ultimately went on to replace Adams in 1829.

siderodromophobia *(n.)* the fear of rail travel

In 1879, an article appeared in the *Medical Times and Gazette* discussing a peculiar medical condition all but unique to employees and passengers of the ever-expanding Victorian railway industry:

> *Siderodromophobia* . . . [is] a more or less intense spinal irritation, coupled with a hysterical condition and a morbid disinclination for work, which, as the result of shock, occurs among railway employees, who, in consequence of their occupation, are specially predisposed to it.

First recognised by a German physician named Johannes Rigler among railway employees who had been involved in crashes, *siderodromophobia* was essentially a combination of whiplash and post-traumatic stress disorder – a damaging combination of physical and psychological disorders, common in those who have experienced high-speed travel accidents.

But in coining the word itself, Rigler brought together three Greek roots meaning 'iron', *sideros*; 'road' or 'way', *dromos*; and 'fear', *phobia*, a reference to the psychological impact of the accidents. As the *–phobia* suffix became ever more familiar to English throughout the twentieth century (and increasingly associated with irrational aversions rather than psychological trauma), this original meaning drifted into obscurity, so that today *siderodromophobia* is merely the irrational fear of train travel.

Either way, it's a word with a clear connection to today's date: on 25 July 1814, George Stephenson's first steam locomotive, a 'travelling engine' named *Blücher* developed at Killingworth Colliery outside Newcastle upon Tyne, ran successfully for the first time. The vast expansion of the railways of Victorian England had begun.

Sardoodledom *(n.)*   well-made but contrived or
trivial works for theatre

The playwright and critic George Bernard Shaw was born on
26 July 1856. The author of more than sixty plays, novels and
countless essays, Shaw established himself as an exceptional turn-
of-the-century writer whose works covered subjects and genres
as diverse as comedy and satire, art and music, and political and
social debate. Shaw also remains the only person in history to have
won both a Nobel Prize (Literature, 1925) and an Academy Award
(Best Adapted Screenplay, for his own play, *Pygmalion*, in 1938).

Known for his often-controversial opinions, Shaw
railed against everything from English spelling to William
Shakespeare. Indeed, Shaw coined the word *bardolatry* in 1901
to refer to what he saw as the undue reverence other writers had
for Shakespeare: 'With the single exception of Homer,' he once
wrote, 'there is no eminent writer, not even Sir Walter Scott,
whom I despise so entirely as I despise Shakespear [*sic*].' Among
Shaw's other coinages:

- *clever-clever* (adj.) anxious to be considered clever
- *impossibilism* (v.) belief in ideas that cannot be put into
  practice
- *moodle* (v.) to idle time away, to dawdle
- *nonentitise* (v.) to make into a nonentity

In 1895, Shaw also coined the word *Sardoodledom*, used to
describe well-made but ultimately trivial or morally objection-
able theatrical works. Based around the dismissive term *doodle*,
the word was a slight against one of Shaw's contemporaries,
French playwright Victorien Sardou, whose stagey and often
contrived plays Shaw considered 'claptrap'.

misocapnist *(n.)*   someone who hates tobacco smoke

The explorer and adventurer Sir Walter Raleigh arrived back in Britain from a trip to North America on 27 July 1586 – and, according to folklore, had with him the very first tobacco ever introduced to England. One version of this tale even has one of Raleigh's servants, on discovering his master smoking a pipe, throwing a pail of water over him in the mistaken belief that he was on fire.

In fact, tobacco had been brought to England a little earlier than this date might suggest: through Columbus's travels to the New World a century earlier, the Spanish had already begun smoking tobacco and through them the practice had spread across much of western Europe by the early 1500s. The tobacco Raleigh had with him was probably the first brought from England's own colonies, most likely Virginia – but it almost certainly wasn't the first in English history.

Raleigh nevertheless enjoyed tobacco, and is credited with popularising smoking in England throughout his lifetime. When he finally fell foul of James I and was executed in 1618, he left a small box of tobacco in his cell, engraved on which was a Latin inscription meaning: 'It was my companion at that most miserable time.' Not everyone, however, is such a fan.

A *misocapnist* is someone who hates cigarette smoke. Dating from the early nineteenth century, *misocapnist* brings together a Greek word for smoke, *capnos*, with the same prefix, *miso–*, as found in words like *misogyny* and *misanthrope*, which derives from the Greek word for 'hatred', *misos*.

underprospect *(n.)*   an aerial view

On 28 July 1858, a French photographer and amateur balloonist named Gaspard-Félix Tournachon – known by the nickname 'Nadar' – floated in a tethered balloon to a height of more than 250 feet above the village of Petit-Bicêtre on the outskirts of Paris. There, he began to take a series of photographs of the surrounding countryside.

It was a fairly remarkable achievement: not only had Nadar constructed the balloon himself, but permanent photography had been introduced by the French inventor Joseph Nicéphore Niépce only three decades earlier, and while photographic technology had progressed in that time it was still in its relative infancy. Ultimately, the so-called 'collodion wet-plate process' that Nadar used to produce his aerial photographs still involved applying fresh emulsion to a glass plate immediately before use, and developing the plate immediately after the photograph was taken. All of which, due to the time pressures entailed in the height and speed of Nadar's flight, had to be done in the basket of his balloon.

Sadly, while many of Nadar's photographs have survived, those he took on this day have not. His place in photographic history was still assured: his was the first aerial photograph ever taken.

An aerial view like that which Nadar captured has been known as a *bird's-eye view* since the late eighteenth century – an expression credited to the English politician and author Horace Walpole. Earlier still, the Elizabethan poet and scholar Sir Philip Sidney coined the term *underprospect* to refer to an aerial view in *The Countess of Pembroke's Arcadia*, a vast work of prose published in 1590.

denary *(n.)*   a group of ten

When it first emerged in the language in the fifteenth century, the word *denary* was used as an English name for a Roman coin called a *denarius* – a Latin word literally meaning 'containing ten', as Roman *denarii* were each equivalent to ten more valuable coins called *asses*. By the seventeenth century, however, *denary* was being used more generally in English to mean simply a group or set of ten, or else a tenth part of something – and it's that meaning that concerns us today.

On 29 July 2005, NASA announced the discovery of the largest planet yet found outside the known solar system to orbit our sun. Spotted by a team of astronomers at the California Institute of Technology, the planet was slightly larger than Pluto and resided for much of its orbit in the so-called Kuiper Belt, a dark region of space where it is believed many hundreds of rocks and dwarf planets orbit the sun on the fringes of its gravitational pull. It was originally given the technical placeholder name 2003 UB_{313}, but was later named Eris after a Greek goddess personifying discord and strife; its single orbital moon was given the name of Eris's daughter in Greek myth, Dysnomia. Both bodies orbit the sun at a distance of 96.3 astronomical units – equal to almost 9 billion miles.

At the time of its discovery, the sheer size of Eris meant that it was briefly labelled the tenth planet in the solar system, but that title wasn't to last. The following year, NASA redefined the criteria determining precisely what constitutes a planet, and Eris fell into the category of 'minor planet' – as did its neighbour in our solar system, Pluto.

whither *(v.)* to move with great force, to buffet like
the wind

Emily Brontë was born on 30 July 1818. She began her career
writing poetry before publishing her only novel, *Wuthering
Heights*, in 1847. It is thought that Emily had started work on
a second novel when she suddenly took ill attending her brother
Branwell's funeral service the following September, and never
recovered. She died on 19 December 1848, aged just thirty.

Emily's untimely death meant she was never able to enjoy the
success her novel eventually attained. On its release, *Wuthering
Heights* had divided its Victorian critics: some admired its innova-
tive structure, use of language and the author's courage in tackling
sensitive subjects like gender and psychological cruelty, but others
considered it an unreadable mishmash of styles and macabre
set pieces. 'It is a compound of vulgar depravity and unnatural
horrors,' wrote one reviewer. 'How a human being could have
attempted such a book as the present without committing suicide
before he had finished a dozen chapters, is a mystery.'

Nevertheless, *Wuthering Heights* has since become a clas-
sic of English literature. But one question remains: what does
wuthering actually mean? According to the novel itself:

> Wuthering Heights is the name of Mr Heathcliff's
> dwelling; 'Wuthering' being a significant provincial
> adjective, descriptive of the atmospheric tumult to
> which its station is exposed.

Wuthering comes from a Yorkshire dialect verb, *wuther*, which
is itself thought to be a derivative of an older dialect word,
whither, meaning 'to knock or move forcefully' – or as in this
instance, 'to buffet like the wind'.

rumbullion *(n.)*   a glass or drink of rum

Known as 'Black Tot Day', 31 July 1970 was the last day on which sailors in the British Royal Navy were issued with a daily ration, or 'tot', of rum – a tradition that had been established as far back as 1655.

Curiously, no one is entirely sure where the name *rum* comes from. Its earliest record dates from the mid 1600s, when the name *rum* originally appeared on a list of 'Barbados liquors' imported for sale in colonial America. Before then, *rum* had been an adjective, meaning 'good' or 'fine', which made *rum bouse* especially fine wine or liquor among sixteenth-century drinkers. It's possible that this meaning simply shifted across when rum first became available in the seventeenth century – or, alternatively, there might be something else going on.

Before rum was called *rum* it was apparently known as *rumbullion*, a name attested slightly earlier in the language than *rum*, and which was also used as a dialect word for an uproar or tumult. As the *Oxford English Dictionary* suggests, the name *rumbullion* could have become attached to the drink 'on account of its effect on its drinkers', and from there *rumbullion* might simply have shortened to *rum*, and the name stuck.

Casting doubt on this theory, as a word for a riotous tumult *rumbullion* is not recorded in written English any time before the nineteenth century. Although it's possible that it was in spoken use long before then, the lack of written evidence makes it hard to pinpoint this as the definitive origin of a glass of *rum*. Ultimately, the word remains something of a mystery.

Yorkshire mile *(n.)*   a proverbially long distance

The first day of August is the anniversary of both the emancipation of slaves in the British Empire in 1834 (the result of a campaign by the Yorkshire philanthropist William Wilberforce), and of the Battle of Minden in 1759, a key conflict in the Seven Years War (in which many troops from Yorkshire fought). As a result, 1 August is now celebrated as Yorkshire Day.

In terms of language, Yorkshire has a rich and distinctive dialect – already attested so far here with words like *twarvlement* (25 February), *head-languager* (14 March) and *shivviness* (27 May). Other words we owe to the Yorkshire region include:

- *brackle* (adj.) unsettled, changeable; used to describe the weather, it literally means 'broken'
- *collyfoble* (v.) to talk secretly together
- *meat-yabble* (adj.) having a good appetite. *Meat* originally meant simply 'food', a meaning that remains in place in some English dialects. Ultimately if you're *meat-yabble* – literally 'meatable' – then you have a robust appetite.
- *muckytrollops* (n.) an untidy woman
- *oaf-rocked* (adj.) weak as an adult due to a sheltered or pampered childhood. *Oaf* here is either a corruption of 'half' (in the sense that a weak adult was only 'half-rocked', or improperly cared for as a child), or 'elf' (derived from an old piece of folklore that claims elves would steal human children and replace them with their own 'changelings').

Elsewhere in the dictionary, a *Yorkshire mile* is a proverbially long distance – supposedly a reference to the tireless, fast-paced horses of Yorkshire that can travel a mile much more swiftly and more comfortably than those from elsewhere.

kelter *(n.)*   a hand of cards of little value or use

In 1865, the legendary frontiersman James 'Wild Bill' Hickok fought a duel with a fellow gambler named Davis Tutt, whom he killed with a single shot through the heart. Charged with murder, Hickok was eventually acquitted – a verdict that caused a public outcry and brought Hickok to national attention. In an interview with *Harper's Magazine*, he later claimed to have killed hundreds more men and grandly boasted of his other exaggerated exploits out West – all of which, whether true or not, gave rise to his legendary gunslinging persona.

On 2 August 1876, Hickok was playing poker in Nuttal & Mann's Saloon in Deadwood, modern-day South Dakota, when a man named Jack McCall entered, shouted 'Damn you! Take that!' and shot Hickok at point-blank range in the back of the head. McCall, it later emerged, had lost heavily against Hickok at cards the previous day.

The hand of cards Hickok was holding at the time of his death – both the aces and 8s of spades and clubs, plus an unknown hole card – ultimately became known as the *dead man's hand*, but Hickok's isn't the only poker hand with its own name. A *big dog* is a run of cards from an ace down to a 9. A *big cat* is a run from king to 8. A *little cat* is a run from 8 to 3, and a *little dog* is a run from 7 to 2.

A *kelter* or *kilter*, meanwhile, is a hand of cards containing little of any real value. Its name dates from the late 1800s and is thought to come from the earlier use of *kelter* to mean 'rubbish' or 'refuse'.

letterling *(n.)*   a short letter or note

John Rut was an English mariner who, in 1527, was chosen by Henry VIII to command an expedition to North America in search of the Northwest Passage. Setting sail from Plymouth, Rut's ship, *Mary Guilford*, arrived off the coast of northern Canada in July, but was held back by sea ice and forced to head south to St John's, Newfoundland. From there, Rut continued south along the American coast to Florida (perhaps the first European to sail the entire Eastern Seaboard) before heading home later that year. No record of him exists after his return to England in 1528.

Although Rut failed to locate the Northwest Passage, his voyage to America nevertheless earned its place in history for another, somewhat unexpected, reason. While in Newfoundland, Rut wrote a letter to Henry VIII on 3 August 1527:

> Pleasing your Honourable Grace to hear of your servant John Rut with all his company here in good health . . . We entered into a good harbour called St. John and there we found eleven saile of Normans [Norman French boats] and one Brittaine [Breton] and two Portugal barks all a-fishing . . . written in hast 1527, by your servant John Rut to his uttermost of his power.

The note was the first letter ever sent to Europe from North America.

A letter 'written in haste' has been known as a *scrawl* since the mid 1600s in English, while one sent in haste is a *dispatchment*. A *letterling*, meanwhile, is a short letter or note, a word first used in English in the late eighteenth century – although the terms *letteret*, *letterlet* and *epistolet* have also been used over the centuries.

Sebastianist *(n.)*   someone who believes something unbelievable

In 1578, the Kingdom of Portugal embarked on a risky crusade against Morocco, led by the country's twenty-four-year-old King Sebastian. Against the best counsel of his advisers, Sebastian headed deep into the Moroccan desert and, on 4 August 1578, is presumed to have been killed in battle at Alcácer Quibir, or else captured and executed shortly after.

When news of the young king's death broke back in Portugal, many people found it difficult to accept, and as a result rumours that Sebastian had merely disappeared during the battle and would one day return home to Portugal began to spread. As the decades passed, the legend of the lost king continued to grow as imposters and pretenders to the throne claiming to be Sebastian came and went, and still the belief that the king would return endured – to the extent that when John IV of Portugal was crowned in 1640, he had to agree to surrender the throne should Sebastian ever return, despite the fact that by then Sebastian would have been well into his eighties.

By the 1700s, more than a century after his death, *Sebastianism* had become a pseudo-mystical cult, whose members believed the king would rise from the dead to return Portugal to its former glory. Despite the cult's increasingly impossible expectations, its numbers nevertheless continued to grow – most notably after a renowned *Sebastianist* supporter supposedly predicted an earthquake that struck Lisbon in 1755.

Today, understandably, the cult of *Sebastianism* has largely been abandoned, nevertheless the term *Sebastianist* remains in place in an allusive sense, referring to someone who steadfastly believes something that is inherently unbelievable or impossible.

Proteusian *(adj.)*   able to change shape at will; variable, inconstant

In Greek mythology, Proteus was a god of the sea, considered by some versions of his story to be the eldest son of Poseidon; the name *Proteus* literally means 'first-born'.

But because the sea and its waters can take on immensely different characters from one day or one location to the next, Proteus was said to be able to change his shape at will and take on vastly different appearances when so required. This shape-shifting ability is the origin of both the sixteenth-century adjective *protean*, meaning 'capable of changing shape', or more figuratively 'fickle', 'inconstant' or 'unreliable', and its later equivalent *Proteusian*. But in medical and anatomical contexts, *Proteusian* has one more meaning that connects it to this date.

Joseph Merrick was born on 5 August 1862 in Leicester, England. Due to severe abnormalities of his body, Merrick became better known across Victorian England as The Elephant Man, and spent much of his youth and young adulthood being exhibited as a curiosity as part of a travelling freak show. It was during this time that Merrick was befriended by an acclaimed English surgeon, Sir Frederick Treves, who remained his physician and close companion for the rest of his life.

Merrick is believed to have suffered from a rare genetic disorder that causes an incurable overgrowth of bodily tissues, including the bones, skin and muscles, to produce large swellings and protuberances all over the body. And because these growths vastly alter the usual shape and appearance of the human body, the condition is best known today as *Proteus syndrome*.

wamble-cropped *(adj.)*   nauseated

In 1552, a Latin word for an upset stomach, *stomachichus*, was given a bizarre translation in a Latin–English dictionary:

> Wamble cropped. *Stomachichus.*
> Wamble stomaked, to be. *Nauseo.*
> Wamblyng of stomake, or disposition, or will to vomit.
> *Nausea.*

Wamble-cropped was a sixteenth-century word meaning 'afflicted with nausea'. Earlier still, *wamble* was a Middle English verb referring to the queasy rolling of the contents of the stomach, which has been traced as far back as the fourteenth century. Neither word has ever been much used in the language, and both have long fallen by the linguistic wayside except for in a handful of local dialects: as late as 1905, the *English Dialect Dictionary* listed *wambliness* as 'an uneasiness or upheaval of the stomach'.

Unfortunately for Russian cosmonaut Gherman Titov, *wamble-cropped* is an apt word for today. As well as becoming the second man to orbit the earth, when the twenty-five-year-old was sent into space aboard *Vostok 2* on 6 August 1961 – just four months after Yuri Gagarin – he earned himself the fairly undignified distinction of being the first human to vomit in space.

Whereas Gagarin's spaceflight had entailed only one complete orbit of the earth (flick back to 12 April for more on that), Titov was sent up for seventeen. After only a few hours in space, however, he reported feeling nauseated and suddenly vomited. Nevertheless, despite his nausea Titov managed to complete his flight and returned safely to earth – whereupon he reportedly broke all space pilot protocol (and arguably the protocol of anyone feeling sick) and promptly downed a bottle of beer.

schoenobatist *(n.)*   a tightrope walker

As far back as the seventeenth century, tightrope walkers were known as *funambulists* or *funambules*, a name derived from the Latin word for 'rope', *funis*. The Greek for 'rope', *skoinos*, is the origin of the later term *schoenobatist*, which first appeared in English in the early nineteenth century. Admittedly, any one of these words would suit today, as on 7 August 1974, French high-wire artist Philippe Petit famously crossed a tightrope between the towers of the World Trade Center in New York.

Petit's stunt was the culmination of six years of covert planning; astonishingly, it was entirely unauthorised. Posing as construction workers, the night before the stunt Petit and his team rode a freight elevator to the 110th floor of the World Trade Center, and used a bow and arrow to fire a fishing line attached to a rope, in turn attached to a 200-foot steel high-wire, across the gap between the two buildings. At 7 o'clock the following morning, Petit began his walk.

Incredibly, Petit crossed the wire a total of eight times, during which he danced, knelt, lay down and even saluted onlookers from a quarter of a mile above the ground. Although Petit's performance had been unlicensed, the stunt proved so astounding that the district attorney dropped all charges against him – on the condition that Petit give a free tightrope performance for children in Central Park. Understandably, he agreed.

climb-tack *(n.)*   a cat that likes to walk on shelves

Established by the International Fund for Animal Welfare in 2002, 8 August is International Cat Day.

The dictionary provides us with quite a few suitably feline words to mark the occasion. According to the *English Dialect Dictionary* (Vol. I, 1898), *climb-tack* is an old word for a cat that is 'over-fond of investigating the contents of the larder-shelves'. In this instance, *tack* is probably derived from *tackle*, which has been used since the fourteenth century, at least in English dialects, to mean 'equipment', 'utensils' or 'furniture'.

A *cloor* is a cat scratch, while a *cumlin-cat* is a cat that spontaneously takes up residence at a different house – *cumlin* being a Scots dialect corruption of *comeling*, meaning 'newcomer'.

Popularised by Shakespeare, *grimalkin* is a seventeenth-century word for a cat that literally means 'grey-haired woman'. *Baudrons* is another old epithet for a cat, originating in Scotland and perhaps derived from a Gaelic word meaning 'frolicsome', as is *Tibert*, the name of a cat that appeared in the old medieval folk tale of Reynard the Fox.

Puss and all its derivatives were probably originally onomatopoeic, meant to either imitate the sound of a cat, or used to represent a hissing sound used to attract or shoo a cat. The same applies to *miauler*, a seventeenth-century word for a cat, as well as forms like *mewler* and *miaower*, which date from the early 1600s. As for *mog* or *moggie*, it probably began life as a variation of the girl's name *Maggie* – though precisely how or why it should have come to be attached to cats is unclear.

paction *(n.)*   the action of making a pact; bargaining, agreement

On 9 August 1721, a Scottish surgeon named Charles Maitland carried out what would now be considered a highly controversial experiment – but one that is also a landmark in the history of medicine.

Maitland had sought a licence to perform a series of experimental smallpox inoculations, or 'variolations', on the inmates of Newgate Prison in London. On this date, that licence was granted, and with the help of the physician and scholar Sir Hans Sloane (turn back to 7 June for more on him), Maitland set to work treating six prisoners with his experimental cure. Making a small incision in the volunteer's skin, Maitland applied a small 'pledget' or wad of absorbent cotton that had been steeped in matter extracted from the pustules of a smallpox patient, and awaited the results.

As grim a procedure as Maitland's experiment may sound, it should be noted that it was not entirely one-sided: the prisoners involved in the trial were all told in return that they would have their crimes pardoned – should they survive the treatment, of course. Happily, all six did.

The act of making or entering into a bargain or agreement like that which led to Maitland's experiment is known as *paction*, originally a legal term dating from the fifteenth century that later came to refer to any casual or unofficial agreement, as opposed to a legally binding contract. Both *paction* and *pact* itself derive from their Latin equivalent, *pactum*, meaning 'agreement' or 'covenant', which in turn comes from the verb *pacisci*, meaning 'to make a bargain'.

repdigit *(n.)*   a number composed of a single repeated figure

In an ordinary calendar year, 10 August is the 222nd day of the year – and 222 is an example of a *repdigit*, a number composed of repeated instances of the same single figure. Also known as a *monodigit*, a *repdigit* is etymologically – and quite literally – a 'repeated digit'.

As far as *repdigits* go, perhaps the most famous are 666, the biblical 'number of the beast' according to the Book of Revelation, and 999, the emergency services number in the UK, Ireland and much of the British Commonwealth. A longer example is 999999, a string of digits better known as the Feynman Point.

The 'Feynman' behind the Feynman Point is the American theoretical physicist and Nobel Prize winner Richard Feynman. According to mathematical legend, while delivering a lecture at the California Institute of Technology, Feynman joked that he would one day like to memorise pi up to the point, 762 decimal places in, where there are six consecutive nines. At that point, he would stop his recital from memory and simply state '999999 – and so on', implying that the famously irrational number suddenly, 762 places in, became nothing more than an infinite chain of 9s. (Incidentally, another six consecutive 9s crop up in the 193,034th to 193,039th decimal places of pi – but memorising up to that point would be quite some feat.)

Sadly, there is little evidence that Feynman ever actually made this joke, and in fact the earliest account of it credits it to fellow scientist Douglas Hofstadter. Nevertheless, it is Feynman's name that has ended up being attached to this particular *repdigit*, and it's his name that has remained in place ever since.

rusticate *(v.)*   to live in the countryside, to live a
quiet rural life

When it first appeared in the language in the early 1500s,
rusticate was an adjective meaning 'countrified', 'rural' or 'uncul-
tured'. By the mid 1600s, however, it had come to be used as
a verb, meaning 'to live in or wander the countryside'. And if
that's the lifestyle for you, it might be worth remembering a
curious tale from the life of William Wordsworth.

Wordsworth – along with fellow poets Samuel Taylor
Coleridge and Robert Southey – is famously classed as one of
the Lake Poets, whose work is linked inextricably with England's
Lake District. But in his youth he spent much of his time
abroad, and then for four years lived with Coleridge in the village of Nether Stowey in Somerset.

By that time, both men were established poets and would
wander the countryside around the village making copious
notes and sketches for use in their writing. But, at the height
of Britain's Napoleonic tensions with France, this curious behaviour soon brought them to the attention of the locals.

On 11 August 1797, one resident of Nether Stowey sent a letter to the Home Office reporting the suspicious behaviour of an
'emigrant' family who had moved into the area. The Home Office
was quick to respond and, suspecting them to be French spies,
posted a detective to the area to investigate. The report he compiled explained that the 'suspects', Coleridge and Wordsworth,
were 'disaffected Englishmen' who were part of a 'set of violent
democrats', sympathetic with the situation in France.

Happily, the investigation went no further and by 1799
Wordsworth was back in Cumbria with sister Dorothy and wife
Mary. For a time, however, his love of *rusticating* almost landed
him in deep trouble.

jeopard *(v.)* to stake a bet

The word *jeopardy* was borrowed into English from French in the early fourteenth century, and derives from a *jeu parti*, or literally a 'divided game' – that is, one with equal or uncertain odds. By the late 1300s, however, *jeopardy* had inspired a derivative verb in English, *jeopard*, which was variously used to mean 'to expose to risk', 'to hazard or imperil', 'to venture' or, in the sense that concerns us today, 'to stake a bet'.

Green Eggs and Ham, one of the most popular works by the children's author Dr Seuss (pseudonym of the writer and illustrator Theodor Seuss Geisel) was published on 12 August 1960. The book was written at the behest of Seuss's publisher, Bennett Cerf, who had noted that Seuss's earlier title, *The Cat in the Hat* (1957), had been written using a vocabulary of just over 200 words. In response, he proposed a bet that Seuss could not write a book using fifty different words or less.

It's fair to say that Seuss more than met the challenge: in its entirety, *Green Eggs and Ham* is written using nothing more than the words *a, am, and, anywhere, are, be, boat, box, car, could, dark, do, eat, eggs, fox, goat, good, green, ham, here, house, I, if, in, let, like, may, me, mouse, not, on, or, rain, Sam, say, see, so, thank, that, the, them, there, they, train, tree, try, will, with, would* and *you*.

Cerf may have lost the bet, but there was at least a silver lining: *Green Eggs and Ham* went on to sell more than 8 million copies worldwide.

cankerfret *(n.)* a corroded surface on metal

Arguably most familiar today as a word for a sore or ulcer, the word *canker* derives from the same root as *cancer* – which, despite appearances, derives in turn from the same Latin word for a crab that now forms part of our zodiac. As bizarre as that may sound, the association between sores, tumours and crustaceans is actually a particularly ancient one, with physicians as long ago as Ancient Greece noting the similarity between swollen nodules on the skin and the hard and often bumpy or uneven shells of crabs.

As a term for an insidiously destructive or damaging condition, however, in the fifteenth century *canker* came to be used of any form of corrosion, like verdigris or rust, that affects the surface of a metal and slowly spreads across it, eating away at it and largely rendering it useless. By the sixteenth century, that word had come to be extended into *cankerfret* – the word *fret* appearing here in an old-fashioned sense of 'a gnawing or wearing away'. In this sense, *cankerfret* was initially used as a verb meaning 'to corrode', but by the early 1600s had come to be used as a noun describing the corrosion or the corroded surface itself.

What does all this have to do with today's date? It was on 13 August 1913 that the English chemist Harry Brearley produced a batch of metal in an electric metallurgy furnace in Sheffield comprised primarily of iron, with 0.24 per cent of its weight made from carbon, and 12.8 per cent chromium: Brearley had produced the world's first true stainless steel.

beautyhood *(n.)*   the state of being beautiful; the time of life when a person is most beautiful

In 1908, an English entrepreneur named Robert Forsyth, manager of the seaside pleasure pier in Folkestone, Kent, hit upon an idea that would not only bring crowds of tourists flocking to the town, but could potentially attract the attention of media from all around the world. His brainwave was the Folkestone Beauty Pageant – a beauty contest that, unlike those that were common in seaside towns up and down the country, would be open to competitors from all over the world.

Despite the contest's global reach, however, the winner was the decidedly homegrown Miss Nellie Jarman, who had travelled from nowhere more far-flung than East Molesey in Surrey to take part. And despite Forsyth's hopes of garnering the town some appreciative publicity, the competition was reportedly hijacked by suffragettes who, according to a contemporary report in the *Folkestone Express*, occupied the entire first two rows of the audience, each wearing 'a large sailor hat with a red band on which the legend appeared, "Votes for Women!"'

Appropriate for the day on which the world's first international beauty pageant was held, the word *beautyhood* was coined in the early nineteenth century to refer to what the *Oxford English Dictionary* defines as 'the state of being beautiful', or 'the time of life during which one is beautiful'.

circumduction *(n.)*   a longwinded, roundabout
route or course of action

The word *circumduction* derives from a Latin verb, *circumducere*, variously meaning 'to show or guide around', or more figuratively, 'to prolong', 'to talk loquaciously', 'to swindle' or 'to nullify or cancel a law' (by effectively 'drawing a line' around it). Since it first appeared in the language in the late 1500s, *circumduction* has been used in many of these senses in English (and still survives in the legal sense of the annulment of a law), but only one concerns us today: a *circumduction* is a longwinded, time-consuming, roundabout route.

Prior to 15 August 1914, a *circumduction* was the only course of action facing a vessel looking to sail from the Atlantic to the Pacific Ocean. But the opening of the Panama Canal on this day saved precious time, avoided the notoriously perilous Cape Horn at the southern tip of South America, and vastly shortened the length of a journey from one ocean into the next.

In constructing the canal, more than 200 million cubic yards of material – enough to bury the island of Manhattan under 12 feet of earth – had to be removed, a task that took thirty-four years to complete. French engineers initially broke ground in January 1881 but after financial problems and a workforce decimated by tropical diseases brought work to a halt, the United States stepped in to take over construction in 1904. As challenging as the project was, however, on its completion the benefits became clear: a ship sailing from New York to San Francisco instantly had the length of its journey cut by more than 7,800 miles.

pennif *(n.)* a banknote

Banknotes were introduced in China during the Tang dynasty, 618–907 AD, and were in use there long before the practice caught on in Europe and elsewhere. China may have pioneered the practice, but not all of the country's leaders fully understood it: in 1425, the emperor gave out so much paper cash as rewards that the value of the currency plummeted, leading to the hastily arranged reintroduction of copper coinage. The problem failed to resolve itself, however, and in 1455 banknotes were banned altogether – it would be another several hundred years before China would reinstate them.

Another curious tale from this period took place on 16 August 1384, when a case of an arguing couple who had torn some banknotes during a domestic fight was brought before the Hongwu Emperor, founder of China's Ming dynasty. At the time, banknotes were protected by the same laws given to government documents, and destroying or defacing them was a crime punishable with 100 lashes. Happily, in his wisdom the emperor dismissed the case as a domestic disagreement and pardoned the couple.

Banknotes arrived in England in the late seventeenth century, with the first pound-sterling notes produced shortly after the establishment of the Bank of England in 1694. Originally – as they still are in America – they were known as *bills*, not notes, and over time came to be nicknamed *screeves, screens, stiffs, flimsies, toadskins* and, perhaps strangest of all, *pennif.*

First used in nineteenth-century slang, *pennif* was invented by reversing the earlier slang word *finnip* or *finn*, meaning 'a five-pound note', which was itself supposedly derived from a mispronunciation of the German word for 'five', *fünf.*

unrecking *(adj.)*   not paying attention, unheeding

To *reck* – a particularly ancient verb dating back to the Old English period – is to take notice or pay attention to something; derived from that, to be *unrecking* is to be careless or unobservant.

Unrecking is a word with tragic associations to today's date, as it was on 17 August 1896 that the first pedestrian involved in a motor accident was killed in London. Bridget Driscoll, a forty-four-year-old Irishwoman, had visited the Crystal Palace exhibition in London and was crossing the road outside with her teenage daughter May when she was struck by a car that was being driven as part of an exhibition of newly designed motor vehicles. The driver, a Londoner named Arthur Edsall, reportedly shouted, 'Stand back!' and rang an alarm bell as Bridget stepped inattentively into the road, but it was too late.

Or, at least, that is one version of the story. Conflicting accounts abounded at the inquiry into the accident, with some claiming that it was Edsall's *unrecking* driving that had caused the crash. Giving evidence to the inquest, Bridget's daughter claimed the driver 'did not seem to understand what he was doing', and had zigzagged around the road prior to the accident. Another witness, Florence Ashmore, claimed the car was going at 'a tremendous pace, like a fire engine'. But in his defence, Edsall stated he had rung the car's warning bell to alert Driscoll, and that, for the purpose of the exhibition, the car's speed had been limited to around half the maximum speed – namely, 4 mph.

Whatever the truth, a verdict of accidental death was recorded, with the coroner, Percy Morrison, ominously noting during that inquest that he hoped 'such a thing would never happen again'.

jugglery *(n.)*   feigned magic or witchcraft

When the word *juggler* was borrowed into English from French in the early twelfth century, it originally referred to a jester or clown who could entertain with songs, anecdotes, dances or magic tricks; the word *juggle*, in this fairly general meaning, can be traced back to a Latin word for a joke or jest. In the sense of someone who is particularly nimble or dextrous, *juggler* was also used at this time to mean a sorcerer or magician, or else someone skilled in conjuring or sleight of hand. And, by extension, that made *jugglery* another word for pretended magic or witchcraft.

On the subject of witchcraft, all but two of the supposed Pendle Witches were tried at a court in Lancaster on 18 August 1612. The Pendle witch trials are among the most famous in British history, in part because so many of those involved were eventually executed, and in part because a number of those involved genuinely believed they had supernatural powers.

The trials began when a young woman named Alizon Device from Pendle, Lancashire, was accused of cursing a local shopkeeper. Alizon was eventually arrested, along with of several members of her family (including her grandmother, Elizabeth Southerns, a notorious practitioner of witchcraft who went by the name of 'Demdike'); several members of another local family, the Redfernes (with whom the Devices had apparently had a long-standing feud); and many of the families' closest friends. The first to be tried was a young woman named Jennet Preston, who was found guilty and executed in York on 29 July; the last to be tried was Alizon Device herself, who, like her grandmother, was reportedly convinced that she indeed had powers of witchcraft and openly admitted her guilt. In all, ten people were hanged as a result.

colewort *(n.)*   cabbage, kale, greens; proverbially,
old news

Cole is an Old English word for cabbage or any similar vege-
table, which, like the names *kale* and *cauliflower*, probably
derives from the Latin word for a stalk, *caulis*. Of similar age,
wort has been used as a generic name for a plant – and, in
particular, one that is hearty or edible, or else has healing or
restorative powers – since the early Old English period, and
has been unearthed in horticultural documents dating from
the reign of King Alfred in the ninth century AD. Put together,
colewort is a fourteenth-century word for cabbage, and in particular any cabbage-like plant that does not have a central core
or heart, like kale or greens. The word is the origin of the peculiar expression *coleworts twice sodden* – literally, 'twice-soaked' or
'twice-boiled cabbage' – which has been used since the sixteenth
century as a proverbial response to being told old news (much
like *G. H.*, for more on which flick back to 23 April).

As old news goes, one of the most infamous examples
occurred on 19 August 1848, when the *New York Herald*
broke the news to its readers that gold had been discovered in
California. The news, unfortunately, came seven months too
late: gold had indeed been discovered in California, but on
24 January.

The *Herald* may have come late to the party, but by breaking
the news on the Eastern Seaboard, it nevertheless kept interest
in the California Gold Rush going for several more months.
Eventually, as a result of the discovery of gold, one per cent
of the entire population of the United States had relocated to
California.

melliturgy *(n.)* bee-keeping; the production of honey by bees

The Greek word for a honeybee was *melissa*, which is not only now used as a popular girl's name, but is the origin a number of bee- and honey-related words. Among the most familiar is *mellifluous* or *mellifluent*, adjectives describing sweet or pleasing sounds (or, less often, written texts) that quite literally 'flow like honey'. Less familiar are the adjectives *mellisaean* (meaning 'relating to or resembling bees') and *melligineous* or *melliform* (meaning 'honey-like'). To *mellificate*, likewise, is to produce honey, while the production of honey by bees, or the act of beekeeping itself, is known as *melliturgy*.

Dating from the early seventeenth century, *melliturgy* combines the Greek word *melissa* with the Greek suffix *–ourgia* or *–ourgos*, which in turn is related to *ergos*, the Greek word for 'work'. That suffix is used in English to form words, like *melliturgy*, bearing some sense of manufacture or production, among them relatively familiar terms like *metallurgy* and *dramaturgy*, as well as a number of more obscure examples like *demonurgy* ('the invoking of demons using sorcery'), *auturgy* ('independent work or action'), *siderurgy* ('the manufacture of iron and steel') and *thaumaturgy* ('the saintly working of wonders or miracles').

Connected to both *melliturgy* and *thaumaturgy*, 20 August is the feast day of a little-known twelfth-century saint named Bernard of Clairvaux: thanks to his supposedly sweet style of preaching, St Bernard is now considered the patron saint of beekeepers.

cyllenian *(adj.)*   pertaining to theft or thieving

According to Greek mythology, a cave high on Mount Cyllene in Greece was the birthplace of the Greek god Hermes; according to Roman mythology, it was the birthplace of his Roman equivalent, Mercury. Both were considered messenger gods of communication and correspondence, and were often depicted as wearing winged sandals or helmets that gave them impossible swiftness. But because of their reputation as being fleet of foot, both Hermes and Mercury were also considered patrons of thieves and thievery, and ultimately the adjective *cyllenian* came to refer to anything relating to or akin to theft.

A notoriously audacious act of thievery took place on 21 August 1911, when an Italian thief named Vincenzo Perugia stole Da Vinci's *Mona Lisa* from the Louvre in Paris.

Perugia had moved to Paris three years earlier. On the day in question, he dressed in the plain white overalls all employees of the Louvre were required to wear at the time, and hid out of sight until the gallery closed. Under cover of darkness, he then slipped the *Mona Lisa* from its frame, and the following morning walked casually back out again with the world's most famous painting hidden under his smock.

The painting remained missing – and Perugia remained undiscovered – for the next two years, until he finally broke cover and contacted Alfredo Geri, an art dealer in Florence, offering to bring the painting to him for half a million Italian lire. Perugia travelled from Paris with the painting secreted in the false bottom of his suitcase, and arrived at Geri's art gallery. There, he was persuaded to leave the painting so that Geri could assess whether or not it was a forgery; Perugia was arrested later that day.

desulture *(n.)* the act of vaulting from one horse
to another

The performer in a circus who simultaneously rides two horses,
vaulting between them as they ride, is properly called a *desultor*,
while the act of jumping between horses is known as *desulture*:

> *Desultores* . . . Persons of agility of body, who used to
> leap from one horse to another, at the Horse Races in
> the Circensian Games.
>
> Nathan Bailey, *The Universal Etymological*
> *English Dictionary, Volume II* (1727)

Both of these words derive from the Latin *desilire*, a verb literally meaning 'to jump down', which in the sense of someone
casually skipping from one task to another is also the origin
of the adjective *desultory*, meaning 'unfocused' or 'superficial'.

In the sense of someone switching between one horse and
another, however, it's worth remembering that the Battle of
Bosworth Field was fought on 22 August 1485. The final significant clash of the Wars of the Roses, the battle proved a decisive
victory for the Lancastrian cause, thereby ending the reign of
the House of York with the defeat of King Richard III, and
establishing the rule of the Tudor dynasty with the triumphant
Henry VII.

According to Shakespeare's version of events, the battle
famously ended with King Richard, unseated from his mount,
staggering around the battlefield looking for another to ride
into battle: 'A horse! a horse! my kingdom for a horse!' But as
famous as this line – and indeed this event – has now become,
it was just a Shakespearean invention.

consanguinate *(v.)* to sympathise, to have an affinity
with or fondness for

On 23 August 1973, Jan-Erik Olsson attempted to rob a bank
in Norrmalmstorg, a square in central Stockholm. When the
police arrived, Olsson opened fire, and from there the situation
quickly escalated into a hostage incident. Olsson requested to be
brought more guns and ammunition, a car, 3 million Swedish
kronor and his friend Clark Olofsson – together, the pair barricaded their four hostages in the bank's inner vault and prepared
to wait.

Hours, and eventually days, ticked by until on 26 August
the police finally drilled through the roof of the vault from
an apartment above the bank. Despite Olsson stating that he
would kill the hostages if gas was pumped into the vault as
part of a rescue attempt, the attack went ahead two days later;
Olsson and Olofsson surrendered after half an hour.

After almost a week's detention, the hostages were released
safely – but in the aftermath some reportedly claimed that they
were more afraid of the police's actions than those of Olsson.
The sympathy they came to have for their captors eventually
led to the term *Stockholm syndrome* being coined to describe
this incident, and any similar situation in which the victims
eventually come to have sympathy for those responsible for
their incarceration.

To sympathise or have an affinity for something or someone
is to *consanguinate*, a seventeenth-century word derived from
an earlier term, *consanguine*, for a blood relative: just like words
such as *sanguiduct*, *sanguisugent* and *consanguineous* before them
(turn back to 26 May for more of those), at the root of both
consanguinate and *consanguine* is *sanguis*, the Latin for 'blood'.

manusculpt *(n.)*   a handmade inscription

The Graffito of Esmet-Akhom, the last known inscription ever written in Egyptian hieroglyphics, can be found inscribed beside a gate in the Temple of Isis at Philae, in southern Egypt. Originally an island in the River Nile, Philae now stands in the centre of Lake Nasser, behind the Aswan Dam. The temple was the last place in Egypt where the Ancient Egyptian religion is known to have still been practised.

According to the inscription itself – written by, and now named in honour of, Esmet-Akhom, one of the last documented priests at the temple – it was inscribed on the stone 'on the birthday of Osiris in the year 110' of the Roman Emperor Diocletian, a date corresponding to what we would now call 24 August 394 AD. The inscription itself, accompanied by a large image of a king wearing an elaborate crown, is not particularly clear but it is believed to be concerned with a visit to the temple by a pagan tribe from outside the area, and was written to honour the goddess Isis herself.

A handmade or hand-carved inscription, precisely like that of the Esmet-Akhom Graffito, can also be known as a *manusculpt*, a word that was coined by the English essayist Thomas de Quincey in the mid nineteenth century. Although the word has sincere Latin roots (it brings together the Latin words for 'hand', *manus*, and 'carve', *sculpere*) de Quincey nevertheless used the word as a fairly frivolous alternative to a *manuscript* – which is literally a handwritten document.

equestrienne *(n.)*   a female horse rider

The Latin word for 'horse', *equus*, sits at the root of the word *equestrian*, which has been used to describe anything pertaining to horse riding, or else as another word for a horse rider, since the mid seventeenth century. A now seldom-used feminine form of *equestrian*, *equestrienne*, followed in 1864 – although perhaps it should have been employed four decades earlier.

On 25 August 1804, Alicia Meynell rode a horse named Vingarillo in a race at York Race Course. Her only opponent was Captain William Flint, her brother-in-law.

The pair had conceived of the race while out riding one day, when a light-hearted argument over who had the better horse ended in a short race down a bridle path outside the city, which Meynell easily won. Unhappy with the result, Flint challenged her to a 'proper' race at the nearby race course, which Meynell gamely accepted. The race would make her the first female jockey to compete on an English racecourse in history.

As soon as the race was announced, bets began to be taken not just on the winner, but on everything from whether Meynell would ride side-saddle, to what she would wear on the day. Meynell, it's fair to say, did not disappoint: according to reports, she arrived ready to race wearing a yellow leopard-spotted dress with blue sleeves and a large blue cap. Captain Flint, in comparison, dressed all in white.

Sadly, after leading for three of the race's four miles, Meynell and Vingarillo began to flag, leaving Flint to take the lead and eventually win. She may have lost, but Meynell kept her good humour: an open letter later appeared in the *York Herald*, claiming that Flint had won the race by foul play – as a gentleman should always escort a lady riding side-saddle.

viaticated *(adj.)*   fully prepared for a journey

Derived from *via*, a Latin word for a street, the word *viaticum* was variously used in its native Latin to refer to cash used to cover the cost of a journey, or to general provisions or supplies for a long trip. Those meanings were still intact when the word was first adopted into English in the mid sixteenth century, but by then the word had also picked up a stricter meaning, referring to a more metaphorical journey: a *viaticum* is also the name given to the Christian Eucharist as administered to someone receiving the last rites.

It's the travelling, wayfaring version of *viaticum* that lies at the root of the adjective *viaticated*, which the English lexicographer Nathan Bailey defined as 'furnished with things necessary for a journey' in his 1727 *Universal Etymological English Dictionary* – and it's this definition that ties this word in with today's date.

On 26 August 1768, the explorer James Cook set sail on his first expedition to the Pacific Ocean aboard HMS *Endeavour*. Cook's voyage was to take three years, but his ship was fully prepared.

The *Endeavour* had begun life as a collier named *Earl of Pembroke*, but having been acquired by the Navy it had been refitted with cabins, storerooms, ten cannon and a vast set of oars, should they be required for use in calmer seas. For the journey, the ship's store contained 6,000 pieces of pork and 9 tons of bread, 3 tons of sauerkraut, 1 ton of raisins and vast quantities of cheese, dried peas, sugar and oatmeal. To wash all that down, the *Endeavour* housed 250 barrels of beer, 44 barrels of brandy and 17 barrels of rum. Cook, it's fair to say, was fully *viaticated*.

escarmouche *(n.)* a brief skirmish or fit of anger

Escarmouche is a French word for a brief military engagement or skirmish or, figuratively, an angry argument or exchange. The word was borrowed directly into English from French in the fifteenth century, and by the mid sixteenth century had come to be used as a verb, meaning 'to fight' or 'to quarrel'.

As a word for a battle or military engagement, *escarmouche* is also an apt choice of word for today: the shortest war in history was fought, in its entirety, on 27 August 1896.

The war was sparked by the death of Hamad bin Thuwaini, the fifth sultan of the island of Zanzibar, off the east coast of Africa, two days earlier. The colonial British had supported a pro-British candidate, Hamoud bin Mohammed, as his successor, but before his accession could go ahead an anti-British candidate, Khalid bin Barghash, swept to power and installed himself as sultan. The British refused to accept Khalid's claim to the throne, citing a treaty signed several decades earlier that had stipulated that a new sultan could take to the throne only with express permission from Great Britain. Khalid was given an ultimatum to leave the palace by 9 o'clock on the morning of 27 August; instead, he and his forces barricaded themselves in the palace. To the British, this was a declaration of war.

The British assembled an impressive armoury including two gunboats, three cruisers and a body of 150 marines offshore, backed up by almost 1,000 local Zanzibari recruits. In their way were more than 2,500 of Khalid's loyal supporters. When the ultimatum expired, the attack on the sultan's palace commenced at 9.02 a.m. By 9.40 a.m., it was all over. Khalid fled the palace, and with help he eventually escaped to the mainland. The Anglo-Zanzibar War had lasted just thirty-eight minutes.

petty-dancers *(n.)*   the aurora borealis, the northern lights

Essentially, *aurora borealis* and *northern lights* both mean the same thing: *aurora* is the Latin for 'dawn' or 'sunrise', and was also the name of a Roman goddess personifying daybreak, while *borealis* means 'northern' in Latin, and derives from the name of the Ancient Greek personification of the north wind, *Boreas*. Both terms first appeared in English in the early eighteenth century to describe the luminous, multi-coloured displays caused by solar winds disturbing the magnetosphere high in the earth's upper atmosphere.

This bizarre phenomenon has also been known as *north-shine*, *fire-flaught* (a *flaught* being a flash of light), *northern morning* and even *dancing goats* over time, but among the earliest recorded names was *petty-dancers*, a term from the mid seventeenth century that still survives in some dialects of English today. The origin of the term is debatable, but it's likely that *petty* is actually a reduced form of *pretty*.

Whatever you choose to call them, the *aurora borealis* is typically seen in the night sky only at areas of especially high latitude – or, for that matter, especially low latitude, at which point they're known as the *aurora australis*, or 'southern lights'. But on 28 August 1859, an enormous solar storm began which threw such a massive amount of material from the sun towards earth that it produced auroras as far south as the Caribbean, and as far north as Queensland. In some places, the night sky became so bright that it appeared like daytime: according to one report, gold miners in the Rocky Mountains became so disorientated that they immediately awoke and started to prepare breakfast.

The storm lasted almost a full week, before dying away on 2 September.

after-roll *(n.)* a later roll of thunder or swell of the sea after a storm; a later event or consequence

The volcano on the Indonesian island of Krakatoa began to erupt on the afternoon of 26 August 1883. The eruption grew to its fiercest late the following morning, when three-quarters of the volcano collapsed in on itself in a series of colossal explosions, each louder and more powerful than the last. Contemporary reports claim the sound of the eruption could be heard clearly as far away as Perth, Western Australia, while sailors in the Sunda Strait, between Java and Sumatra, had their eardrums damaged despite being some 40 miles out at sea.

The eruption produced landslides, clouds of volcanic ash and tsunamis, some more than 150 feet tall, that claimed the lives of more than 30,000 people and effected coastlines as far away as South Africa. Indeed, the after-effects of the eruption could be felt all over the world – including in Britain.

On 29 August 1883, three days after the eruption had begun, a noticeable series of swells was recorded by tidal gauges in the English Channel. Precisely what caused these swells is debatable: although some reports claim that they were the remnants of the tsunamis caused by Krakatoa, it's unlikely that the waves could have travelled so far in just three days. Instead, it seems probable that they were whipped up by enormous pockets of air, thrown and buffeted with great force by the explosion.

Whatever the cause of the swells, they are essentially examples of *after-rolls* – swells or surges of the sea that follow a storm, or else later rolls of thunder that follow previous ones. The term was coined in the sixteenth century but has since come to be used figuratively of any later consequence or after-effect, especially of a substantial or devastating event.

anabiosis *(n.)* a revival, a coming back to life

Mary Shelley was born on 30 August 1797. The daughter of philosopher William Godwin, in 1814 she began an intense romance with one of her father's protégés, the poet Percy Bysshe Shelley, but the couple's relationship was a tragic one. Shelley's first wife, Harriet, committed suicide shortly after they met. Mary then lost three children with Percy, and then, in 1822, Percy drowned when his sailing boat sank during a storm off the coast of Tuscany. Mary herself died in 1851, having been plagued for the last decade of her life by a mystery ailment now believed to have been a brain tumour. She was just fifty-three years old.

Despite writing several novels, short stories, travelogues, poems, children's stories and countless articles and reviews, much of her work has been eclipsed by her horror novel *Frankenstein*. In 1816, while holidaying in Switzerland, Mary, Percy, Lord Byron and the novelist John Polidori arranged a competition to see who could write the best horror story. Mary later dreamt of a scientist who created life from death and was horrified by what he had done; *Frankenstein* was published two years later.

The process of returning to life can properly be called *anabiosis*, a biological term coined in the nineteenth century and formed from Greek roots meaning 'again', *ana*, and 'life', *bios*. An *anabiotic* revival, however, is not strictly one along the lines of Dr Frankenstein's experiment: the term is often applied to plants or animals that can return to life from intense external hardships, like plants growing after droughts or wildfires, or insects that can survive being frozen solid in the depths of winter.

intershock *(v.)*   to collide, to hit or strike together

Strictly speaking, a *collision* is an impact of two objects that are both moving; if one of the objects involved is stationary, the impact is an *allision*. Understandably, that fairly finicky discrepancy is rarely observed in everyday English, but it remains an important distinction in legal contexts where, for instance, it helps to determine liability in accidents. But why use the word *collision* at all, when you can use *intershock*?

Adopted directly from its French equivalent, *s'entrechoquer*, in the early 1600s, in English *intershock* is used both as a noun, meaning 'a strong hit or collision', and as a verb meaning 'to collide' or 'to strike together'. And either one of those meanings would make it a fitting choice of word for today.

On 31 August 1979, a comet named Howard-Koomen-Michels smashed directly into the surface of the sun. The collision was the first of its kind ever witnessed by astronomers, as most comets that come within any close distance to the sun – known as 'sungrazers' – either break up or vaporise entirely before they reach the solar surface. The impact of Howard-Koomen-Michels, however, produced a monumental amount of energy, estimated at the time to be equivalent to 1,000 times the energy used by the United States in an entire year.

sceptredom *(n.)*   the reign of a king; royal power or sovereignty

The word *sceptre* – the name of the ornamental and often jewel-encrusted staff or wand held as a symbol of royal power – derives via French and Latin from its Greek equivalent, *skeptron*. In its native Greek, *skeptron* was used both to mean a sceptre or baton carried as a symbol of power, and as another word for a walking stick or staff, or a prop used to support a lame or ailing person. In that sense, *sceptre* derives ultimately from the Greek verb *skepto*, meaning 'to lean upon' or 'to press one thing against another'.

The word *sceptredom* was coined by the English author and pamphleteer Thomas Nashe, who used it in his final work *Lenten Stuff* (1599). Nashe intended the word to mean 'the reign of a king', or 'a period of royal control', but later writers broadened its meaning and applied it to the power or entire sovereignty of a reigning monarch. In either sense, the word is an apt choice for today: on 1 September 1715, King Louis XIV of France died at the age of seventy-six.

Louis had ascended to the French throne on 14 May 1643 when he was just four-and-a-half years old. His reign of 72 years and 110 days – during which time he developed the Palace of Versailles as the seat of the royal court, and oversaw France's involvement in three major wars – not only set the record in his native France, but makes Louis the longest reigning monarch of any sovereign state in the history of Europe.

ucalegon *(n.)*   a neighbour whose house is on fire

It's fair to say the English language contains its share of niche and all but unusable words. According to the *English Dialect Dictionary* (1905), for instance, to *spanghew* is to inflate a frog and bowl it across the surface of a pond. To *feague* is to insert a live eel up a horse's backside in order to make it appear more sprightly. A *rum-snoozer* is a drunk who falls asleep in a brothel. And a *ucalegon* is a neighbour whose house is on fire.

The word *ucalegon* is an allusion to a character who appears in both Homer's *Iliad* and Virgil's *Aeneid*. One of the counsellors of the city of Troy, Ucalegon – whose name essentially means 'unworrying' in Greek – had his house set on fire when the city was sacked by the Achaeans:

> Then Hector's faith was manifestly clear'd,
> And Grecian frauds in open light appear'd.
> The palace of Deiphobus ascends
> In smoky flames, and catches on his friends.
> Ucalegon burns next: the seas are bright
> With splendour not their own, and shine with Trojan light.
>   Virgil's *Aeneid* (II, 307–12)

From there, Ucalegon's name dropped into allusive use in English in the late seventeenth century.

On the subject of burning cities, the Great Fire of London started shortly after midnight on 2 September 1666 in the bakery of a man named Thomas Farriner on Pudding Lane, close to the northern end of London Bridge. The fire burned until the following Wednesday, during which time more than 10,000 homes and almost 100 churches were destroyed, leaving perhaps as many as 70,000 of the city's population homeless.

ambilaevous *(adj.)*   equally clumsy in both hands

If you're *ambidextrous*, then you're equally agile or nimble with both hands and can display perfect adroitness with both your left and right sides. If you're *ambilaevous*, then you're equally clumsy with both hands.

Both these adjectives – one much more familiar than the other – date from the mid seventeenth century in English and have at their roots a Latin prefix, *ambi–*, meaning 'both', plus the Latin words for 'right', *dexter*, and 'left', *laevus*. Being clumsily *ambilaevous* implies being literally 'left-handed on both sides' but, as unfair as that may seem, this isn't the only term to somewhat slight the left hand in comparison to the right. In the mid nineteenth century an equivalent term, *ambisinistrous*, was coined from another Latin word for the left hand, *sinister* – which became so unfavourably associated with contrariness and misfortune that it came to be used in English to mean 'ominous' or 'threatening' in its own right.

With left-handedness and right-handedness in mind – and switching deftly or not so deftly between the two – today is 'H-Day', the day on which the entire Swedish road network switched from driving on the left to driving on the right. H-Day (the H standing for the Swedish word *Högertrafik*, literally 'right-traffic') was initially hugely unpopular with the Swedish people, 83 per cent of whom voted against the change in a referendum in 1955. Nevertheless, by the mid 1960s the sheer number of left-hand drive cars on Sweden's roads – and the left-handedness of Sweden's immediate neighbours, Norway and Finland – led to the decision being forced through by parliament, paving the way for H-Day on 3 September 1967.

potmeal *(n.)*   a drinking session

Although things did not end well for the explorer Henry Hudson at the end of his final voyage in 1610 (turn back to 22 June to find out why), the previous year marked one of his most successful explorations. As captain of a Dutch ship named the *Half Moon*, Hudson sailed from Amsterdam to the Arctic, then down past Newfoundland and the east coast of Canada, and on 4 September 1609 sailed into New York Harbour – and there discovered the island of Manhattan.

What happened next has become the subject of a long-standing bit of American folklore. According to the tale, Hudson met with a group of Native Americans while exploring the island and invited them back to the *Half Moon* for a restorative glass of brandy. The natives, however, had never drunk such potent liquor before and soon fell into a drunken stupor. From then on, they referred to the island where their carousing had taken place as *Mannahattanik* – 'the place where we were all drunk'.

Sadly, it's unlikely this tale of Hudson's overzealous hospitality is genuine; instead, Manhattan is thought to take its name from a Lenape word meaning 'island of hills'. Nevertheless, it's a popular anecdote – and leads us neatly on to today's word.

Potmeal is a seventeenth-century word for a drinking bout, derived from the somewhat old-fashioned use of 'pot' to mean 'tankard' or 'drinking vessel'. Derived from the same root, a *pot parliament* is a group of drinkers (mid 1500s); a *pot-quarrel* is a drunken argument (late 1500s); a *pot-ally* is a drinking companion (early 1600s); and a *pot-leech* is a heavy or insatiable drinker (mid 1600s).

pogonophobia *(n.)*   a hatred or dislike of beards

The Greek word for 'beard', *pogon*, is the origin of a surprising number of English words. If you're *pogonate*, for instance, then you're bearded – a word that was originally used as an epithet for the Roman emperor Constantine the Great. *Pogonotrophy* is beard growth, while *pogonotomy* is the trimming of a beard. The *pogonion* is the foremost point of the chin. And *pogoniasis* is excessive beard growth, especially in someone, like a child or a woman, who should really remain *imberbic* (that is, beardless).

First used in the mid nineteenth century, *pogonophobia* is an intense dislike of beards – and on this date, one of the most famous figures in European history took his dislike of beards one step further.

On 5 September 1698, Peter I of Russia imposed a beard tax. Depending on the status and standing of the wearer, the tax worked out at anywhere from 30 to 100 roubles a year: once paid, the wearer would be handed a silver 'beard token' to prove that their *pogonotrophy* was entirely legal.

The emperor's rule was brought in to ally Russian culture more closely with the European culture he admired. His counsel of advisers, however, objected to Peter's attempt to 'Europeanise' his court and pushed for Russia to follow the conventional ideals of old Slavic culture. The clash prompted Peter to introduce levies on several aspects of traditional Russian life: besides beards, fishing, bathing and even beekeeping were all taxed, partly as a means of westernising the Russian way of life, and partly as a means of filling the deficit in his budget. Perhaps thanks more to its economic rather than cultural benefits, the Russian beard tax was not repealed until 1772.

airquake *(n.)*   an air tremor; a sonic boom

If an *earthquake* is a tremor in the earth, then an *airquake* is a tremor or shockwave felt in the air. For such a contemporary-sounding word, it's surprising to find that the word *airquake* was first used way back in 1746, when the Irish cleric and philosopher George Berkeley wrote of a series of tremors that had recently been reported in London:

> Having observed it hath been offered . . . that the late shocks felt in and about London were not caused by an earthquake . . . I take it upon me to affirm the contrary . . . We are not to think the late shocks merely an air-quake (as they call it), on account of signs and changes in the air, such being usually observed to attend earthquakes . . . I see nothing in the natural constitution of London, or the parts adjacent, that should render an earthquake impossible or improbable.

Berkeley would go on to be proved right: a powerful earthquake struck London in March 1750. But from Berkeley's description, we can deduce that an *airquake* was originally some kind of earthquake-like event that appeared to affect the atmosphere more greatly than the earth.

By the late twentieth century, however, all that had changed: as aviation technology improved, the word *airquake* came to be attached to the shockwaves and 'booms' associated with supersonic flight. And on 6 September 1948, RAF test pilot John Derry became the first Briton to break the sound barrier, when he lost control of the de Havilland DH 108 he was flying and dived 10,000 feet through the sky at supersonic speed. Happily, he survived.

prosopopoeia *(n.)* personification, the application of human characteristics to an inanimate thing

On 7 September 1813, the nickname 'Uncle Sam' was used to refer to the United States in print for the very first time in an editorial in the *Troy Post*, a local newspaper printed in Troy, New York. The name quickly caught on, and before long had been given an accompanying caricature, often depicted with grey hair and a beard, and a red, white and blue striped top hat and tails.

Despite Uncle Sam's often fairly garish appearance, legend has it that he was based on a real person. Samuel Wilson was a New York meat packer who, according to the story, supplied barrels of meat to the US Army during the War of 1812. His supplies were stamped with the letters 'US', and a joke quickly emerged among troops that the barrels belonged to 'Uncle Sam'. The local press soon picked up on the quip, thereby popularising the nickname in and around New York, and it has remained in use ever since.

The personification of something that is inanimate can be properly known as *prosopopoeia*, a term from rhetoric that covers a number of figures of speech in which inanimate objects are given human characteristics. As well as referring to anthropomorphised characters that represent concepts or entities, like Uncle Sam, Britannia and France's Marianne, *prosopopoeia* also refers to a technique in which a voice is given to an inanimate object (as in Shakespeare's 'The iron tongue of midnight hath told twelve', from *A Midsummer Night's Dream*).

Prosopopoeia literally means 'to make a face' in Greek.

petrifact *(n.)*   a stone artefact or statue

In the early 1400s, the overseers of Florence Cathedral struck upon an idea to place statues of Old Testament characters atop twelve buttresses on the cathedral roof. The first, a terra-cotta figure of Joshua, was completed by Donatello in 1410, and the project continued apace until 1463, when an Italian Renaissance sculptor named Agostino di Duccio was commissioned to provide a statue of David.

At great expense to the cathedral, an enormous slab of marble was purchased and transported to Florence, and Agostino set to work hewing away several vast chunks to produce a vaguely human form – but, for some reason, the project suddenly collapsed. Agostino's involvement in the commission ceased, and although it was handed over to fellow sculptor Antonio Rossellino, he never started work on it. The marble lay dormant in the cathedral workshop for more than twenty-five years, until finally interest in the project re-emerged. In 1501, a twenty-six-year-old artist named Michelangelo Buonarroti won the commission – beating stiff competition from Leonardo da Vinci. His masterpiece statue of David was unveiled on 8 September 1504 in the Piazza della Signoria, a square in front of the Palazzo Vecchio, in Florence.

It is worth remembering on a day on which what is arguably one of the world's most famous statues was unveiled, a *petrifact* is a stone statue or object. Based on the word *artefact* combined with the Latin word for 'stone', *petra*, the word *petrifact* was coined in the late nineteenth century. As well as referring to stone statues and relics, it can also refer to objects that have been literally *petrified* – that is, turned to stone.

agerasia *(n.)* a more youthful appearance than one's true age

At the height of the First World War, Admiral John Arbuthnot Fisher, the former head of the British Navy, sent a letter to Winston Churchill, who was by then the government's Minister for Munitions. 'I hear that a new order of Knighthood is on the tapis,' he wrote. 'O. M. G. (Oh! My! God!) – Shower it on the Admiralty!'

Fisher's letter was dated 9 September 1917 – and provides us with the earliest known record of the abbreviation *OMG*.

The fact that the now ubiquitous slang term *OMG* is likely a little under a century older than many people realise makes *agerasia* a fitting word for today. Derived from a Greek word for 'eternal youth', *agerasia* first appeared in English in the early eighteenth century, when it was defined as 'vigorous old age' in a 1706 collection, *The New World of Words*. On the rare occasion that it falls into use today, however, *agerasia* (pronounced 'adge-uh-*ray*-zee-ah', incidentally) tends to be used of the faculty of looking younger than one really is. Or, put another way, it refers to things that are older than they seem.

Alongside *OMG*, other words that could fall into this category include *dude*, which was used of a priggish, dandyish gentleman as early as 1877; *hipster* and *fangirl*, which date from 1938 and 1934 respectively; and *unfriend*, which despite having connotations of Facebook fallouts was first used as a verb by Thomas Fuller in 1659:

> I hope, Sir, that we are not mutually un-friended by this difference which hath happened betwixt us.
>
> Letter to Peter Heylin, 1659

pot-valour *(n.)*   courage or boldness induced by drinking

Shortly before 1 o'clock in the morning on 10 September 1897, a London cab driver named George Smith crashed his car into the wall of a building in Westminster. According to an article in the *Morning Post*, Smith 'swerved from one side of the road to the other, and ran across the footway into 165 New Bond Street, breaking the water pipe and the beading of the window'. Smith was taken to a local police station, where it was discovered he had been driving at a heady 8 mph when he had crashed. But as the magistrate overseeing his case explained to him, 'You are not charged with driving furiously, but with being drunk.'

Smith, who was fined 20 shillings, later apologised and admitted to having had 'two or three glasses of beer', explaining in his defence that it was 'the first time I have been charged with being drunk in charge of a cab'. In fact, it was the first time in history that anyone had ever been charged with drink driving.

The recklessness or misplaced confidence that made Smith get behind the wheel of his cab that night might best be described as *pot-valour*, a term from the first half of the seventeenth century for courage or rash boldness induced by drink. Along similar lines, the word *pot-proof-armour* was coined by the Scots writer and translator Thomas Urquhart in 1653, to refer to drink as a source of courage, while the German language has perhaps one of the best ill-advised dipsomaniac words in the form of *schnapsidee* – a crazy or impractical idea that seems ingenious when you're drunk.

Septembrise *(v.)*   to murder someone for political reasons

In September 1792, a series of brutal murders took place across Paris. Almost a month after the overthrow of the monarchy – and three years after the start of the French Revolution – rumours had begun to spread among Paris's increasingly anxious population that the political prisoners now held in the city's jails were on the verge of rising up and forming a counter-revolutionary force that threatened to put an end to the Republican cause. Adding pressure to the situation, news broke that the Duke of Brunswick's Prussian army had invaded eastern France and was heading towards the capital seeking to reinstate the king; if Brunswick were to reach Paris, he could free the prisoners and bolster his already vast forces. The solution was simple: the political prisoners had to be killed.

For five nights, prison after prison across Paris was stormed, and their inmates executed. Most of those killed were merely petty criminals and other non-political prisoners, killed indiscriminately with little chance to plead their case. In total, more than 1,000 prisoners were murdered.

The September Massacres, as they became known, eventually led to the coining of the word *septembrise*, meaning 'to murder for political reasons', which first appeared in print in English just two years after the events in Paris.

On the subject of which, Gyorgy Markov died on 11 September 1978, four days after having been stabbed in the leg with an umbrella containing a pellet of ricin while waiting at a bus stop in London. A Bulgarian dissident writer and broadcaster who had worked for the BBC World Service, Markov's murder was believed by some to be linked via the Bulgarian Secret Service to the Russian KGB.

serendipitist *(n.)* someone who benefits from serendipity or a serendipitous event

Serendipity, meaning 'happenchance' or 'providence', was coined in 1754 by the English writer Horace Walpole. Writing to his friend, the diplomat Horace Mann, Walpole explained that he coined the word based on an old Persian folk tale, *The Three Princes of Serendip*, the title characters of which were 'always making discoveries, by accidents and sagacity, of things they were not in quest of'. *Serendip*, incidentally, is an old name for the island of Sri Lanka.

A *serendipitist*, meanwhile, is someone who enjoys or benefits from serendipity or else from some fortunate, serendipitous occurrence. And one of the most extraordinary serendipitous discoveries in recent times took place on this date.

On 12 September 1940, eighteen-year-old Marcel Ravidat stumbled across the entrance to a cave system while walking in a valley near the village of Montignac, Dordogne. Wanting to explore further, he returned later with three friends, and together they descended into the caves. To their amazement, they found that the cave walls were decorated with an extraordinary array of some 2,000 painted images, depicting human figures, animals, plants and abstract designs. Ravidat had discovered the now world-famous Lascaux Caves.

Named after the valley in which they are located, the Lascaux cave paintings are estimated to have been made during the late Stone Age, roughly 18,000 years ago.

epinicion *(n.)*   a song or poem of victory

During the War of 1812, two American lawyers, Francis Scott Key and John Skinner, were invited aboard a British ship, HMS *Tonnant*, to discuss the release of prisoners of war. While the negotiations continued, the British fleet moved along the coast towards Baltimore, a major port the British were intent on attacking. Now aware of the British fleet's intent, Key and Skinner were prohibited from leaving the ship – and so, on the night of 13 September 1814, they could do nothing but watch as the city was bombarded.

By the following morning, however, the British had been defeated. As he left the ship, Key noticed the American flag still flying above the local garrison, Fort McHenry, and when he returned home composed a poem to commemorate the event:

O say can you see, by the dawn's early light,
What so proudly we hailed at the twilight's last gleaming,
Whose broad stripes and bright stars through the perilous fight,
O'er the ramparts we watched, were so gallantly streaming?
And the rockets' red glare, the bombs bursting in air,
Gave proof through the night that our flag was still there.

Entitled 'Defence of Fort M'Henry', the poem soon came to the attention of a local music publisher, Thomas Carr, who set the lyrics to the tune of a popular melody, 'To Anacreon in Heaven'. Now known as 'The Star-Spangled Banner', it was made the national anthem of the USA in 1931.

A poem written in honour of a victory is an *epinicion*, a term first used in English in the early 1600s, but which has its roots in a Greek word, *epinikion*, for an ode sung in honour of a victor in the Olympian games. The word literally means 'upon victory'.

charette *(n.)* a period of intense work or creative activity undertaken to meet a deadline

According to etymological legend, it was not unusual for architecture and design students at the École de Beaux-Arts in Paris to work furiously together as the deadline for their work approached at the end of each term. The students' projects, however, were not handwritten essays or dissertations, but often heavy and somewhat bulky sculptures and scale models, which would have to be collected from their workshops using a small wheeled cart or wagon known as a *charette*. The students' energetic, last-minute flurry of work ultimately became known as working *en charette* – or literally 'in the cart'.

In this sense, *charette* dates from the mid nineteenth century in its native French, and fell into use in English in reference to an intense period of working activity or creativity – a fine example of which came to a head on this date.

In July 1741, the composer George Frideric Handel received a new libretto from his friend and collaborator Charles Jennens. A devout Christian, Jennens adapted his lyrics from the King James Bible and the Book of Common Prayer, telling the stories of the prophet Isaiah and the enunciation, crucifixion and resurrection of Jesus. Handel set to work composing music for the text the following month, and by 14 September 1741 had produced all 259 pages of music, comprising a vast fifty-three-movement oratorio for choir and orchestra. The work – Handel's masterpiece oratorio, *Messiah* – had been completed in just twenty-four days.

miraculate *(v.)*   to produce by a miracle

To *miraculate*, a seldom-used word coined in the seventeenth century by an English clergyman and preacher named Thomas Adams, is to produce something by means of a miracle.

Both *miracle* and *miraculate* are descended from the Latin *miraculum*, meaning 'object of wonder', which itself derives from a Latin verb meaning 'to marvel at'. Any one of these would make a suitable word for today, thanks to a bizarre feat of *miraculation* that took place in Italy in the mid sixteenth century.

According to legend, early on the morning of 15 September 1530, three mysterious women appeared in the grounds of a Dominican friary in Soriano Calabro in southern Italy. None of the women spoke, but one merely handed the sacristan of the friary a rolled-up canvas before departing. The women, it was later claimed, were the Virgin Mary, St Catherine and Mary Magdalene; the painting was of St Dominic, the twelfth-century priest who founded the Dominican order of monks.

The friars promptly put the artwork on display, where it soon attracted the attention of the local townspeople. As word of its supposedly miraculous appearance spread, the portrait of *St Dominic in Soriano* acquired a reputation for having miraculous properties of its own, and over the following century more than a thousand miracles were directly attributed to the painting. As a result, in 1644 Pope Innocent XII established a feast day on 15 September celebrating not the life of St Dominic (whose feast day is 8 August), but the painting itself.

Sadly, the painting is believed to have been destroyed in an earthquake sometime later, and its feast day is no longer observed.

perfretation *(n.)*   a sea voyage or crossing

A *perfretation* is a sea crossing, a word dating from the seventeenth century in English and derived from *fretum*, a Latin word for a strait or channel. To *transfrete*, likewise, is to cross a strait or sea – and given the events of this day, either word would make an appropriate choice for today.

In 1620, the *Mayflower* – the ship that transported the first Pilgrims to America – docked at Southampton to rendezvous with her sister ship, the *Speedwell*, before they both set off on their voyage to the New World. The *Speedwell*, however, soon proved unseaworthy and both ships were forced to return to Dartmouth on the coast of Devon for repairs. From there they headed out into the Atlantic, but again the *Speedwell* quickly sprung a leak and the ships were forced to return to England, this time to Plymouth, where the problematic *Speedwell* was sold and its 102 passengers, crew and provisions loaded on to the *Mayflower*. Finally, the *Mayflower* alone departed England and headed to America – but not before it had made one final stop.

While the Pilgrims' journey from Plymouth, England, to Plymouth, Massachusetts, is one of the most famous in history, it is less well known that the *Mayflower* was forced to stop at the small Cornish town of Newlyn on 16 September 1620. The reason for the break in the journey is debated, but a widely held theory is that the drinking water picked up at Plymouth had been contaminated, and fresh water had to be acquired before the journey could continue. The *Mayflower* reputedly refreshed its supply at Newlyn – its final stop before, at long last, departing for America.

mamamouchi *(n.)*   someone who believes themselves
more important than they really are

On 17 September 1859, Joshua Norton sent a letter to a local
newspaper in San Francisco, California:

> At the peremptory request and desire of a large majority
> of the citizens of these United States, I, Joshua Norton,
> formerly of Algoa Bay, Cape of Good Hope, and now
> for the last 9 years and 10 months past of S. F., Cal.,
> declare and proclaim myself Emperor of these U. S.

Norton, who was born in England in 1818, was a businessman who had lost his money investing in a failed Peruvian rice
enterprise. A four-year protracted court case attempting to void
the contract and recoup his losses had left him disillusioned
with the legal and political structures of the United States, and
ultimately, in sheer frustration, he proclaimed himself emperor.
Over the years that followed, he continued to issue imperial
decrees, calling for everything from the abolition of Congress to
the construction of a tunnel below San Francisco Bay. Through
his sheer audacity, Norton soon became a popular local eccen-
tric, and when he died suddenly in 1880, some 30,000 people
attended his funeral.

Someone who believes themselves more important than
they truly are is a *mamamouchi*, a word coined by the French
playwright Molière as a suitably magnificent-sounding title
bestowed on one of the characters in his 1670 comedy *Le
Bourgeois Gentilhomme*. From there, the world soon fell into
broader use in English, and is defined by the *Oxford English
Dictionary* as both a 'pompous-sounding title' and 'a person
assuming such a title – a pretender to elevated dignity'.

scugways *(adv.)* clandestinely; with a hidden
purpose or ulterior motive

To do something *scugways* is to do it clandestinely, with an ulterior motive, or from a hidden vantage point.

Scugways is an old Scots dialect word that derives from an earlier Scots term, *scug*, thought to be descended from an ancient Scandinavian word for a shadow. As a verb, *scug* or *scogue* can be used to mean 'to conceal', 'to hide' or 'to skulk', while as a noun it variously means 'a two-faced, underhand person', 'a false pretence or insincere excuse' or 'a piece of subterfuge' – an infamous example of which took place on this day.

Late in the evening of 18 September 1931, an explosion struck a railway track near the city of Mukden (modern-day Shenyang) in Manchuria, China. The line – like much of the city at the time – was controlled by Japan, and the Japanese government was quick to blame the explosion on Chinese nationalists. Although the explosion failed to destroy the track (a train reportedly passed over it without knowing of the problem just minutes later), Japan seized the propagandising opportunity. A full invasion of Manchuria was organised, and within six months the Imperial Japanese Army had taken control of the entire region, and established a puppet state named Manchukuo.

The explosion that had sparked the invasion, however, had been staged. Reportedly, a lieutenant among the Japanese army officers had rigged a small amount of dynamite in the hope that the explosion would act as a pretext for war. Whether or not he acted alone remains hotly debated. Nevertheless, international condemnation of the act was quick to follow, and the ruse eventually led to Japan being internationally isolated and, two years later, withdrawing from the League of Nations.

omniparity *(n.)* universal equality

On 19 September 1893, Lord Glasgow, Governor of New Zealand, signed into law a new act that gave all women the right to vote in parliamentary elections: New Zealand ultimately became the first self-governing territory in the world to give women the vote.

The first election in which women could cast their votes followed just two months later – as did the election of Scottish-born mayoral candidate Elizabeth Yates, who, as Mayor of Onehunga, a suburb of Auckland, became the first female mayor in the entire British Empire in November 1893.

Universal equality can be known as *omniparity* or *comparity*, words coined in the mid 1600s and rooted in the Latin word for 'equality', *paritas*. Equal power or force, likewise, has been known as *equipollence* (literally 'equally strong') since the fourteenth century, while the act of making something equal can be known as *adequation*, and absolute equality of civil rights is *panpolism*, a term adopted into English in the mid nineteenth century from the writings of the German socialist writer Karl Marlo.

New Zealand's step towards equality was still a few steps short of global *omniparity*. The constituent states of Australia and the USA began to extend the franchise to women shortly after, soon followed by a handful of European countries, but the process was staggered in many places and painfully slow in others. Britain, for instance, only extended the right to vote to property-owning women over thirty in 1918, before the law was extended to include all women a decade later. The last European country to grant women the right to vote, Liechtenstein, did so only in 1984.

cohonestation *(n.)* the act of honouring with your company

Derived ultimately from a Latin word meaning 'to grace' or 'to honour', *cohonestation* is a seventeenth-century word for the act of visiting or honouring someone with your company. And on this date in 1860, a landmark royal *cohonestation* took place.

After a regiment of troops from Nova Scotia fought alongside Britain at the Siege of Sevastapol in 1855, the Canadian government requested that Queen Victoria pay a state visit to Canada. The prospect of the lengthy sea voyage such a trip would entail did not appeal to the queen, and nor did Canada's subsequent suggestion that one of her young children be sent in her stead. But by 1860, growing diplomatic pressure from her government (and the increasingly unruly behaviour of her eldest son, eighteen-year-old Edward, the Prince of Wales) forced Victoria's hand.

A trip was arranged in which Edward would not only tour Canada but – in an effort to bolster the relationship between the two countries, and much to the queen's distaste – visit the United States.

Edward departed England in July and arrived in Canada to dedicate a new bridge across the St Lawrence and to lay the cornerstone of a new parliament building in Ottawa. From there, he boarded a ferry at Windsor, Ontario, and crossed the Detroit River to Michigan, arriving in the United States on 20 September 1860, to become the first British royal to visit America since its independence.

After Victoria's death in 1901, her son succeeded her as King Edward VII; it wasn't until 1939 that George VI became the first reigning monarch to visit the US.

otacust *(n.)*   a spy, an eavesdropper

At the Battle of Long Island in August 1776 – the first major conflict of the American Revolutionary War – a decisive British victory led to much of the island falling under British control, while George Washington's American troops were pushed back to Manhattan. In a desperate need to know the British forces' next move, Washington asked for a volunteer to head behind enemy lines and gather intelligence. The mission would be a perilous one, but a young captain named Nathan Hale put himself forward. A plan was hatched for him to pose as an itinerant schoolteacher (his job before he had enlisted in a Connecticut militia the previous year), and on 12 September, Hale crossed to the mainland and made his way to Long Island.

Before Hale had a chance to relay any information, however, the British attacked once more. New York City – then just the southern tip of Manhattan – fell to the British, and Washington was pushed back to the island's northern end. Precisely what happened to Hale, however, is unclear: some reports say that he was recognised by his cousin, a supporter of the British cause, who turned him in to the authorities, while others say he was tricked by a British major, Robert Rogers, into divulging his true identity. Either way, on 21 September 1776 he was arrested, questioned and sentenced to death. He was hanged the following morning.

First used in English in the seventeenth century, *otacust* is seldom-used word for a spy or eavesdropper, derived, via French and Latin, from a Greek word literally meaning 'listener'. At its root are Greek words meaning 'ear', *ous*, and 'hearing' or 'audible', *akoustos* – which, despite appearances, is enough to make *otacust* a distant etymological cousin of words *otalgia* ('earache') and *acoustic*.

monomachy *(n.)*   a fight between two lone combatants; a duel

The Greek word for a battle or fight, *makhe*, sits at the root of a number of fairly obscure words relating to combat or confrontation. A *tauromachy*, for instance, is a bullfight, while *alectryomachy* is a formal word for cockfighting dating from the seventeenth century. A *logomachy* is a literal war of words. *Chiromachy* is hand-to-hand combat, while a *pygmachy* is a fight using clubs or bludgeons. And, first used in the mid 1500s, a *monomachy* is a fight between two individual combatants – or, more specifically, a duel.

A notable duel in English history took place on 22 September 1598, when the playwright and actor Ben Jonson killed Gabriel Spenser, a fellow actor, in a sword fight on Hoxton Fields, London. Precisely what sparked the duel is unclear, but Jonson later claimed Spenser had initiated it (and that he had the benefit of a longer sword). Spenser struck first, hitting Jonson on his arm, but Jonson somehow fought back and fatally stabbed his opponent in his right side. An inquest later recorded that Spenser had died of a stab wound six inches deep.

Jonson admitted to the killing, but his education saved him from being executed himself: at the time, a legal loophole called 'benefit of clergy' allowed anyone who could demonstrate their literacy by reading from the Latin Bible to escape capital punishment. Instead, Jonson was merely briefly imprisoned, had his possessions seized, and was branded with a letter T on his thumb – a reference to the Tyburn gallows, where Jonson would otherwise have been sent to be hanged.

Neptunist *(n.)*   a sailor or mariner

Neptunist is an old epithet for a sailor, first recorded in English in the late sixteenth century. It derives unsurprisingly from the name of the Roman god of the sea, whose name is also borne by the eighth planet in the solar system, Neptune.

Neptune was discovered on 23 September 1846 by the German astronomer Johann Gottfried Galle – although the notion that there was an eighth planet in the solar system, beyond the orbit of Uranus, had been postulated for almost a century.

As early as the 1780s, the Finnish-Swedish astronomer Anders Lexell noticed irregularities in Uranus's orbit that he realised could only be caused by the gravitational pull of a neighbouring planet. That theory took a step forward in the 1820s, when the French astronomer Alexis Bouvard noticed that predictions on the location of Uranus in the sky, based purely on Newton's laws of motion and gravitation, failed to match actual observations. And by the early 1840s, so much data on Uranus's bizarre orbit had been collected that Urbain le Verrier, a mathematician based in Paris, was able to calculate the size and position of the still undiscovered eighth planet using mathematics alone. Le Verrier sent his predictions to Galle – he discovered Neptune the same night that the letter arrived, and found Le Verrier's predictions to be less than one degree out.

In naming the new planet, a number of classical mytho-logical names were suggested in keeping with the remainder of the solar system. Janus, the Roman god of entrances, and Oceanus, the Titan personifying the great river meant to encir-cle the earth, were both suggested, but Le Verrier opted for Neptune, the name of the Roman god of the sea, supposedly in reference to Neptune's rich sea-blue colour.

bishop's-finger *(n.)*   a signpost

On 24 September 1909, Thomas M. Flaherty of Pittsburgh, Pennsylvania, filed a patent application for a 'signal for crossings'. Flaherty's invention comprised a large horizontal metal arrow, pivoted at the top of a post, that could be positioned at crossroads and junctions and turned electronically by an operator at the side of a road to indicate the direction of the flow of traffic. Flaherty's was the first design for a traffic signal received by the US patent office; his patent was granted two years later.

A signpost at a junction or crossroads that uses an arrangement of wooden posts or arrows to indicate the direction of travel has been known as a *fingerpost* in English since the early eighteenth century – the name alluding to the fact that such signs and signals were often carved to resemble a finger, pointing in the direction of their eventual destination. In the later eighteenth and early nineteenth centuries, however, these signposts came to be known as *bishop's-fingers*, a term that largely survives in English today only as a traditional name for a pub or roadside tavern.

Conversely, the English lexicographer Francis Grose's *Classical Dictionary of the Vulgar Tongue* (1785) listed the word *fingerpost* as an eighteenth-century slang nickname for a parson. And the origin of both terms is meant as something of a slight against the sanctimonious or hypocritical behaviour of some clergymen. As Grose explains:

> *FINGER POST.* A parson: so called, because he points out a way to others which he never goes himself. Like the finger post, he points out a way he has never been, and probably will never go, i.e. the way to heaven.

theic *(n.)*   an excessive drinker of tea

On 25 September 1660, the diarist Samuel Pepys met with a friend, Sir Robert Ford, to discuss politics and international relations – and to try a drink he had never tried before:

> We talked together of the interest of this kingdom to have a peace with Spain and a war with France and Holland . . . And afterwards I did send for a cup of tee (a China drink) of which I never had drank before, and went away.

Whether Pepys enjoyed his 'tee' is unclear; the only other reference in his diary comes seven years later, when he returned home to find 'find my wife making of tea, a drink which Mr Pelling [an apothecary] tells her is good for her cold and defluxions'.

The Latin word for 'tea', *thea*, is the origin of *theism*, a word coined in the mid nineteenth century to refer to an excessive appetite for tea and all the medical problems supposedly caused by it; an excessive tea-drinker, meanwhile, is a *theic*. According to one description of the tea-drinking scourge, *theism* could be blamed for everything from hearing voices to irritability:

> America and England are the two countries that are afflicted most with the maladies arising from the excessive consumption of tea . . . The predominance of nervous symptoms is a characteristic of theism . . . Perversion of the sense of hearing is not at all an uncommon symptom – patients report hearing voices that have no real or objective existence. The irritability that overtakes women so frequently may sometimes be clearly traced to an excessive indulgence in afternoon tea.
>
> *Scientific American*, 1886

palaestra *(n.)*   a place for debate or a battle of wits

A *palaestra* is literally a 'wrestling-place'. Derived from the Greek word for 'wrestle', *palaiein*, it originally referred to a school or training area in Ancient Greece where wrestling could be taught, before its meaning broadened to refer to a gymnasium or any place of athletic combat or exercise. It was this more general meaning that was first adopted into English, via Latin, in the early fifteenth century – but before long the word had begun to be used more figuratively to describe any place of confrontation or combat. By the eighteenth and nineteenth centuries, the original and now historical meanings of *palaestra* had all but disappeared, leaving a word for an intellectual battleground or arena for debate.

Fittingly, the very first US presidential debate took place on 26 September 1960. The debate between Massachusetts Senator John F. Kennedy and the incumbent Vice President of the United States Richard Nixon was broadcast live on television and radio to an audience of millions – almost two out of every three American households tuned in.

Although Nixon reportedly fared well with radio listeners, on television it was a different story; he refused to wear make-up and sweated profusely, and having continued campaigning until the day of the debate (as well as not being fully recovered from a recent stay in hospital with an infected knee) appeared unshaven and exhausted. Kennedy's telegenic good looks and charm, meanwhile, helped him win the debate among viewers – and eventually, by a margin of just 100,000 votes, the 1960 election.

anonym *(n.)*   someone who wishes to remain anonymous; a pseudonym

On 27 September 1888, a menacing letter arrived at the offices of the Central News Agency in London. Written in red ink and addressed 'Dear Boss', it read:

> I keep on hearing the police have caught me but they wont fix me just yet . . . Grand work the last job was. I gave the lady no time to squeal. How can they catch me now. I love my work and want to start again . . . The next job I do I shall clip the ladys ears off and send to the police officers just for jolly wouldn't you . . . My knife's so nice and sharp I want to get to work right away if I get a chance. Good Luck. Yours truly Jack the Ripper.

The letter – which the news agency printed and passed on to police the following day – was originally believed to be a hoax. But when prostitute Catherine Eddowes was found murdered in the corner of Mitre Square, Whitechapel, just two days later with one of her ears removed, the 'Dear Boss' letter was taken seriously by police.

This letter also marked the first time that the Whitechapel killer (or else, the hoaxer) referred to himself as 'Jack the Ripper'.

A pseudonym like this can also be known as an *anonym*, a term first used in nineteenth-century English and derived, like its much more familiar cousin *anonymous*, from a Greek word literally meaning 'without a name'. Unlike *pseudonym*, however, *anonym* can also be used to refer to the person whose name is withheld, and who wishes to remain nameless. Precisely who that was in the Jack the Ripper case was famously never discovered.

brocard *(n.)*   an elementary principle, a short proverbial rule or maxim

Traditionally, 28 September 551 BC is the date given as the birthdate of Confucius.

Born in Qufu, northeast China, Confucius excelled in his studies as a young man and eventually became a teacher. Through his work he advocated a well-grounded and comprehensive education system for all, not just the children of the wealthiest families, and made much of his belief that learning was character-building to the individual, as well as beneficial to all of society. In his later life, he served in a variety of governmental positions before his increasing dissatisfaction with his superiors' lack of interest in his suggestions led him – with an ever-growing circle of students and followers around him – to leave Qufu for a life of exile. He returned a decade later to resume his teaching, and died in 479 BC.

After his death, many of Confucius' students collated their notes of conversations they had had with their mentor into an anthology known by the Chinese title *Lunyu*, literally 'edited conversations'. To English speakers, however, the work is best known as Confucius' *Analects* – a collection of his most notable sayings, rules, ideals and maxims.

A *brocard*, too, is a rule or maxim. The word derives from a Latin form of the name of Bishop Burchard of Worms, a tenth-century cleric who compiled a vast twenty-volume collection of ecclesiastical rules and principles known as the *Decretum*, or 'Decree'. His work grew so well known across medieval Europe that eventually his name became synonymous with any basic rule or doctrine, and in that sense was adopted into English in the mid seventeenth century.

jingle-boy *(n.)*   a rich man

On 29 September 1916, American oil tycoon John D. Rockefeller's personal fortune surpassed the $1 billion mark, making him the first dollar billionaire in history. According to a report in the *Chicago Tribune*, the previous day a rush on oil sales had pushed shares in Rockefeller's Standard Oil Company of New Jersey up to a price of $2,000 each, over 250 per cent more than their price five years earlier. Rockefeller owned a quarter of the company's shares – as well as a quarter stake in the thirty-three other individual enterprises his Standard Oil company had splintered into in 1911 – which pushed his personal wealth into the billions and made him the richest man in the world.

The word *billionaire* had entered the language only fifty years earlier, when the American writer Oliver Wendell Holmes apparently invented it for his 1861 novel *Elsie Venner*. Holmes modelled the word on the earlier *millionaire*, which had been borrowed directly into English from French in the late 1700s; before then, anyone with a personal wealth measuring in the millions was known by the decidedly more English-sounding word *millionary*.

Even earlier still, however, in seventeenth-century slang a notably wealthy man was known as a *jingle-boy* – literally, someone who had enough coins in his pocket for them to jingle as he walked.

paregoric *(adj.)*   painkilling, analgesic

Something that is *paregoric* has the ability to relieve or deaden pain. First used in English in the late 1600s, the word derives via Latin from a Greek word, *paregorikos*, literally meaning 'soothing'. That in turn is comprised of two Greek roots meaning 'beside', *para*, and 'to speak' or 'to speak in public', *agoreuein*, the implication being that a *paregoric* drug or preparation is as soothing or ameliorating as someone talking soothingly and calmly.

In the early eighteenth century, the word *paregoric* was temporarily plucked from obscurity as the name of an 'asthmatic elixir' developed by German chemist Jakob le Mort, which comprised a mixture of opium and various traditional herbal and chemical remedies, including honey, liquorice and camphor. The product remained readily available as a household treatment for everything from diarrhoea to toothache right through to the late nineteenth and early twentieth centuries, when regulation of its narcotic ingredients led to its disappearance from pharmacy shelves – largely taking the word *paregoric* with it.

On the subject of pain relief, it was on 30 September 1846 that the anaesthetic properties of ether were first demonstrated by an American dentist named William Morton, who administered the drug to one of his patients before performing an entirely painless tooth extraction. News of Morton's experiment quickly spread, and the following month Morton publicly assisted in an operation at Massachusetts General Hospital in Boston, the success of which kick-started the widespread use of ether as an anaesthetic in the later nineteenth century. The room in which the operation took place is now appropriately known as the 'Ether Dome'.

polly-in-the-cottage *(n.)* a man who helps with housework

Besides all its more familiar meanings, the word *cot* is a seventeenth-century term for someone who lives in a rural 'cot' or cottage – or, more broadly, someone who enjoys a quiet, disconnected rural life. But through association with the stereotypically unsophisticated characters who live in isolation in the countryside, detached from more cosmopolitan society, *cot* eventually came to be used as a byword for a rustic fool or a 'country bumpkin' – and in that sense inspired a host of uncomplimentary terms for henpecked or unmasculine men.

Polly-cot, cot-betty, molly-cot, cot-quean and, more fully, *polly-in-the-cottage* are all old dialect terms for men or husbands who either meddle in their wives' affairs, or like to carry out domestic chores and housework. Mostly dating from the seventeenth and eighteenth centuries (although a *Dictionary of the Canting Crew* defined a *cotquean* as 'a man that meddles with women's matters' as early as 1699), in words like these *molly, polly* and *betty* are all used simply as typically feminine names, while *quean* is simply an old English word for a woman or daughter.

Wife-carl, likewise, is an old Scots dialect word for a man who takes on traditionally female chores, as is *hussy-fellow* – a man who, according to the *Scottish National Dictionary*, 'interferes with or undertakes women's duties'.

What do all these household words have to do with today? Well, it was on 1 October 1861 that *Mrs Beeton's Book of Household Management* was published in England for the first time.

beaglepuss *(n.)* a pair of novelty glasses with a fake nose, eyebrows and moustache attached

Groucho Marx was born in New York, on 2 October 1890.

Having left school aged twelve, Marx joined his brothers in a vaudeville singing group, but when a runaway mule interrupted a performance in 1912 he was quick to pick up on the bizarreness of the incident and began cracking jokes between songs. Seeing a future in comedy, the Marx Brothers began to work more jokes into their act, and quickly proved hugely popular. They made their Broadway debut in the mid 1920s, and a contract with Paramount Pictures followed: together, they made more than a dozen comedy films, including *Animal Crackers* (1930), *Duck Soup* (1933) and *A Day at the Races* (1937). After moving into television and radio in later years, Groucho died in 1977 at the age of eighty-six.

It was during one of the brothers' Broadway shows that Groucho arrived late to the theatre one night and, without time to apply the fake moustache he needed for his part, smeared a black line of greasepaint on to his top lip and eyebrows. The look eventually became his trademark – and inspired the Franco-American Novelty Company of New York to produce their own version.

In the mid 1940s, the company began producing novelty glasses with a fake nose, black eyebrows and a moustache attached. Although better known as 'Groucho glasses', these novelty glasses were originally sold under the name *beaglepuss*, a nonsense word based around the old slang use of *puss* to mean 'face'. The term stuck for a time and eventually found its way into the dictionary – but today, these novelties remain better known by the name of the comic icon who inspired them.

trucidation *(n.)*   an especially cruel killing or murder

The grim word *trucidation* first appeared in the language in the early 1600s, followed shortly after by a verb, *contrucidate*, meaning 'to wound' or 'to slay'. Both have at their roots the Latin verb *trucidare*, meaning 'to kill' or 'to cut to pieces', which in turn brings together the Latin *trux*, meaning 'harsh' or 'brutal' (the origin of *truculent* behaviour) and *caedere*, meaning 'to cut' (from which *deciduous* trees and *caesarean* sections both take their names).

And as 'cuts' go, you can't get much more 'savage' than those doled out on a rebellious medieval prince today in 1283.

Dafydd ap Gruffydd was the last ruler of independent Wales before the country was conquered by Edward I. Having fought for much of his life against his brother Llywelyn for control of the kingdom of Gwynedd, in 1274 Dafydd joined forces with Edward to challenge his brother once more. The result was the Treaty of Aberconwy in 1277, which divided Gwynedd between the two brothers and the English crown. Dafydd, however, grew dissatisfied with his lot and in 1282 he attacked Hawarden Castle, a stronghold in Edward's newly acquired Welsh territory. The king was furious.

Edward raised an army and conquered Wales. Llywelyn was killed, and Dafydd – who had assumed Llywelyn's title as Prince of Wales – was captured and condemned to death for high treason. On 3 October 1283, Dafydd was dragged through the streets of Shrewsbury by a horse, then hanged, revived, disembowelled, his entrails then burnt in front of him, and then his body cut into four quarters and sent to the four corners of Edward's kingdom: Dafydd was the first nobleman in recorded history to suffer being hanged, drawn and quartered.

smoot *(n.)* a unit of length equal to five feet, seven inches

As little-used and insanely precise units of measurement go, the likes of *beard-second*, *microfortnight* and the others that made the list on 10 April are among the most peculiar. But arguably most peculiar of all is the *smoot*, a unit of length or distance defined by the *American Heritage Dictionary* as 'equal to precisely five feet, seven inches'.

Why such a precise size? Well, it just so happens that Oliver R. Smoot, the MIT-educated Chairman of the American National Standards Institute and namesake of the *smoot*, stands five feet, seven inches tall.

On 4 October 1958, Smoot and some of his Lambda Chi Alpha fraternity brothers decided to pull a prank that involved measuring the length of the Harvard Bridge, connecting Boston and Cambridge, Massachusetts, using Smoot's five-foot-seven frame as the measuring tape. Smoot lay down, repeatedly, the entire length of the bridge while his fellow pranksters marked his height on the pavement in chalk and, by the end of the experiment, the bridge was found to be 364.4 smoots long – or a little under 2,035 feet.

Smoot's prank quickly became legendary. To this day, graffiti on the Harvard Bridge still divides it up into various Smoot-sized sections, and in 2008, Oliver Smoot returned to MIT to take part in a celebration marking its fiftieth anniversary – although apparently he stopped short of remeasuring the bridge.

weather-sharp *(n.)*   a weather forecaster

We're more likely to call them *weather forecasters* today, but *weather-sharp*, dating from the late 1800s, is the earlier term for those who predict the weather. Before then, terms as impressive as *weather-wizard* and *weather-spy* (both late 1500s), *weather-monger* (mid 1600s) and *weather-maker* (mid 1800s) were all in use, while weather forecasts themselves were once somewhat grandly known as *weather-prophecies*. And any one of these would be an apt choice for today, thanks to the remarkable predictions of Stephen Martin Saxby.

Saxby was a lieutenant in the Royal Navy in the mid nineteenth century who used a pseudoscience known as 'meteorological astrology' – the theory that the positions of the stars and planets affect the weather on earth – to predict the weather, often months in advance. Saxby's *weather-prophecies*, however, went largely ignored, so that when he published an open letter in London's *Standard* in December 1868 warning of exceptionally high tides coinciding with the north Atlantic hurricane season the following October, his predictions fell on deaf ears. But sure enough, the following October, a powerful hurricane struck the eastern coast of North America.

The storm skirted the east coast of America and made landfall in Canada shortly after midnight on 5 October 1869, driving a 6½-foot storm surge up on to land. At Burncoat Head, Nova Scotia, the tide was swept up to a staggering height of 71 feet, a world record that has yet to be broken. The 'Saxby Gale', as it is now known, claimed the lives of at least thirty-seven people.

latrocination *(n.)*   robbery, theft

Latrocination is a formal word for theft or robbery that first crept into the language in the mid seventeenth century. It derives from a Latin word literally meaning 'to rob on a highway', which in turn is descended from the Latin *latron*, meaning 'mercenary' or 'brigand'. The crime of *larceny*, despite appearances, is a distant etymological cousin.

On 6 October 1866 a gang of four *latrocinating* brothers known as the Reno Gang committed the very first robbery of a moving train in history. The brothers' audacious stunt proved a landmark in US crime: previous train robberies had been committed only on cars resting in stations, but the Renos singled out a train en route across the notoriously lawless and sparsely populated western United States, taking its drivers entirely by surprise. The brothers made off with $10,000 from an O&M Adams Express Company train just outside Seymour, Indiana – but their crime spree was not to last. And oddly, it would end almost where it had started.

Two years later, in July 1868, the Reno Gang was captured and arrested in a sting operation organised by Chicago's Pinkerton detective agency. While being taken to jail by train, however, the gang's prison transport stopped in the middle of the track a few miles outside Seymour, where the prisoners were taken off the train and hanged from a nearby tree. The remaining gang members were apprehended shortly after – but they too were killed at the hands of vigilantes. By December, the Reno Gang was no more.

earthshine *(n.)* the reflection of sunlight on to an otherwise dark part of the moon

On clear nights, sunlight striking the earth can be reflected back on to the moon, making that part of the moon that should be in the earth's shadow visible. This phenomenon is known as *earthshine*, and accounts for the fact that on nights when, for instance, only a crescent moon should be visible in the sky, a brightly lit and clearly visible crescent moon will be accompanied by the darkened, but still faintly visible, remainder of the moon.

The phenomenon of *earthshine* (or *planetshine* when it affects other bodies in the solar system) has been known and described for centuries; even as early as the 1400s, Leonardo da Vinci commented on it and hypothesised that both the earth and the moon must be capable of reflecting sunlight at the same time. But the term *earthshine* has been with us only since the early nineteenth century, when the visibility of 'that part of the moon which receives no light directly from the sun' was mentioned in an appropriately titled *Library of Useful Knowledge*.

'That part of the moon which receives no light directly from the sun', incidentally, became much more visible on 7 October 1959 when the Soviet space probe *Luna 3* took the first photographs of the dark side of the moon. The images the probe sent back to earth covered roughly one-third of the moon's surface that remains permanently turned away and out of sight. But technology advanced so quickly through the 1960s that the very first atlas of the entire lunar surface was produced in 1967.

blunder-a-whack *(n.)*   someone whose carelessness
has caused a disaster

According to the *English Dialect Dictionary* (Vol. I, 1898), a *blunder-guts* is a clumsy, blundering person, and a *blunder-skull* is an empty-headed fool. An 1862 dictionary, *The Dialect of Leeds and its Neighbourhood*, listed the word *blunder-a-whack*, defined as 'one whose carelessness has brought on disastrous consequences'. And, of the three, it's this last word that arguably best suits today's date.

According to folklore, on Sunday 8 October 1871 a cow kicked over a lantern in the barn of Catherine O'Leary, an Irish immigrant in Chicago. The flames from the lantern quickly ignited the straw in Mrs O'Leary's barn, and from there spread to the surrounding buildings. By the time the fire had burned itself out the following Tuesday, more than 17,000 buildings had been destroyed, at least 200 people had lost their lives, and a further 100,000 people were homeless. The Great Chicago Fire destroyed more than three square miles of the entire city.

Whether or not Mrs O'Leary's absentminded placing of her lantern by her cow's leg did indeed spark a fire that caused $200 million worth of damage is open to debate, with alternative theories placing the blame on everything from an ember blown from a sparking chimney stack to a burning comet. But it's the tale of Mrs O'Leary's cow – a phrase now used allusively to refer to 'an unwitting agent of disaster', according to *Merriam-Webster* – that has become the most well-established legend. Folk etymologists will even have you believe Mrs O'Leary had given her cow a shot of bourbon to stimulate its milk production – but no matter who tells you, no, this isn't the origin of the word *firewater*.

umbratical *(adj.)*   disguised, cloaked

From his accession in 1189 (turn back to 6 July for that) to his death in 1199 (and head to 25 March for that), it's thought Richard I might have spent as little as six months in England. That's partly because he chose to live in France rather than rainy old England, and partly because he was for a long time held prisoner by the king of Germany. And partly it's because he spent much of his ten-year reign on the Third Crusade.

Determined to take Jerusalem from the Muslim leader Saladin, Richard departed for the Holy Land in 1190 and arrived the following June. City after city fell under European control, but Jerusalem remained out of Richard's grasp. The Crusaders staged several attacks on the city over the months that followed, but all attempts were unsuccessful and after a year of stalemate, Richard and Saladin came to an awkward truce. On 9 October 1192, the king left for home. To escape without fear of capture, Richard travelled in disguise: some records state that he travelled as a Knight Templar, others that he passed himself off as a merchant. But, whatever the truth, his disguise wasn't good enough to stop him from being recognised in Vienna and imprisoned by Henry VI of Germany (4 February will tell you more about that).

If you're cloaked or disguised, incidentally, then you're *umbratical*, a word derived from *umbra*, a Latin word for 'shadow'. *Umbratical* was first used in English in the seventeenth century, when it was also used to mean 'remaining in seclusion', or 'serving as a poor representation or replacement' – in the sense that an object may provide only a 'shadow' of the real thing.

go-to-meeting *(adj.)*   of clothes – smart, formal

The 'meeting' that crops up in the late eighteenth-century word *go-to-meeting* is a church meeting or congregation. In relation to smart clothes or formal attire, *go-to-meeting* literally refers to a person's 'Sunday best' – their smartest, or most elegant or impressive outfit or garment, which would be saved for attending church.

Through that association, *go-to-meeting* later came to be used to describe devout, churchgoing folk, and later to anyone who spends an inordinate amount of time attending parish gatherings or assemblies, but its original and literal meaning was that of a person's outfit. And on the subject of smart clothes, 10 October 1886 was the date on which the tuxedo dinner jacket not only debuted in the United States, but earned its name.

According to legend, the very first tuxedo was fashioned on London's Savile Row in 1860 at the request of Queen Victoria's eldest son, Prince Edward, the future King Edward VII. Edward wanted a short-fitting evening jacket that could be worn both at formal and informal dinner parties, and in response his tailor, Henry Poole, produced a relatively simple, tailless black and white dress suit which the prince debuted at a party at Sandringham House later that year. The design quickly caught on, and in 1886 came to the attention of an American socialite, James Potter, who was invited by the prince to spend a weekend at Sandringham. Potter had a tuxedo made for him during his stay in England, and debuted the outfit at the Tuxedo Park Country Club in New York later that year.

Xanthippe *(n.)* a scolding, quarrelsome woman

Traditionally, 11 October is the feast day of St Gummarus, an eighth-century Belgian saint now considered the patron saint of childless couples, separated spouses and difficult marriages.

How did St Gummarus come to be so commemorated? Most accounts of his life claim that his wife Guinmarie was shrewish and argumentative, and abusive to the servants in their employ. After a long military service, Gummarus returned home to his wife but found their relationship had soured in his absence, and the couple eventually separated. Gummarus left for a life of solitude and eventually founded an abbey in Lier, Belgium – the city of which he is now the patron saint.

While Guinmarie is not a celebrated enough character to have her name adopted into the language, one of history's more infamous scolding spouses is: Xanthippe, the wife of the Greek philosopher Socrates. Xenophon, one of his students, famously referred to her as 'the most difficult woman not just of this generation . . . but of all the generations past and yet to come' in his *Symposium* (*c.*368 BC). Precisely what Xanthippe did to deserve such a reputation is unclear (many of Xenophon's contemporaries were considerably kinder in their recollections of her), but nevertheless Xanthippe's name ended up in the dictionary as an allusive reference to a henpecking, argumentative spouse:

> Be she as foul as was Florentius' love,
> As old as Sibyl and as curst and shrewd
> As Socrates' Xanthippe, or worse,
> She moves me not, or not removes at least
> Affection's edge in me, were she as rough
> As are the swelling Adriatic seas.
>
> *The Taming of the Shrew* (*c.*1592)

love-light *(n.)*   a romantic glimmer in a person's eyes; an infatuation

On 12 October 1786, the future US President Thomas Jefferson wrote an aching love letter to a young artist he had met while in Paris named Maria Cosway. Jefferson's letter, known as his 'Dialogue Between the Head and the Heart', contains some of his most emotive and revealing writing:

> My Dear Madam,
> – Having performed the last sad office of handing you into your carriage at the pavillon de St. Denis, and seen the wheels get actually into motion, I turned on my heel & walked, more dead than alive, to the opposite door, where my own was awaiting me . . . Seated by my fireside, solitary & sad, the following dialogue took place between my Head & my Heart:
> Head. Well, friend, you seem to be in a pretty trim.
> Heart. I am indeed the most wretched of all earthly beings. Overwhelmed with grief, every fibre of my frame distended beyond its natural powers to bear, I would willingly meet whatever catastrophe should leave me no more to feel or to fear.

By the time the pair met, Jefferson was a widower, but Cosway was married. Their relationship was destined to go nowhere, but his infatuation was unquenchable: once, while walking with Cosway through a Paris park, Jefferson jumped over a stone fountain in his excitement. He fell and broke his wrist.

Besides jumping over fountains, a sure sign of infatuation is a *love-light* – a term coined in the mid nineteenth century for the radiant spark or glimmer that can be seen in a lover's eyes.

quinie *(n.)* a cornerstone, the first stone laid in a
building

Long before it came to be attached to money, a *coin* was originally a block forming the corner of a building, or else one of the
wedge-shaped stones forming part of an archway. In that sense,
the word derives from the Latin word for 'wedge', *cuneus*, and
was borrowed into the language from French in the mid 1300s.

But because wedge-shaped dies were once used to impress
designs on to coins, a monetary meaning soon developed and
established itself as the dominant meaning of the word in the
fifteenth and sixteenth centuries. This earlier architectural
meaning of *coin* is, meanwhile, still retained in the *coign* or
quoin of a building – words used to refer to angles or corners,
or to the cornerstones and keystones, of buildings.

And from *quoin* came *quinie*, a dialect word for a cornerstone, or the first stone laid in erecting buildings.

Arguably one of the most famous buildings in the world
had its *quinie* laid on this day in 1792. By that time, President
George Washington had been in office for a little over a year,
during which time he had overseen the choice of a site fit for
a purpose-built capital city. And the centrepiece of this new
capital was to be a grand mansion house, the principal residence
of the president of the United States.

An Irish architect, James Hoban, was tasked with designing
the mansion. Construction work began with the laying of the
cornerstone on 13 October 1792, but the project took another
eight years to complete. Sadly, George Washington died one
year before completion, and was never able to live in the house
he commissioned. Instead, his successor John Adams became
the first president to live in what would eventually become
known as the White House.

Parthian *(adj.)*   describing or akin to a shot fired while in retreat

The Battle of Hastings was fought on 14 October 1066. Exhausted and depleted from fighting the Battle of Stamford Bridge just nineteen days earlier, the English King Harold's forces were eventually overcome by those of the invading Norman King William when they began to implement an ingenious and effective tactic. Reportedly, William's troops pretended to flee from the battle in panic, and as their English attackers pursued them, the Normans suddenly turned back and resumed fighting.

> The Normans and their allies, observing that they could not overcome an enemy which was so numerous and so solidly drawn up, without severe losses, retreated, simulating flight as a trick . . . Suddenly the Normans reined in their horses, intercepted and surrounded [the English] and killed them to the last man.
>
> William of Poitiers, *Gesta Guillelmi* (*c.*1071)

The Normans weren't the first to use such a tactic; fighters in ancient Parthia, a region of northeast Iran, were known to continue firing arrows at their enemies while retreating from the battlefield. The ploy proved so effective that the adjective *Parthian* ultimately came to be used of any shot or attack employed while in retreat, or in the dying moments of an engagement.

In that sense, the word first appeared in English in the mid seventeenth century, but while the technique they employed remained familiar, the Parthians themselves did not. Ultimately, the word *Parthian* became corrupted, and steadily drifted closer to a much more familiar term – so that today this kind of last-minute attack or sally is typically known as a *parting shot.*

aerogram *(n.)*   a message sent by radio

In the early days of radio communication, messages sent by radio were known as *aerograms*. The word was first introduced in a newspaper article of 1890, which imagined a futuristic world where communication across vast distances would be commonplace, but by the turn of the century the word had fallen into wider use. Since then, however, *aerogram* has come to refer to any communiqué delivered or sent through the air – and today it is more likely to be used of a letter sent by airmail rather than by radio.

A memorable first in the world of radio communication took place on 15 October 1910, when US journalist and aeronaut Walter Wellman attempted to cross the Atlantic in his airship, the *America*. Setting off from New Jersey, the *America* only got as far as Bermuda before a series of problems forced it to turn back. But while the mission was a failure, Wellman and his crew did at least achieve one aviation first: on board was the first ever in-flight radio system. And also on board was Wellman's pet cat, Kiddo.

Kiddo, it soon emerged, wasn't quite as comfortable being airborne as Wellman might have hoped. According to the ship's navigator, Murray Simon, before long he was running all over the cockpit 'like a squirrel in a cage'. In desperation, radio operator Jack Irwin picked up his radio set and relayed perhaps the very first in-flight message in aviation history: 'Roy, come and get this goddamn cat!'

Happily, Kiddo soon calmed down and became a perfect travel companion. Simon later claimed he even went on to become a surprisingly useful addition to the crew, advising that, 'You must never cross the Atlantic in an airship without a cat.'

idioticon *(n.)*   a dictionary of a minority or
geographically localised language

Derived from a Greek word, *idios*, meaning 'personal' or 'particular to oneself', an *idioticon* is essentially a lexicon of idiomatic language – that is, a dictionary dedicated to the language of one particular region or group of people.

The lexicographer Noah Webster, author of the very first dictionary of exclusively American English, was born in Hartford, Connecticut, on 16 October 1758. It wasn't until he was seventy years old that Webster secured his place in linguistic history with the publication of his two-volume *American Dictionary of the English Language* in 1828. The dictionary had taken him twenty-two years to complete, but for good reason: in that time he had learned twenty-six different languages and assembled a collection of 70,000 words, more than any other dictionary in history. Indeed, around half of the words in Webster's *American Dictionary* had never been included in an English dictionary before – including some very specific Americanisms like *squash*, *skunk*, *hickory*, *chowder* and *applesauce*.

In writing his dictionary, Webster took the opportunity to implement a series of proposed spelling reforms, reordering words like *centre* and *fibre* to *center* and *fiber*, shortening words like *colour* and *axe* to *color* and *ax*, and simplifying words like *plough* and *manoeuvre* to *plow* and *maneuver*. Although not all of his reforms caught on (he also suggested dropping the E from *nightmare*, changing *soup* and *steady* to *soop* and *steddy*, and reworking *daughter* and *machine* as *dawter* and *masheen*), Webster's dictionary nevertheless helped to implement many of the spelling differences that still divide British and American English to this day.

tourbillion *(n.)*   a whirlwind

The Latin word for a whirlwind was *turbo* – although in the sense of something that spins or rotates at great speed, *turbo* could also be used to refer to a whirlpool or eddying current, a rotating spool or spindle, and even a child's spinning top. The word *turbine* is now derived from the same root, as are the little-used words *turbinate*, a verb meaning 'to spin like a top', and *tourbillion*, a word for a tornado or whirlwind that was borrowed into English from French in the mid fifteenth century.

Tornado, meanwhile, is thought to be a corruption of the Spanish word for a thunderstorm, *tronada*. It originally referred merely to a violent rainstorm or gale before the word came to be specifically attached to whirlwinds in the early 1600s. But the tornados themselves have been written of for several centuries longer than that – including one that struck the city of London on 17 October 1091.

The storm of 1091 demolished the original wooden London Bridge, as well as hundreds of homes, churches and other buildings across the city. Thought to be equivalent to what would now be a category F4 storm (with winds approaching 260 mph), the storm struck with such force that four rafters from the roof of St Mary-le-Bow Church – each measuring 26 feet long – were driven so deeply into the ground below that only 4 feet remained visible above the surface. Despite the ferocity of the storm and the extent of the damage, however, there were only two reported fatalities.

nappishness *(n.)*   sleepiness; a tendency to nap

In the mid 1830s, Herman Melville enlisted as a cabin boy on a merchant ship, the *St Lawrence*, and travelled from America to Britain in 1839. Over the years that followed, he enlisted with the crews of several more vessels and travelled extensively – during which time he was involved in a mutiny and imprisoned, spent time with a tribe of cannibals, and worked as a beachcomber in Tahiti. He returned to New York to begin writing about his travels in 1844, and published a semi-autobiographical account of his adventures, *Typee: A Peep at Polynesian Life*, two years later.

But it is for his masterpiece *Moby-Dick* – published on 18 October 1851 – that Melville is best known. In writing the book, Melville not only called upon his own experiences of working on a Pacific whaling ship, but was inspired by the story of a ship named the *Essex* that had been attacked by a sperm whale in 1820 (flick ahead to 20 November for that one). Melville is known to have met the son of one of the *Essex*'s surviving crewmembers, and after the publication of *Moby-Dick* met its captain, George Pollard – whom he later described as 'one of the most extraordinary men I have ever met'.

Moby-Dick is also credited with introducing a fairly niche set of words into the English language, including *cetology*, the study of whales, and *plum-puddinger*, naval slang for a voyage short enough to carry fresh fruit and other spoilable provisions. Among the more useful terms *Moby-Dick* introduced to the language, however, is *nappishness* – another word for sleepiness, or an inclination to nap.

auripotent *(n.)*   rich and powerful

The Latin word for gold was *aurum*, which is not only responsible for the chemical symbol for gold, Au, but is today found at the root of a host of suitably golden words. *Aurigraphy*, for instance, is the act of writing or engraving on gold. Something that is *auriphrygiate* is embroidered or fringed with golden threads. Anything *aureoline* or *aurelian* is golden coloured, while an *auricomous* person has golden hair. *Aureity* is goldenness, or the collective qualities possessed by gold. And if you're *auripotent* then you're rich in gold – which, thanks to a discovery on 19 October 1872, the prospector Bernhardt Holtermann certainly was.

Born in Germany in 1838, Holtermann emigrated to Australia when he was twenty and began prospecting in Hill End, New South Wales, in 1861. There he teamed up with a fellow Prussian emigrant, Hugo Beyers, and in 1872, after several luckless years, their partnership, the Star of Hope Gold Mining Company, struck upon a rich seam of gold containing an enormous single specimen of gold known as the Holtermann Nugget.

Measuring almost 5 feet long and weighing in at a staggering 630 lbs, the Holtermann Nugget – not a true nugget in the strictest sense, but rather a massive deposit of gold encased in quartz rock – contained 3,000 troy ounces (equivalent to more than 200 lbs) of pure gold. It remains the single largest specimen of gold ever found on earth.

After unsuccessfully bidding to buy the nugget outright, Holtermann resigned from the partnership the following year, but had still secured his fortune.

limitrophe *(n.)*   a borderland, a neighbouring country

On 20 October 1818, Great Britain and the United States signed a treaty that established the 49th parallel – the line of latitude lying 49° north of the equator – as the permanent land border between the United States and British North America (now Canada). According to the treaty, it was agreed that the border should follow 'a line drawn from the most north-western point of the Lake of the Woods' in Ontario, and travel due west along the 49th parallel 'until the said line shall intersect . . . the Stony Mountains', as the Rocky Mountains were known at the time.

As part of the deal, both countries agreed to share control of Oregon County (a disputed territory in the Pacific Northwest), with both ceding territory to the other elsewhere: the US handed the northernmost stretches of Missouri Territory, which it had claimed as part of the Louisiana Purchase, to Britain, while in return Britain ceded the southernmost stretches of one its major Canadian territories, Prince Rupert's Land. The changes marked both countries' last major territorial losses in North America.

A borderland, or a neighbouring country on the opposite side of a border, can be known as a *limitrophe*, a word first used in English in the mid sixteenth century. Although adopted from French (wherein it was once an adjective describing anywhere located on or near a boundary or frontier), *limitrophe* was originally a Latin word referring to a borderland region set aside for the training and support of troops. In that sense, it combines the Latin word for a boundary line, *limitem*, with a suffix derived from a Greek word, *trophe*, meaning 'nourishment'.

stradametrical *(adj.)* pertaining to the size and measurement of streets and roads

A *metre* was originally defined as 1/10,000,000th of half of one meridian – one ten-millionth of the distance between the equator and the North Pole. But over the centuries that definition has been refined several times and has steadily become more complex.

In 1799, a platinum bar that had been used to measure the meridian was placed in the French National Archives and used as the international standard for the metre. Copies of this bar were sent worldwide as the metric system came to be adopted internationally, but they were subject to wear and torsion, and with little guarantee that they were being used effectively, a new standard had to be introduced.

In 1889, a tougher, specially cast X-shaped bar was produced, on to which two marks were etched to indicate the precise size of one metre. As technology progressed, the temperature, pressure and metallic composition of this bar were standardised, before a measurement based on a solid object was abandoned altogether. In 1960, one metre became 1,650,763.73 wavelengths of an atom of krypton-86 radiation. Then, at the General Conference on Weights and Measures on 21 October 1983, even this remarkable precision was improved on: the international standard for one metre is now the length travelled by light in a vacuum in 1/299,792,458th of a second.

Mercifully, the story behind the word *metre* is a lot simpler than its definition. *Metre* is a French derivative of the Greek *metron*, meaning 'measure', from which words like *metronome*, *trigonometry* and *parameter* are all likewise derived – as is the adjective *stradametrical*, a term introduced in the nineteenth century to refer to the measurement of streets and roads.

brolly-hop *(n.)*   a parachute jump

On 22 October 1797, a French balloonist and daredevil named André-Jacques Garnerin performed the world's first successful parachute jump.

Floating in a gondola hanging beneath a hot-air balloon, Garnerin climbed to a height of 3,000 feet above the Parc Monceau in central Paris. He then cut the ties attaching his basket to the balloon, which floated skyward, and as the gondola began its descent, his homemade 23-foot canvas parachute unfurled above him. The descent was far from smooth, and the basket swung violently as it fell, but Garnerin managed to make a bumpy but nevertheless successful landing in the grounds of the park and stepped from the gondola uninjured.

Over the years that followed, Garnerin continued to improve his hot-air-balloon parachute designs, and gave regular demonstrations of his prototypes to ever larger crowds; in 1798, he courted controversy by asking a woman named Citoyenne Henri to accompany him on one of his flights.

Sadly, after a lifetime of surviving perilous falls, in 1823 Garnerin was struck by a falling beam while constructing a new balloon in his workshop and was killed. His place in history as the world's first successful parachutist, however, was secured.

To British Royal Air Force parachutists in the first half of the twentieth century, parachuting became known as *brolly-hopping*, while a *brolly-hop* was a parachute jump. First recorded in 1932, the term – alluding to the umbrella-like canopy of the parachute – grew in popularity during the Second World War but had largely disappeared by the 1950s.

thrimble *(n.)*   to grudgingly repay a debt

At its independence in 1776, the United States was already in debt, and in 1789 that situation worsened when America assumed liability for $75 million of debts accumulated during the Revolutionary War. Concerted efforts brought that figure down to its lowest in history – $37,000 – by the mid 1830s, but spending on the military sent it spiralling back to the $1 billion mark by the time of the Civil War. By the mid 1970s, debts had reached $500 billion, and on 23 October 1981, it was announced that the national debt of the United States had surpassed the $1 trillion mark for the very first time; half of that figure had been accumulated in just seven years.

To repay a debt – and, specifically, to do so reluctantly – is to *thrimble* or *thrumble*, an English dialect word dating back to the mid sixteenth century. Thought to be derived from an earlier word, *thrum*, for a multitude or throng of people, on its earliest appearance in the language *thrimble* meant 'to squeeze or press together', like people standing in a dense crowd, or 'to jostle' or 'to push your way through'.

By the early seventeenth century, that meaning had broadened (perhaps with influence from the word *thumb*) to come to mean 'to press or crush between the fingers' and then 'to toy or fiddle with something in your hands'. From there one last meaning developed in the late eighteenth century: according to the *English Dialect Dictionary* (Vol. VI, 1905), to *thrimble* is 'to finger or handle anything as if reluctant to part with it' and, ultimately, 'to dole or pay out money grudgingly or reluctantly'.

hardiment *(n.)*   courageousness, audacity; a daring exploit or stunt

Before it came to mean 'resilient' or 'robust', *hardy* meant 'courageous', and it's from this original meaning that the word *hardiment* developed in the early fifteenth century. Originally simply another word for boldness or bravery, by the early 1500s *hardiment* had come to be used more specifically of a singular act of courage, audacity or heroism, and ultimately a daring stunt or exploit. And as daring exploits go, the one that took place today is up there with the most extraordinary – not least because of the somewhat unlikely character who performed it.

On 24 October 1901, the first person in history went over the edge of Niagara Falls in a barrel and survived. That person was sixty-three-year-old music teacher Annie Edson Taylor.

Hoping the stunt would bring her fame and fortune, Taylor had an elongated oak and iron barrel especially constructed for her that was lined with mattresses and fitted with a short breathing tube and safety straps to keep her in place. After she had clambered inside, the barrel was sealed, the pressure inside compressed using a bicycle pump and the hole plugged with a cork. It was then set adrift and bobbed its way down the Niagara River and over the Canadian side of the famous Horseshoe Falls.

Twenty minutes later, the barrel was pulled from the waters by a rescue boat and Taylor was found alive and uninjured except for a small cut on her head. The stunt earned her the nickname 'Queen of the Mist' – but, alas, not the fame and fortune she desired. She died in poverty in 1921.

polyanthea *(n.)*   a literary collection, an anthology

Geoffrey Chaucer died on 25 October 1400.

Chaucer's written work includes a verse retelling of *Troilus and Cressida*, English translations of works by renowned Latin and French scholars and philosophers, and a non-fiction account of the workings of an astrolabe, an elaborate mechanical device used by navigators and astronomers. But it is for his *Canterbury Tales* that he is obviously best known today: an anthology of twenty-four tales related by a group of pilgrims en route to Canterbury to visit the shrine of Thomas Becket.

An *anthology* is literally 'a collection of flowers'. The word derives from the same root – the Greek for 'flower', *anthos* – as words like *dianthus* and *chrysanthemum*. But this isn't the only book that treats its contents as 'flowers' in a literary garden:

- *florilegium* (n.) Latin for 'flower-gathering', *florilegium* dates from the 1600s and refers to what the *Oxford English Dictionary* calls 'a collection of the flowers of literature'
- *polyanthea* (n.) from the Greek for 'many flowers', *polyanthea* has been used since the early 1600s to refer to a choice collection of poems or literary works
- *pomander* (n.) originally a container of scented flowers used to freshen clothes, *pomander* was also used to refer to a choice collection of prayers or poems in the sixteenth century
- *spicilegy* (n.) from the Latin for an ear of corn, a *spicilegy* is a literal 'harvest' of literary extracts
- *sylva* (n.) from a Latin word meaning 'tree', *sylva* came to refer to a treatise on horticultural matters in the seventeenth century, and from there any choice collection of written work

xenotransplantation *(n.)*   the transplantation of
non-human material into
a human patient

In 1984, a girl named Stephanie Fae Beauclair was born three weeks prematurely in a hospital in California. Although outwardly healthy, Fae was found to have a heart defect known as hypoplastic left-heart syndrome, a condition in which the left-hand side of the heart is fatally underdeveloped. The only cure was a transplant, but heart transplant surgery was still in its relative infancy (the first successful heart transplant had been performed only in 1967) and a dearth of donors meant that such a procedure on an infant patient was all but unheard of. Fae's doctor, Leonard Bailey, however, had an alternative.

He had spent many years researching *xenotransplantation* – transplant procedures performed between different species. Ultimately, on 26 October 1984, twelve-day-old baby Fae Beauclair received a donor heart from a baboon in an extraordinary landmark in the history of medicine.

Remarkably, the heart began to beat almost immediately, and Fae's condition initially improved – but sadly it did not last and she died two weeks later on 16 November. The fact that she had survived both her condition and the procedure as long as she had, however, was nevertheless considered an extraordinary achievement.

The term *xenotransplantation* was coined back in 1968 to describe transplants of this type, although an earlier term, *xenograft*, had been in use since 1961. The words derive from the same Greek root – *xenos*, meaning 'stranger' – as words like *xenon*, *xenophobia* and *xenodochy* (flick back to 13 February for more on that). As for Dr Bailey, he went on to perform the first successful infant transplant, using a human donor, the following year.

ananym *(n.)*   a word formed by reversing the letters of an existing word

Dylan Thomas was born on 27 October 1914. Alongside works like 'Do not go gentle into that good night' and *A Child's Christmas in Wales*, Thomas is best remembered for his 1954 play *Under Milk Wood*, set in the fictional Welsh town of Llareggub – a name Thomas famously invented by reversing the letters of 'bugger all'.

Words formed by reversing existing ones are known as *ananyms*, a word combining Greek roots meaning 'back', *ana*, and 'name', *onyma*. Most ananyms tend either to be fictional inventions (like Llareggub), or proper nouns, like Oprah Winfrey's Harpo production company, the towns of Adanac in Canada and Saxet in Texas, and Dioretsa, an asteroid with a retrograde orbit. But a handful of *ananyms* have found their way into the dictionary.

The *mho*, for instance, is the name of a unit of electrical conductance, coined in opposition to the *ohm*, a unit of resistance. Physicists also have at their disposal units called the *yrneh* (derived from the *henry*) and the *daraf* (as opposed to the *farad*), and in 1921 US engineer Frank Bunker Gilbreth invented the *therblig*, a unit of work in a time-and-motion study.

Perhaps the most familiar ananym is *yob*, first recorded as a reversal of the word 'boy' in a *Dictionary of Modern Slang* compiled by John Camden Hotten in 1859. In fact, Hotten's dictionary included a glossary of 'back-slang', a peculiar trend that emerged among market sellers in Victorian England that involved coining new buzzwords by reversing everyday ones. A cabbage, ultimately, became an *edgabac*, and an orange an *edgenaro*, while after a day's trading a seller might treat himself to a *top o'reeb* (a 'pot of beer') and end up *kennurd* ('drunk').

Rechabite *(n.)*   a person who abstains from alcohol

According to the Old Testament, the Rechabites were a nomadic clan descended from a strict Israelite figurehead named Rechab, who lived sometime in the mid ninth century BC. Rechab's followers were prohibited from living in houses and towns, forbidden to practise agriculture and cultivate the land, and were obliged to follow a total abstinence from alcohol. As the prophet Jeremiah explained:

> I set before the sons of the house of the Rechabites pots full of wine, and cups, and I said unto them, 'Drink ye wine.' But they said, 'We will drink no wine: for Jonadab, the son of Rechab our father, commanded us, saying, "Ye shall drink no wine, neither ye, nor your sons for ever."'

By the seventeenth century, this biblical account of the Rechabites' strictly teetotal lifestyle had led to their name becoming a byword for anyone who followed an equally strict lifestyle of abstinence.

The word remained in relative obscurity until 1835, when the Independent Order of Rechabites was founded on the back of the burgeoning temperance movement. Members of the Order met in lodges known as 'tents' (a reference to the Rechabites' nomadic existence and avoidance of towns) and were obliged to take a pledge resolving to completely abstain from alcohol. Rechabite organisations were soon emerging all over the world: founded in 1842, America's Independent Order of Rechabites boasted almost a million members by the turn of the century – just in time for the National Prohibition Act to be enacted in the United States on 28 October 1919.

boswellise *(v.)* to write a detailed account of another's life or deeds; to praise or eulogise greatly

In 1837, the Scottish writer and editor John Gibson Lockhart published his eulogising *Memoirs of the Life of Sir Walter Scott* – the renowned Scottish novelist who just so happened to be his father-in-law. In it, Lockhart spoke of 'several literary gentlemen' who had sent him their own reminiscences of Scott's life, which Lockhart explained were 'designed to Boswellize Scott'. Ironically, in apparently coining the word *boswellise* (his *Memoirs* provide the word's earliest known record) Lockhart name-checked the author of another glowing literary biography, James Boswell.

Boswell was born in Edinburgh on 29 October 1740. When he was twenty-two years old, he happened to bump into the writer and lexicographer Samuel Johnson in a bookshop, and the pair quickly became firm friends. Boswell was by all accounts captivated by Johnson's quick wit and intellect, and soon began to take notes of his witticisms and anecdotes, and to record their meetings in a journal – which before long had expanded across several volumes. Boswell's fanatical note-taking even became the subject of one of Johnson's typically sardonic comments, when he wrote to a friend joking that 'one would think the man had been hired to spy upon me'.

After Johnson's death in 1784, Boswell quickly set about collating his notes and journals, and published *The Life of Samuel Johnson* in 1791. Although it largely covered only the twenty-two years that he and Johnson had been friends (Johnson was fifty-three years old when they met), Boswell's *Life of Johnson* soon proved immensely popular – while the relentlessly reverent terms in which Boswell describes Johnson throughout the book eventually gave rise to the word *boswellise* in the early nineteenth century.

panshite *(n.)*   a state of panic, confusion, or uproar

Panshit or *panshite* is a fairly questionably spelled Scots dialect word for what the *Scottish National Dictionary* defines as 'a flurry, to-do, state of excitement, panic, or muddle'. Quite where such a peculiar word comes from is a mystery, but the dictionary's theory is certainly a plausible one: *panshit* might be a local corruption of *pansheet* or *panshard*, meaning 'a shard of broken pottery'. The association with panic or disorder, so the theory goes, may have come from 'the practice of breaking and throwing these in large quantities into houses on Shrove Tuesday', presumably in some age-old custom that is now, thankfully, as obsolete as the word *panshit* itself.

On the subject of panic and disorder, it was on 30 October 1938 that Orson Welles' infamous dramatisation of H. G. Wells' novel *The War of the Worlds* (1898) was first broadcast. Updated for a twentieth-century American audience, Welles' version of the story was written as a series of news broadcasts reporting a violent Martian invasion in near real time. From reports of distant explosions on the surface of Mars to a crowd of onlookers being vaporised by a ray gun fired from an alien craft, the events of the invasion steadily escalate until an attack on New York City describes terrified people jumping 'like rats' into the East River and tourists in Times Square 'falling like flies'. Finally, radio static is interrupted by a broadcaster ominously asking, 'Isn't there anyone on the air? Isn't there – anyone?'

Welles' broadcast was chillingly effective – in fact, almost too effective. The following morning, the *New York Times* ran with the front-page headline, 'Radio Listeners in Panic, Taking War Drama as Fact'.

demonagerie *(n.)*   a demonic menagerie

As 31 October is Halloween, it might be worth bearing in mind that a *demonagerie* – a term coined in the mid nineteenth century – is a literal 'demonic menagerie', a collection of monsters or demonic spirits. As for precisely what might constitute a *demonagerie*, the dictionary has more than its fair share of ghosts, ghouls and monsters.

The 'mare' of *nightmare*, for instance, is a spirit supposed to crouch on the chest of a sleeping person and give them bad dreams or a feeling of suffocation as they sleep. An *ephialtes* is a demon supposed to personify the nightmare itself, whose name is thought to derive from a Greek word literally meaning 'to leap upon'.

A *tenebrio* is literally a night spirit, the name of which comes from a Latin word meaning 'darkness' (and for that reason can also be used of a prowler or burglar who operates under cover of darkness). A *fetch* is the ghostly double of a living person, also known by the German word *doppelgänger*, literally 'double-goer'. *Loup-garou* and *turnskin* are both old words for werewolves. And the word *carrion* originally meant 'dead body', and as such was also used in fifteenth-century English to refer to a reanimated corpse.

As for demons, *burlow-beanie* is an old Scots dialect word for a seven-headed, fire-breathing demon, one of which was said to have worked in the service of King Arthur. A *titivil* is a demon who supposedly collected all the mumbled or mispronounced words from church services and carried them back to Hell. And *Belial* – a name derived from a Hebrew word meaning 'worthlessness' or 'uselessness' – is an ancient epithet for the Devil himself.

laqueary *(n.)*   a ceiling, the roof of a room

Thomas Blount's early English dictionary *Glossographia* (1656) defined a *laqueary* simply as 'the roof of a chamber'. Precisely how that meaning came about is difficult to say – not least because the word *laqueary* or *laquearia* derives from a Latin word, *laqueus*, for a hangman's noose.

It could be that *laqueary* somewhat grimly alludes to a noose being hung from the rafters of an open-ceilinged room. Or perhaps it could be that the bare beams of an open ceiling might be supposed to resemble the tough wooden struts of a hangman's gallows. Or perhaps there's something less macabre going on.

According to a nineteenth-century *Encyclopaedia of Architecture* (1842), there are two types of decorated ceilings: those with sunken wooden or fretwork panels consisting of 'compartments sunk or hollowed, without spaces or bands between', which are known as *lacunaria*; and those that are divided up and decorated with moulded bands, which are known as *laquearia*. The moulded or carved designs used on ornate *laqueary* ceilings would often take the form of twisted ropes or cords – like a wooden string of brocade – and so perhaps the name *laqueary* alludes to the resemblance between these traditional rope-like designs and the literal Latin hangman's noose.

Whatever the origin of the term, there is another way to decorate a ceiling, of course.

The Sistine Chapel, with its epic ceiling of biblical frescos by Leonardo da Vinci, was opened to the public for the first time after its completion on 1 November 1512. Fifteen years later, da Vinci would be commissioned to return to the chapel to add his *Last Judgement* to the wall behind the chapel's altar.

spurcity *(n.)*   obscenity, uncleanness

Descended from a Latin word, *spurcus*, meaning 'foul' or 'impure', *spurcity* is an early seventeenth-century word for obscenity. The verb *conspurcate*, meaning 'to defile' or 'befoul', and the adjective *spurcidal*, meaning 'speaking dishonestly or bawdily', both derive from the same root.

On 2 November 1960 a landmark legal case over an instance of *spurcity* came to an end when Penguin Books was found not guilty of obscenity for publishing an unabridged edition of D. H. Lawrence's novel *Lady Chatterley's Lover*.

Written in the mid 1920s, *Lady Chatterley's Lover* was first published in Italy in 1928, but it wasn't until 1932 that an edition was published in the UK. Even then, British readers were left with a heavily expurgated version of the text that played down the novel's controversial content (a tempestuous affair between the wife of a paralysed landowner and his gamekeeper) and Lawrence's unabashed use of taboo language (including both the F- and C-words).

When an unabridged text of the novel was finally published in 1960, it was Lawrence's four-letter language – and Penguin Books' determinedness not to censor it – that saw the publisher charged with obscenity. After a verdict of not guilty was reached, Penguin included this dedication in the book's second uncensored edition in 1961:

> For having published this book, Penguin Books was prosecuted under the Obscene Publications Act . . . This edition is therefore dedicated to the twelve jurors, three women and nine men, who returned a verdict of 'not guilty' and thus made D. H. Lawrence's last novel available for the first time to the public in the United Kingdom.

dragsman *(n.)*   a thief who steals from vehicles

In Victorian slang, a *dragsman* was a thief who specialised in stealing from 'drags' – a kind of elaborate stagecoach, usually drawn by four horses, with seats both inside and on top.

Born in New York sometime around 1830, Charles E. Boles was one of the most notorious *dragsmen* of nineteenth-century America. After unsuccessfully trying his luck as a gold prospector in California, Boles turned to a life of crime and began targeting stagecoaches ferrying gold from isolated mines to banks and storehouses in the nearby towns. Boles is thought to have robbed his first coach in 1875, disguising himself with an old flour bag pulled over his head, and giving the illusion that he had 'backup' by placing sticks in a nearby bush to look like rifle barrels.

In 1877, he robbed a coach outside Point Arena on the California coast, and left behind a bizarre calling card:

> I've labored long and hard for bread,
> For honor, and for riches,
> But on my corns too long you've tread,
> You fine-haired sons of bitches.

Signed 'Black Bart', this was one of a number of short verses Boles left at the scenes of his crimes – but on 3 November 1883, he left behind something that would eventually lead to his downfall. Wounded during a robbery outside the town of Copperopolis, Boles fled, leaving behind a handkerchief with a laundry mark attached. He was quickly tracked down and imprisoned.

Despite his notoriety, Boles had never shot anyone nor robbed a stagecoach passenger of their belongings during his spree; he was released from prison after four years for good behaviour and was pardoned.

leggism *(n.)* swindling; cheating at games or gambling

Francis Grose's *Dictionary of the Vulgar Tongue* (1785) defined a 'black-legs' as 'a gambler or sharper on the turf or in the cock-pit', and postulated that the word might perhaps refer to 'their appearing generally in boots, or else from game-cocks whose legs are always black'.

Whatever the origin, by the turn of the nineteenth century *black-legs* had shortened merely to *leg*, and by the mid 1840s had inspired the slang term *leggism*, referring to the actions or practices of a swindling gambler. And as *legs* and *leggism* go, one of the most notorious in history had his comeuppance today.

Born in 1882, Arnold Rothstein began gambling as a teenager in New York and had soon become not only proficient but rich. By his early twenties he had opened his own casino, and as his fortune and suspiciously unbroken 'lucky streak' continued to build, he expanded his empire to include property, racehorses, nightclubs and moneylending. He used his immense wealth and power to bribe the police and the New York courts, and was even suspected of arranging to fix the 1919 Baseball World Series. Reportedly, he never carried less than $200,000 with him at all times.

But on 4 November 1928, Rothstein's luck ran out. During a poker game against three of the New York underworld's kingpins, Rothstein racked up an immense debt and refused to pay out. Later that evening, he was found fatally shot at the service entrance of the Park Central Hotel in Manhattan; according to legend, when asked who had shot him he reportedly held his finger to his lips. He died two days later.

quaquaversally *(adv.)*   moving, pointing or
protruding in all directions

When a firework explodes in the sky on 5 November – celebrated as Guy Fawkes Night in the UK – the outward movement
of something in all possible directions from a centralised point
is known as *quaquaversality*. Ultimately, something described
as *quaquaversal* moves or expands outwards in the same manner, while anything that moves *quaquaversally* does do in all
directions.

The word *quaquaversal* was coined in the late seventeenth
century and originally tended to be used only in fairly strict
scientific contexts, to refer to the likes of the seemingly random movements of heavenly bodies, the outward flow of blood
through the body, and the unpredictable geological shift of the
earth or growth of mineral deposits. In those contexts, its use
was contrasted with words like *centroclinal* ('moving inwards
towards a common centre') and *partiversal* ('moving in different
directions through a semicircle').

Although never particularly widely used, in more recent
years this strictly scientific use has broadened, so that on the
occasional instances that *quaquaversal* is employed in print
today, it tends to be used more loosely to mean simply 'wide-
ranging', 'random' or 'sprawling'.

The word *quaquaversal* itself derives from the Latin phrase
quaqua versus, which essentially means 'turned wherever'.
Quaqua is a form of the Latin pronoun *quisquis*, meaning 'who-
ever' or 'whatever', while in this context *versus* literally means
'turned' or 'changed' (the same *versus* we use in English when
two combative parties are literally 'turned' against one another).

four-and-nine *(n.)*   a hat, in particular a cheap or poor quality one

In Victorian slang, a *four-and-nine* was a hat. The term has long since fallen out of use, but at the time was well known enough to be alluded to in a poem by Lewis Carroll ('For it had lost its shape and shine / And it had cost him four and nine') and to inspire a music-hall number ('So round me young and old, if you want a slap-up hat / Don't buy a four and nine') published in 1841.

According to one Victorian dictionary, the term *four-and-nine* emerged from the fact that four shillings and ninepence was the price a noted hat-maker advertised his wares for in the mid 1800s:

> So-called from the price at which an enterprising Bread Street hatter sold his hats, circa 1844, at which date London was hideous with posters displaying a large black and white hat and '4s and 9d' in white letters.
>
> J. S. Farmer and W. E. Henley, *Slang and its Analogues, Past and Present* (1893)

This theory seems sound, with one dictionary even recalling the advertising slogan the hatter apparently used:

> Whene'er to slumber you incline, Take a short nap at 4 and 9.
>
> John Camden Hotten, *A Dictionary of Modern Slang, Cant and Vulgar Words* (1859)

One question remains, though. What does all of this have to do with today's date? Well, on 6 November 1942, the Church of England quietly abolished a long-standing rule that had required all women to wear hats in church.

mysterifical *(adj.)*   mystery-creating

Dating from the early 1600s in English, the word *mysterifical* can be used not only as a synonym for *mysterious*, but also to describe anything or anyone that creates a mystery. With that in mind, today marks the anniversary of one of the most bizarre and enduring mysteries of the nineteenth century.

On 7 November 1872, the brigantine *Mary Celeste* set sail on her final voyage from New York, heading to Genoa, Italy. On board were the ship's captain, Benjamin Briggs, his young wife and infant daughter, and his crew. A month later, the *Mary Celeste* was spotted by the crew of another vessel, the *Dei Gratia*, with her sails oddly arranged and her lifeboat missing, moving erratically through the water off the coast of the Azores in the eastern Atlantic.

The captain of the *Dei Gratia*, David Morehouse, recognised the ship from New York (according to some reports, he was good friends with Captain Briggs and had dined with him the night before the ship set sail) and sent some of his crew aboard to investigate. The last entry in the ship's logbook was dated nine days previously, and recorded a position some 600 miles from where she was found. The cargo was intact, but a vast amount of water had leaked into the hold, causing damage to the hull and to some of the cabins. There was, however, no sign of foul play or disaster – the crew had simply disappeared. Precisely what happened aboard the *Mary Celeste* remains one of maritime history's greatest enigmas.

decussate *(v.)*   to mark with X; to cross or intersect in an X-shape

On 8 November 1895, German physicist Wilhelm Roentgen was working in his laboratory in Würzburg when he happened to notice that the light emitted by a vacuum tube made a screen on the opposite wall fluoresce, despite the tube being shielded with paper. Roentgen theorised that a new kind of ray must be responsible, one that was capable of passing through opaque bodies to reach other solid bodies within them. Not knowing quite what he was dealing with, he called this new phenomenon an X-ray – and the name ultimately stuck.

The letter X has been used to refer to an unknown quantity or entity since the seventeenth century, when the practice was introduced by the mathematician René Descartes: in Descartes's system, *a*, *b* and *c* were used to represent known quantities, while the corresponding final letters of the alphabet, *x*, *y* and *z*, represented those that were unknown. X has been used in place of a kiss since medieval times, when it was originally a hand-drawn cross used to symbolise faith or sincerity (and which would often be kissed by the writer as a mark of reverence). And the Roman numeral X (10) is perhaps built from two Vs (5s) one atop the other – or else, like V itself, it might derive from a technique of double-marking each set of five or ten tally marks.

As for X-related words, to *decuss* or *decussate* is to mark or form a letter X. It derives from *decussis*, a Latin word for a coin worth ten bronze Roman coins, known as an *as*.

parietines *(n.)*   fallen or ruined walls

On 9 November 1989, following a series of revolutions and immense political changes in the former Eastern Bloc nations of Europe, the government of East Germany finally announced that all East German citizens were free to travel to West Berlin and West Germany. Before long, scores of people were clambering over and through the Berlin Wall, and as the day wore on the wall was steadily brought down, piece by piece, by ecstatic Berliners celebrating the end of thirty-eight years of living in a divided city. The fall of the Berlin Wall symbolised the end of the Cold War, ushered in the reunification of Germany and, under Soviet leader Mikhail Gorbachev, a brighter and more open relationship between Russia and the West.

Little still stands of the Berlin Wall today, with the few stone slabs that remain dotted across the city now acting as little more than museum pieces, symbolising the city's gloomier past. And these crumbling remains are fine examples of *parietines* – that is, segments of fallen or ruined walls.

The word *parietines* dates from the early seventeenth century in English, while its roots lie in a Latin word for 'wall', *paries*. That same root is shared by the adjective *parietal*, which can be used in various different contexts to refer to everything from *parietal art* (that is, cave paintings and other artworks painted directly on to walls) to the two *parietal bones* of the human skull (which act as the 'walls' of the cranium, protecting the left and right flanks of the human brain).

indagation *(n.)* investigation, a searching or questing

Derived from Latin, to *indagate* is to search or investigate some-thing, which makes *indagation* a sixteenth-century word for an investigation or tracking. Likewise, if you're *indagacious* then you're investigative or on the hunt for facts or the truth, while someone who does precisely that is an *indagator* (or, should they happen to be female and a fan of Latin gender markers, an *indagatrix*).

One particularly famous *indagation*, by an equally famous *indagator*, came to an end today in 1871.

The Scottish explorer and missionary David Livingstone had travelled to Africa five years earlier on an expedition to locate the source of the Nile. The expedition – Livingstone's third African adventure – was far from successful: his sup-plies were repeatedly stolen, his team of African guides all but deserted him and his letters home went undelivered. By now desperately ill and with little hope of ever contacting the outside world again, Livingstone disappeared into the African jungle. No word of him reached England for several years.

Then, in 1869, the American journalist Henry Morton Stanley was commissioned by the *New York Herald* to travel to Africa to locate Livingstone, whose disappearance had by then become something of a cause célèbre. After two years of *indagating*, on 10 November 1871 Stanley found Livingstone in the town of Ujiji on Lake Tanganyika, famously greeting him with the words 'Dr Livingstone, I presume?' Livingstone's remarkably composed reply is less well remembered: 'Yes; I feel thankful that I am here to welcome you.'

eirenicon *(n.)* a statement or proposal intended to bring peace; an attempt at reconciliation

The Greek word for peace was *eirene*, which is not only the origin of the girl's name *Irene* but also a number of words relating to a theme of peace and reconciliation. An *eirenarch*, for instance, was once a public officer charged with keeping the peace in Ancient Greece, and whose title was adopted into English in the mid 1700s as an inflated title for a local magistrate or bailiff. Something done *eirenically*, likewise, is done in the spirit of peace or compromise. And an *eirenicon*, or *irenicon*, is a statement or act of peace or reconciliation.

In English, *eirenicon* was first used in the early seventeenth century to refer in particular to councils and other assemblies convened to foster peace and settle disagreements between different churches or congregations. But in more general use, the term refers to any attempt to assuage or reconcile differences, or to bring peace to a troubled or hostile situation.

In that sense, the word is particularly worth calling to mind today.

At the eleventh hour on the eleventh day of the eleventh month of 1918, Germany signed an armistice agreement officially ending the hostilities of the Great War. Since then, 11 November has been commemorated as Armistice Day – the date on which the First World War officially came to a close.

perchist *(n.)*   a trapeze artist

The circus *trapeze* takes its name from the mathematical term *trapezium*, which in turn derives from a Greek word literally meaning 'little table'. The term was introduced to mathematics by the Greek geometer Euclid, who used it to refer to any quadrilateral that didn't fit under the heading of a square, a rectangle, a rhombus or a rhomboid. Nowadays, however, the term tends to be applied only to shapes with two parallel sides, like a triangle with its topmost point removed.

Ultimately, the *trapeze* is thought to be so named as early designs of this particular piece of performance equipment probably formed a trapezium shape between their crossbar, ropes and the ceiling above.

A performer on a *trapeze* can be called a *trapezist*. But in the theatrical slang of the early 1900s, *trapeze* artists were jokingly nicknamed *perchists*, a reference to the fact that the acrobats' *trapeze* resembles an enormous perch for birds or a swing. And on this date in 1859, perhaps the very first *perchist* performed his death-defying act for the very first time.

Jules Léotard was born in Toulouse in 1838. After quitting studies to become a lawyer, he set his sights on becoming a circus performer and began practising intrepid high-flying stunts at home using a homemade trapeze constructed from ventilator cords and suspended above the family swimming pool. In his early twenties, he joined the Cirque Napoléon in Paris and it was there that he perfected an act in which he would vault or somersault between two giant *trapezes* suspended high in the air, hanging from the circus roof. On 12 November 1859, he performed his intrepid stunt for the first time – in the streamlined, figure-hugging outfit that eventually came to bear his name.

stone-ginger *(n.)*   a dead cert, a sure thing

Originally, *stone-ginger* was ginger ale that was quite literally sold in stoneware bottles or jugs. But in the unpredictable slang of the 1920s and '30s it came to be used as a quirky byword for a sure thing or an absolute, solid (i.e. 'stone') certainty.

On the subject of certainties, on 13 November 1789 Benjamin Franklin wrote a letter to his friend and fellow scientist Jean-Baptiste LeRoy. Having originally become acquainted through their mutual interest in electricity, Franklin and LeRoy had become good friends during Franklin's time serving as the US ambassador to France. Now back in America, Franklin was worried that he had not heard from Leroy for over a year:

> Are you still living? Or has the mob of Paris mistaken the head of a monopolizer of knowledge for a monopolizer of corn and paraded it about the streets upon a pole? . . . If anything material in that way had occurred, I am persuaded you would have acquainted me with it. However, pray let me hear from you . . . a year's silence between friends must needs give uneasiness. Our new Constitution is now established, and has an appearance that promises permanency; but in this world nothing can be said to be certain, except death and taxes!

Franklin wasn't the first writer to use the now familiar 'death and taxes' metaphor, but it is his phrasing that has since become a popular idiom for certainty or inevitability.

As for LeRoy, he had indeed survived the Revolution and died in 1800 at the age of eighty; and Franklin, after admitting to Leroy that he felt 'thinner and weaker' and 'cannot expect to hold out much longer', died five months later, aged eighty-four.

anfract *(n.)*   a winding, circuitous route

Something that is *anfractuous* is winding or meandering, while *anfractuosity* is intricacy, circuitousness or sinuousness, and an *anfract* is a winding or timewasting route. All three of these come from a Latin word, *anfractus*, for a 'bend' or 'curve', which in turn combines Latin roots meaning 'around', *an–*, and 'break', *fractus*. An *anfractuous* route, ultimately, is one that may wind and bend but does not break, and will eventually arrive at its intended destination.

On 14 November 1889, the pioneering American journalist Nellie Bly set off from New York on an extraordinary trip: an attempt to emulate the trip made by Phileas Fogg in Jules Verne's *Around the World in Eighty Days*.

Bly had just two days' notice to prepare for her 25,000-mile journey, and boarded an Atlantic ocean steamer, the *Augusta Victoria*, with just the dress she had on at the time, a few changes of underwear, an overcoat and a toiletry bag. She arrived in Southampton a few days later, then headed to London and on to Paris (where she accepted an invitation to meet with Jules Verne himself – going without sleep for two days to make sure she caught her connection), then Italy, through the Suez Canal to Ceylon, Singapore, Japan and then back across the Pacific to San Francisco. By then, she was two days behind schedule, but her trip had become such a popular story that the newspaper she worked for, the *New York World*, chartered a private train to bring her back to New York. She arrived on 25 January 1890 – completing her *anfractuous* round-the-world trip in just seventy-two days.

tachygraphy *(n.)*   shorthand; swift handwriting

In his *Dictionary of the English Language* (1755), Samuel Johnson defined the word *tachygraphy* as 'the art or practice of quick writing'. That's certainly the word's literal meaning (it combines Greek roots meaning 'swift', *tachys*, and 'writing', *graphe*), but there's a lot more to *tachygraphy* than merely fast-paced note-taking.

In 1626, an English writer named Thomas Shelton published a book entitled *Tachygraphie* in which he introduced an ingenious and hugely popular system of shorthand. Letters of the alphabet were replaced with simpler shapes and linear symbols, while vowels were dictated by the position of the following consonant: the symbol for L written directly 'north' of the symbol for B, for instance, would spell *ball*, while placing the L north-east, east, south-east or due south of the B would spell *bell*, *bill*, *boll* and *bull* respectively.

Shelton's *tachygraphic* system proved hugely popular, but it was not without its drawbacks. And so, on 15 November 1837, it was replaced by a complex but ultimately more streamlined shorthand system.

It was on that date that Isaac Pitman's *Stenographic Shorthand* was published – a *tachygraphic* textbook in which Pitman outlined a new phonetic shorthand system that ingeniously replaced sounds (like *th* and *sh*) rather than letters (not *T-H* and *S-H*) with an elaborate system of dots, lines and symbols. Although more complicated that Shelton's *tachygraphy* (similar sounds, like *p* and *b*, were differentiated only by the pressure with which they are written, for instance) Pitman's was a faster and more streamlined writing system and consequently was quick to catch on. It remains one of the most widely used shorthand systems in the world today.

arctophile *(n.)*   a collector of teddy bears

The *Arctic* takes its name from the Greek word for 'bear', *arktos*. That's not, despite what folk etymology will have you believe, a reference to the polar bears that live there, but rather a name based on the prominent position of the Great Bear constellation in the northern night sky. *Arktos* is also the origin of a handful of obscure words like *arctician* ('a polar animal' – flick ahead to 29 November for that one), *cynarctomachy* ('a fight between a bear and a dog') and *arctophilia* ('a love of teddy bears'), a proponent of which is called an *arctophile*.

Teddy bears themselves famously take their name from Theodore 'Teddy' Roosevelt – thanks to a memorable caricature printed across America on this day. In the autumn of 1902, Roosevelt embarked on an unsuccessful hunting trip to Mississippi, and when the president didn't manage to shoot anything during the hunt, a young black bear was caught and chained to a tree for Roosevelt to shoot for sport – but the president refused. Instead, he asked for the animal to be released.

Despite showing Roosevelt in a compassionate light, this incident was quickly pounced upon by the press, and a famous satirical cartoon – depicting a bespectacled Roosevelt turning his back on a trembling bear cub, with the caption 'Drawing the line in Mississippi' – appeared in the *Washington Post* on 16 November 1902. Within a matter of weeks, shrewd toyshop owners in New York had started selling toy black bears nicknamed 'teddies' to monopolise on the joke, and before long the trend had spread elsewhere. The surprisingly presidential *teddy bear* has been with us ever since.

cataractine *(adj.)*   resembling a waterfall

The word *cataract* literally means a 'rushing down' in Greek. From there, a Latin equivalent, *cataracta*, later emerged, which was used not only to refer to a flowing cascade of water, but also the grid-like metal portcullis of a castle keep. The use of *cataract* to mean 'waterfall' derives from the first and more literal of these two, while the use of *cataract* as the name of a medical condition affecting the eyes derives from the Latin for 'portcullis', in the sense that the dulling of the eyes places a portcullis-like obstruction to a person's field of vision.

Happily, it's the more picturesque of these two *cataracts* that is the origin of the nineteenth-century adjective *cataractine*, which can be used to describe anything that resembles or has the power of a waterfall.

One of the grandest and most famous of the world's waterfalls was seen by European eyes for the first time on 17 November 1855. Partway through the second of his three trips to Africa (the third of which cropped up on 10 November), David Livingstone heard word of an immense waterfall on the River Zambezi. The locals knew the falls as *Mosi-oa-Tunya*, or 'the smoke that thunders', but when Livingstone set eyes on it he named it in honour of Queen Victoria. He later recalled in his memoirs:

> No one can imagine the beauty of the view from anything witnessed in England. It had never been seen before by European eyes; but scenes so lovely must have been gazed upon by angels in their flight.
>
> David Livingstone, *Missionary Travels* (1857)

bibliopoesy *(n.)*   the creation or publication of books

The Greek word for 'making', *poesis*, lies at the root of a number of words implying some sense of manufacture or creation, a handful of which are surprisingly familiar, and a great many more of which are much more obscure.

At the more familiar end of the spectrum, *onomatopoeia* literally means 'making names', in the sense that by inventing words to echo the sounds we hear around us we are essentially 'naming' them. Likewise, a *poet* is literally a 'maker' or 'composer', while a *poem* is simply something that has been made or created. At the more obscure end of things are words like *epopoeia* ('the writing of epics'), *melopoeia* ('the writing of melodies'), *mythopoesis* ('the creation of myths') and *bibliopoesy*, a nineteenth-century word introduced by the Scottish writer Thomas Carlyle to mean 'the making of books'.

It was on 18 November 1477 that the printer William Caxton printed the first dated book ever produced in England: an edition of a work entitled the *Dictes and Sayings of the Philosophers*. Caxton had learned how to print books while in Bruges, Belgium, where he had moved in his late twenties. Wanting to ply his newfound trade in his home country, he returned to London in 1476 and set up England's first ever printing press at Westminster Abbey. The first book he produced is popularly said to have been an edition of Geoffrey Chaucer's *Canterbury Tales*, but the first book he printed and dated was his *Dictes and Sayings* – giving today's date an important significance in the history of English literature.

archiloquy *(n.)*   the opening of a speech

The *arch–* of words like *archbishop*, *archangel*, *architect* and *archipelago* derives via Latin from a Greek word, *arkos*, meaning 'chief', 'leader' or 'commander'. That makes an *archbishop* literally a 'chief' bishop, an *architect* a 'master builder', and an *archangel* an angel of the highest celestial order. It also makes an *archipelago* literally a 'chief' sea: the word originally referred specifically to Greece's island-strewn Aegean Sea, which was, understandably, the most important sea to the Ancient Greeks.

In the sense of something that leads or commands, however, the prefix *arch–* is also used to create words bearing some sense of being positioned at the first, headmost or opening point of something. So, an *architrave* was originally the topmost beam or section of a column. *Adrenarche* is a medical term for the first appearance of body hair. And an *archiloquy* – a word dating from the seventeenth century in English – is the opening or introduction to a speech.

It was on the afternoon of 19 November 1863, just over four months since the bloody and decisive Battle of Gettysburg had been fought during the American Civil War, that President Abraham Lincoln returned to the site of the battle, and in a newly dedicated Soldiers' National Cemetery delivered a speech beginning with these lines:

> Four score and seven years ago our fathers brought forth on this continent, a new nation, conceived in Liberty, and dedicated to the proposition that all men are created equal.

As *archiloquies* go, Lincoln's Gettysburg Address is perhaps one of the most famous and most memorable in political history.

belue *(n.)*   a great beast or sea monster; a whale

Derived from a Latin word meaning 'brutal' or 'bestial', *belue* is a fifteenth-century word for a giant beast or monster – or, given some early descriptions, a whale:

> This is a great fish in the sea, and is called Belua. He casteth out water at his jaws with vapour of good smell, and other fish . . . pursue him hotly and delighting after the smell, they enter and come in at his jaws: whom he devoureth, and so feedeth himself with them.
>
> John Bossewell, *Workes of Armorie* (1572)

On the subject of monstrous whales, on 20 November 1820 a gigantic sperm whale attacked a whaling ship called the *Essex*, 2,000 miles west of the South American coast, leaving her twenty-man crew stranded in three small, rundown lifeboats. Within a matter of weeks, their food and potable water had been consumed, and the men began to perish.

By February, one of the boats had vanished, while the crews of the remaining two had resorted to cannibalism to survive. Lots were drawn in one to decide who among the men should be killed and eaten, and who should kill them; the victim chosen was the seventeen-year-old cousin of the *Essex*'s captain, George Pollard – who was in the boat with him when he was killed and consumed.

Finally, after ninety-five days at sea, the last of the remaining eight survivors of the *Essex* whaling disaster were rescued. All the men eventually returned to their careers at sea, while their horrific ordeal partly inspired a fellow seafarer and author to write a fictional account of a South Pacific whaleboat (turn back to 18 October for more on that).

trajectile *(n.)*   a projectile, something thrown
forward

Trajectory, meaning 'the path followed by a projectile', derives
from a Latin word, *trajectus*, meaning 'thrown across'. Derived
from the same root, *trajection* is the act of conveying or crossing
a river, while a *traject* is a traversing place or ford where a stretch
of water is safest to cross. A *trajectile*, meanwhile, is something
that is thrown through the air or space; in other words, it's simply a *projectile* – a word that literally means 'thrown forwards'.

Speaking of *projectiles* and *trajectiles*, it was on today's date
that Frenchman Emilio Maîtrejean became the world's first
human cannonball at the Cirque Napoléon in Paris.

Maîtrejean was the son of the circus's founder, Henri
Maîtrejean, and had performed almost his entire life at the circus as part of a troupe of acrobats and trapeze artists (turn back
to 12 November for more on how that all started) using the
stage name Emilio Onra. On a quest to make his performances
even more impressive, in 1871 Maîtrejean concocted the idea of
blasting himself out of a cannon and on to a trapeze bar, more
than 30 feet above the ground, from where he could begin a
routine of high-flying stunts. He constructed a spring-loaded
platform that would hurl him out of a fake cannon barrel amid
a cloud of smoke, and on 21 November 1871, Maîtrejean performed the stunt for the very first time. It soon proved hugely
popular, and before long Maîtrejean's stunt – known as '*l'homme
obus*' or 'the exploding-shell man' – was one of the circus's big-
gest attractions. Imitators were quick to copy Maîtrejean's act,
but his was the very first human cannonball act in circus history.

pseudandry *(n.)*   the use of a male pseudonym by a female writer

Pseudos meant 'falsehood' in Greek, and is ultimately used in English to form words carrying some sense of deception, imitation or spuriousness. In *pseudandry*, it is used alongside the Greek word *andro* to give us literally a 'counterfeit' man – that is, a male name adopted by a female writer.

Pseudandry is certainly nothing new. George Sand was the pen name of French novelist and playwright Amantine Dupin. The Brontë sisters wrote their novels and published an anthology of their poetry under the pseudonyms Currer, Ellis and Acton Bell. And while Louisa May Alcott may have published her masterpiece *Little Women* (1868) under her own name, she wrote a series of somewhat 'unladylike' gothic stories under the androgynous pseudonym A. M. Barnard; Barnard's true identity was not discovered until 1942.

Perhaps the most famous of all the *pseudandrists*, however, was George Eliot. Born Mary Ann Evans on 22 November 1819, Eliot chose her pseudonym during the preparation of her first book, the short-story collection *Scenes of Clerical Life*, in 1857. Eliot wrote to her publisher (who was unaware of her identity) to suggest that her work be published under a male pseudonym, partly to conceal her gender, and partly to throw the eyes of publicity off her private life (at the time, Eliot was an unmarried woman living with a married man, the philosopher George Lewes). Her true identity was revealed two years later when her first full-length novel, *Adam Bede* (1859), became an instant bestseller, but the unmasking seemingly did not affect her success and Eliot went on to become one of the foremost writers – male or female – of her day.

epistolisable *(adj.)* worthy of writing in a letter

Before he established his reputation as an author, the novelist Anthony Trollope worked as a post office clerk and later as a postal surveyor in mid-nineteenth-century London. In that capacity, Trollope was sent to the Channel Islands by the parliamentary secretary to the Post Office, Sir Rowland Hill. He was tasked with investigating what could be done to improve the reliability of the postal service on Jersey and Guernsey, which was often disrupted by bad weather and unpredictable sea crossings.

After surveying the islands, Trollope recommended as a solution something he had seen in Paris – something he called a 'letter-receiving pillar', in which the islanders could place their post ready for collection at the next opportune time. The Post Office took him up on his recommendation and seven cast-iron post boxes – three for Guernsey and four for Jersey – were produced. The first was brought into service in St Helier, the capital of Jersey, on 23 November 1852, and when it proved successful, the boxes were quickly rolled out across the UK.

The Latin word for a letter or item of correspondence was *epistola*, which in turn comes from a Greek word meaning 'to send' or 'to dispatch'. *Epistolary* or letter-based novels take their name from the same root, as do a handful of obscure words like *epistolisable* ('something worthy of being written about in a letter'), *epistolographer* ('a writer of letters') and *epistolophobia* ('the fear of receiving or opening one's mail' – turn back to 3 March for more on that).

vandemonianism *(n.)*   rowdy, unmannerly
behaviour

In the mid seventeenth century, partway through the first of his two voyages to the southern hemisphere, the Dutch explorer Abel Tasman reached the south coast of Australia and on 24 November 1642 became the first European to set eyes on Tasmania. He named the island Van Diemen's Land, in honour of Antonio van Diemen, Governor General of the Dutch East Indies, and spent the next week skirting the island in an attempt to land and claim it for the Dutch crown. In the end, one of his crew had to jump overboard and plant the Dutch flag in the surf before Tasman's expedition departed for New Zealand.

By the early 1800s, Van Diemen's Land had become home to several British penal colonies (some 68,000 convicts were sent to Tasmania in the nineteenth century alone), and by the 1810s the island was becoming increasingly unruly. Criminal escapees fled into the countryside and became bandits. The establishment of rival settlements on the island increased competition for land, food and resources, and raised tensions between the settlers and Aborigines. Ultimately, Van Diemen's Land gained a reputation for lawlessness and brutality – and, as a consequence, the English language gained a word for rowdy, unruly behaviour: *vandemonianism.*

By the mid 1800s, British governance of the island became more ordered. Industries like sheep farming and whaling began to emerge and British entrepreneurs brought money to the island, tempted by the promise of cheap labour and free land. Tensions remained high (not helped by a gender imbalance as high as 16:1 in some male-dominated penal colonies) but steadily the island became increasingly self-sufficient and joined the Commonwealth of Australia in 1901.

flux-ale *(n.)* poor-quality ale; drink that will cause digestive problems

Flux has been used to refer to a rushing flow or flood since it was borrowed into English from French in the fourteenth century. Derived from that, the *Oxford English Dictionary* fairly uncompromisingly defines *flux-ale* as 'ale likely to cause diarrhoea'. And oddly, there's a story concerning *flux-ale* that not only took place on this day, but altered the course of British history.

On 25 November 1120, a vessel called the *White Ship* was chartered to carry Henry I and much of his family and court home to England from France. Keen to travel alone, Henry eventually made other arrangements, while the rest of his court travelled on the *White Ship* as planned. With the king absent, the *White Ship*'s passengers soon took full advantage of the situation and began drinking, but off the coast of Normandy the rowdy and overcrowded ship sank. Of the 300 or so people on board, all but a handful died – including the heir to the English throne, Prince William.

In the aftermath of the disaster, Henry named his daughter Matilda as his new successor. But when the king died in 1135, Matilda proved an unpopular choice, leaving Henry's nephew, Stephen of Blois, to mount his own attempt to steal the throne. The crisis sparked a violent civil war, which saw Matilda's claim to the throne reneged and Stephen sweep to power.

The entire war, however, was a consequence of the ale served aboard the *White Ship*. According to Orderic Vitalis, a twelfth-century historian, King Stephen had been aboard the doomed ship but left before it departed – due to a sudden bout of diarrhoea caused by the copious amounts of *flux-ale* the passengers were drinking.

unweather *(n.)*   bad weather, a storm or tempest

Bad weather can be known as *judgment weather* (so-called as it is proverbially said to be caused by God's displeasure) and *catch-cold* weather (a Scots dialect word attested in the early 1800s). *Dirt-and-greuse* was nineteenth-century slang for the mugginess that precedes a thunderstorm. A *feeding-storm* is a period of bad weather that appears only to worsen. Weather that is *backendish* is unseasonably dull, and better suited to the 'back end' of the year. And *unweather*, or rather *unweder*, was an Anglo-Saxon word for bad or stormy weather that survived into the Middle English period, before largely falling into only occasional or dialect use in modern English.

On the night of 26 November 1703, a period of such extreme *unweather* blew across Britain from the Atlantic that even Queen Anne is recorded as calling it 'a calamity so dreadful and astonishing that the like hath not been seen or felt in the memory of any person living in this our kingdom'. She had first-hand experience, in fact: so many chimneys were toppled in London that the queen had to shelter in the cellar of St James's Palace.

The Great Storm of 1703 remains the most destructive and deadly storm on record in Britain, with well over 8,000 people estimated to have died in one night – 1,500 of whom were seamen drowned in the English Channel. Countless buildings were lost across the country, with reports of windmills burning to the ground when their sails were spun so swiftly that their mechanisms caught fire. The Royal Navy lost thirteen of its ships – while one of its vessels, HMS *Association*, was torn from its dock in Harwich on the Essex coast and blown all the way to Gothenburg.

exsibilation *(n.)*   the hissing or jeering of a
performer from a stage

On 27 November 1911, the audience of a controversial play, premiered at the Maxine Elliott Theatre on Broadway in New York City, erupted into violent protest, hurling rotten vegetables and stink bombs on to the stage:

> By this time everybody who reads the newspapers knows that . . . the most unruly mob ever gathered within the four walls of an American theater threw eggs and vegetables and bad-smelling compounds upon the stage of the immaculate Maxine Elliott on the night of November 27, 1911, when the Irish Players first presented in New York 'The Playboy of the Western World,' by the late JM Synge.
>
> *Munsey's Magazine*, 1912

Synge's play tells the story of a young man claiming to have killed his father, whose behaviour is celebrated not condemned by the people he tells. It sparked outrage on its debut in Dublin in 1907, with audience members taking grave offence at its questionable morals and portrayal of Ireland. The protests continued across the Atlantic when the play debuted in New York in 1911, leading to the malodorous disturbance described above – which is often claimed to provide the first record of a theatre audience hurling vegetables at unpopular actors in the United States.

The dictionary sadly doesn't provide us with a word for pelting vegetables at unpopular performers, but it does give us one for jeering them from the stage: the word *exsibilation* dates from the seventeenth century in English, and derives ultimately from a Latin verb, *sibilare*, meaning 'to hiss'.

lown (*n.*)   a calm or quiet state; an area of calm seas

On 28 November 1520, the Portuguese navigator and explorer Ferdinand Magellan arrived in the Pacific Ocean.

Having left Spain a little over a year earlier, Magellan and his fleet sailed down past Africa and across to South America, searching for an opening that would provide them with a western route to South East Asia. After a number of false starts (Magellan spent days sailing the Rio de Plata estuary in Brazil, wrongly thinking that it would eventually lead him to the other side of the continent) and surviving an attempted mutiny, in October Magellan arrived at the stormy southern tip of South America and set off through the violent oceanic straits that now bear his name. It took him thirty-eight days to navigate a way through, before the seas suddenly opened up into such a vast, calm and clear expanse that Magellan named it the 'Pacific' Ocean – derived from a Latin word, *pacificus*, meaning 'peace-making'.

An expanse of calm water is a *lown*, a word thought to have been borrowed into the language from Scandinavia in the Middle English period. Originally, *lown* was used to mean simply 'tranquillity' or 'stillness' (or else, as an adjective, was used to describe calm or settled weather conditions) but by the fifteenth century it had come to be used more specifically of flat or calm bodies or water, shelters or idyllic refuges, and later calm or unperturbed people or personalities. The word remains in occasional use in some dialects of English, as do derivatives like *lown-warm*, describing calm, summery weather, and *lown-side*, another word for the sheltered or lee side of an object.

arctician *(n.)* a polar animal; a polar explorer

Back on 16 November, we found that the Arctic takes its name from the Greek for 'bear'. And derived from the Arctic is the word *arctician* – a term coined in the early 1800s, originally as a word for any creature well adapted to arctic conditions. But as polar exploration picked up pace in the nineteenth century, *arctician* began to be applied to arctic explorers and travellers, and in that sense the word first appeared in a discussion of the drifting of sea ice and the mysterious movements of ships encased in frozen seas in 1860:

> The extraordinary drift of the *Resolute* [locked in ice in Baffin Bay in 1854] . . . and the mysterious appearance of two ships . . . on a large iceberg near Newfoundland in 1851 . . . have more in connexion with each other . . . than the Arcticians themselves, the best judges, at present admit.
>
> Admiral Robert FitzRoy,
> *Meteorological Papers* (1860)

On 29 November 1929, noted American *arctician* Richard Byrd became the first person in history to fly over the South Pole. Setting off from a base on the Ross Ice Shelf late the previous evening, Byrd and his crew reached the pole at 1 o'clock the following morning. Magnetic compasses proved useless that close to the pole, so Byrd's own expert navigational skills had proved imperative on the flight. But to compensate for any navigational errors, the plane circled the area above the pole to ensure the flight was a success – and to give Byrd the chance to drop a small US flag on to the snow below before returning to base.

astrobleme *(n.)* an eroded impact crater, caused by a meteorite or asteroid

Coined as recently as 1960, *astrobleme* is a term from geology for a crater or scar on the surface of the earth – and in particular an ancient or eroded one – caused by the impact of an object falling from space, like a meteorite. At its root is a Greek word, *blema*, for a projectile, a missile or else a wound caused by the impact of an object that has been hurled or fired. And thanks to a curious and highly improbable event, that's an etymology that has more significance today than any other.

Shortly before 2 o'clock on the afternoon of 30 November 1954, a meteor burst through the earth's atmosphere causing a loud explosion and a vast glowing fireball visible above much of Alabama and its surrounding states. As it fell towards the earth, the meteorite fragmented into at least three sizeable sections, the largest of which, a grapefruit-sized portion of rock weighing 8.5 lbs, was sent spiralling towards the small town of Oak Grove, near Montgomery. There it crashed through the roof of a house, bounced off a wooden console radio and struck thirty-four-year-old Ann Hodges as she slept on her couch. Hodges was badly bruised down the right-hand side of her body by the impact, but survived.

The Sylacauga meteorite – named after the town of Sylacauga, Alabama, above which it had been seen – was the first recorded instance in history of an object from space hitting and injuring a human being. For its significance to science, a portion of the meteorite is now housed in the Smithsonian Museum in Washington DC.

obstrigillation *(n.)*   the action of opposing or
resisting; an act of defiance

At 6 o'clock on the evening of 1 December 1955, Rosa Parks
boarded a bus in downtown Montgomery, Alabama, and sat in
the front row of the section of seats reserved for black passengers. As the bus continued on its route, the whites-only section
filled up and the bus driver, James F. Blake, ordered Parks and
three other black passengers to move to the back of the vehicle
to make room. All except Parks complied; instead, she moved
closer to the window and refused to move. When Blake asked
why, Parks simply replied, 'I don't think I should have to stand
up.'

The police were called to the scene, and Parks was arrested
on charges of disorderly conduct and violating the segregation
laws of Montgomery. At her court appearance a few days later,
she was found guilty and fined $10 – but her act of defiance
had caught on. The black community of Montgomery, who
comprised three-quarters of the local bus company's passengers, organised a boycott of all bus services until the segregation
rules were either slackened or removed entirely. Incredibly, the
boycott lasted a total of 381 days, crippling the bus operator's revenue severely. At a landmark court case the following
year, the segregation of passengers on buses in Montgomery
was found to be unconstitutional and the state ordinances were
repealed.

An act of defiance like that shown by Parks, or else the process of resisting or defying, can be known as an *obstrigillation*,
a word dating from the early 1600s in English. Fittingly, its
roots lie in a Latin word, *strigare*, meaning 'to come to a halt'.

boulevard-journalist *(n.)* an unscrupulous or exploitative journalist

A *boulevard-journalist* is an unscrupulous journalist. The term dates from the early 1850s, when the French President Louis-Napoleon Bonaparte, barred by both the constitution and his own parliament from serving a second term, overruled all opposition and essentially staged a *coup d'état* of his own government to give himself unassailable power across France. Supported by two questionable referenda, in 1852 the president dissolved the French National Assembly, re-established the French Empire and – on the anniversary of his uncle Napoleon Bonaparte's coronation, 2 December – crowned himself Emperor Napoleon III of France. Understandably, not everyone was happy.

But with the politicians of the day now effectively rendered powerless by Napoleon's rule, it fell to the press to oppose the emperor's new regime. Disgruntled writers across Paris were soon publishing and distributing vitriolic journals and pamphlets full of personal slights and angry remonstrations against the newly crowned emperor. The legitimate press labelled these crude newspapers *les journaux des boulevards*, or 'street journals', while those who wrote for them were *les journalistes boulevardiers* – literally 'boulevard journalists'.

The term was borrowed into English after these journals and journalists turned their anger against the British in 1853, when Britain entered into an uncomfortable alliance with the newly reformed French Empire to fight the Crimean War. Although the Crimean campaign proved successful, the subsequent Franco-Prussian War was not, and when Napoleon was captured at the Battle of Sedan in 1870 his empire collapsed. A new French Republic was declared on 4 September, and Napoleon died in exile in England in 1873.

geoplanarian *(n.)*   someone who believes the earth is flat

Derived from the Latin *planus*, meaning 'flat', a *geoplanarian* is an advocate of the Flat Earth theory. Modern proponents of *geoplanarianism* like to call on a famous quote by George Bernard Shaw to show that their theory has a prominent backer:

> In the Middle Ages people believed that the earth was flat, for which they had at least the evidence of their senses: we believe it to be round . . . because modern science has convinced us that nothing that is obvious is true, and that everything that is magical, improbable, extraordinary, gigantic, microscopic, heartless, or outrageous is scientific.
>
> G. B. Shaw, *Saint Joan* (1923)

But the very next line reads, 'I must not, by the way, be taken as implying that the earth is flat, or that all or any of our amazing credulities are delusions or impostures.' G. B. Shaw was not a 'flat-earther' – and thanks to an experiment conducted on 3 December 1736, neither should anyone else be.

On this day, the astronomer Anders Celsius journeyed to Torneå in northern Sweden as part of a two-tier experiment, organised by French mathematician Pierre-Louis Maupertuis, to measure the length of one degree of the meridian, the great circle connecting the north and south poles. While Celsius was in Lapland doing precisely that, a team of French astronomers and mathematicians was en route to Peru to repeat the experiment on the equator. When their results were later compared, they proved Isaac Newton's theory that the earth is an ellipsoid – essentially a slightly misshapen sphere – flattened at its poles.

premonstrance *(n.)*   a portent, an omen

To *premonstrate* is to foreshadow something or point it out before it has happened, while a *premonstrance* is a sign of precisely that – in other words, it's an omen, a portent or a premonition. Omens of events yet to occur can also be known as *foresignifications, presentiments, bodements* and *presagations*, while a specific prophecy or sign of evil yet to come is an *infausting* or a *misboding*.

A notable and somewhat bizarre *premonstrance* occurred in Rome in 1680, when a comet was discovered by the German astronomer Gottfried Kirch. Eventually bright enough to be seen during the daytime according to some reports, the comet began to streak across the sky and remained visible in some locations for several months before vanishing from sight the following spring.

At its closest, Kirch's comet came to within 580,000 miles of the earth, and because of its proximity and obvious appearance in the sky it was soon pounced on by astrologers and doomsayers as a portent of some terrible event to come. On 4 December 1680, they seemingly had their theories backed up when a hen in Rome laid an egg supposedly marked with a comet, stars and religious symbols. The 'comet egg' was examined by Rome's best scholars, who sent it to colleagues in Paris for further analysis of its meaning.

Precisely what happened then is unclear – but, needless to say, Kirch's comet did not bring about the end of the world. Today, it is an estimated 23.9 trillion miles away from earth.

licitation *(n.)* to sell at auction; to sell to the highest bidder

The word *auction* was first used in English in the late sixteenth century, when it was adopted directly into English from Latin; at its root is the Latin verb *augere*, literally meaning 'to increase'.

Before then, sales dictated by the highest price paid were known as *outroops* (literally 'an outcry'), *port-sales* (which has nothing to do with coastal towns and instead derives from an Old English word for a walled market town) and *subhastations* (a legal term referring to a property auction that derives from the Latin word for 'spear', *hasta*; according to etymological legend, Roman slaves would be sold at public auctions, the location of which would be marked by a spear stabbed into the ground).

To *licitate* is to sell something at auction or to advertise for bids, while the act of selling something in this way has been known as *licitation* since the early seventeenth century. Both derive from the Latin *liceri*, meaning 'to bid' or 'to attach a price to', which is also the origin of the equally rare word *pollicitate*, meaning 'to assure' or 'to promise'.

Any one of these would make an apt choice for today's word: on 5 December 1766, the very first sale ever held at Christie's auction house in London took place.

Christie's was founded by the Scottish auctioneer James Christie, whose friendships with some of the most prominent Londoners of the day – including Thomas Gainsborough, who painted Christie's portrait in 1778 – helped to establish Christie's as one of the foremost auctioneers in the city. Among the company's most notable early sales were the contents of Samuel Johnson's library (sold after his death, in 1785) and J. M. W. Turner's painting *Sun Rising through Vapour* – which Turner himself bought at auction for 480 guineas in 1827.

butterboy *(n.)* a new or trainee taxicab driver; a rookie

On 6 December 1897, the world's first motorised taxicabs hit the streets of London. The brainchild of entrepreneur Walter C. Bersey, the fleet of twelve – and later as many as seventy-five – taxis was electric, each powered by two glass plate batteries with a range of around 30 miles, after which they had to be recharged at the London Electric Cab Company station in Lambeth.

As the company's promotional material attested, these electric taxis had many advantages over petrol or steam-powered vehicles. 'There is no smell, no noise, no heat, no vibration, no possible danger, and it has been found that vehicles built on this company's system do not frighten passing horses,' one advertisement claimed, while another stated with great insight:

> Whilst petroleum may become the motive power in country districts, and steam will probably be used for very heavy vehicles, there is no doubt that electricity will be the most advantageous where the traffic can be located within a radius.

Sadly, it wasn't to last. With continued technical problems proving too expensive to fix, Bersey was forced out of business just two years later.

Not that it meant the end of the London taxi, of course. By the turn of the century, numbers of licensed taxicabs on the streets of the capital had already begun to rise, and as the industry continued to grow it developed its own dedicated slang. A *legal*, for instance, is a passenger who pays the exact fare and no tip. A *Mary Ann* is a taximeter. A *linkman* is a hotel doorman. And a *butterboy* is a newly qualified driver, so called because his keenness for the job takes the 'butter' or earnings from other drivers.

hooliness *(n.)*   slowness, gentility; lateness, tardiness

The word *hooly* or *huly* originally meant 'gently' or 'softly' when it first appeared in the language in the fourteenth century, often in the old expression *hooly and fairly*, defined by the *Scottish National Dictionary* as 'slowly and gently but steadily, cautiously'. Over time, however, the word also came to be associated with lateness or tardiness (perhaps the result of an over-cautious or over-guarded approach to something), which makes *hooliness* or *huliness* an equally ancient word for lateness or tardiness. Today, both *hooly* and *hooliness* have long since fallen out of widespread use, but still survive in some dialects of northern England and Scotland.

> Fortunately my thoughts are agreeable; cash difficulties, etc., all provided for, as far as I can see, so that we go on hooly and fairly.
>
> Sir Walter Scott,
> *The Journal of Sir Walter Scott* (1827)

On the subject of lateness or tardiness, it was on 7 December 1968 that Richard Dodd returned a medical textbook on febrile diseases to the University of Cincinnati Medical Library. The book had been borrowed from the library by his great-grandfather in 1823. Happily, the library waived the fine that had been incurred in that time – calculated to be $22,646.

saucerian *(n.)*   a believer in flying saucers; an alien
that travels by saucer-shaped craft

It wasn't until 1947 that the first *flying saucer* was mentioned
in print in an article in *The Times*. The word *saucerian* followed shortly after in 1950, originally as an adjective referring
to saucer-shaped craft, and later as a word for a believer in flying
saucers. The first *unidentified flying object* was also described in
1950, with the abbreviation *UFO* following in 1953, and *ufol-
ogy* – the study of UFOs – in 1959. But the very first record of
what could be called a flying saucer dates from ever so slightly
earlier than that: 8 December 1733.

According to reports, it was an unseasonably warm and
bright Saturday when James Cracker of Fleet, Dorset, saw an
object appear in the sky to the north of the town. He later
recounted:

> Something in the sky which appeared in the north but
> vanished from my sight . . . The weather was warm, the
> sun shone brightly. All of a sudden it reappeared, dart-
> ing in and out of my sight with an amazing coruscation.
> The colour of this phenomenon was like burnished or
> new-washed silver. It shot with speed like a star falling
> in the night. But it had a body much larger and a train
> longer than any shooting star I have seen.

Cracker wasn't alone in seeing the bizarre, fast-moving object.
He later heard from another man, a Mr Edgecombe, who
informed him that 'he and another gentleman had seen this
strange phenomenon at the same time as I had', from roughly
15 miles away.

Precisely what the men saw remains a complete mystery.

hempen-widow *(n.)* a woman whose husband has been hanged

In the late eighteenth century, the site of London's criminal gallows moved from Tyburn, near what is now Oxford Street, to Newgate Prison, where hangings recommenced on 9 December 1783.

Both locations ultimately came to be attached to a number of macabre phrases and expressions. As far back as the sixteenth century, *to preach at Tyburn cross* was a euphemism for being hanged on the Tyburn gallows, which were themselves known as the *Tyburn tree*. Because a *tippet* is a hanging cord or ribbon decorating a hood or headdress, a *Tyburn tippet* was a hangman's noose. A hanging at Tyburn was a *Tyburn stretch*, while the *Tyburn jig* was the 'dancing' legs of a hanged man. And according to an edition of Francis Grose's *Dictionary of the Vulgar Tongue* (1796), a *Tyburn blossom* was 'a young thief or pickpocket', so called because he 'in time will ripen into fruit, borne by the deadly never-green'.

Walking *Newgate fashion*, meanwhile, once meant to walk hand in hand or side by side, like prisoners shackled together. A *Newgate fringe* was a beard worn only around the chin and below the jawline, giving the impression of a noose around the neck. A *Newgate solicitor* was a lawman who frequented prisons on the hunt for new clients. And a *Newgate bird* was a habitual criminal or repeat offender, so called because they were so frequently 'caged'.

As for words for the criminals themselves, turn back to 7 April for more on *crack-ropes*, *wag-halters* and *hang-strings*. But for every one who danced the *Tyburn jig*, there was a *hempen-widow* – a woman whose husband has been hanged.

inkyo *(n.)* the act of resigning or renouncing your position of office

Inkyo is a Japanese word that was first borrowed into English in the late nineteenth century. In its native Japanese, it refers to a custom of stepping down or resigning from some high position at a time dictated by circumstance rather than age: *inkyo* might be used of a manager stepping down from the running of his business once it has attained a certain status, or the head of a household stepping back from the day-to-day running of the family home once their children are of an age to run the home themselves. Although often said merely to mean 'resignation' or 'abdication', *inkyo* literally and somewhat poetically means 'to dwell in the shade'.

A famous example of stepping back from office took place on 10 December 1936 when King Edward VIII signed the Instrument of Abdication, thereby renouncing his claim to the throne in favour of his younger brother Albert, who became King George VI. Edward's decision to abdicate followed his failed attempt to strike a compromise with the British parliament and the Church of England that would have allowed him to remain king while also marrying his lover, the twice-divorced American socialite Wallis Simpson (head back to 3 June for more on that).

Having given up the throne, Edward took on the title Duke of Windsor and married Simpson the following year. They remained together until his death in 1972.

stirrup-cup *(n.)*   one last drink before a departure, a parting glass

So called as it was once a drink handed to a rider as they prepared to leave, a *stirrup-cup* is one final drink before a departure. One final drink can also be called a *bang-of-the-latch* (from the image of a shutting door), a *voidee* (a French borrowing in use since the fourteenth century) and, if it comes immediately before night-time, a *pillow-cup*.

But for one man on this date in the mid 1930s, one last drink really did mean one last drink.

In early December 1934, thirty-nine-year-old Bill Wilson staggered, blind drunk, up the steps of the Charles R. Towns Hospital in New York. This was the fourth time he had been admitted to the hospital while drunk. It would also be his last.

A heavy drinker from the age of twenty-one, Wilson became an alcoholic in his twenties. Before his final admission to the Towns hospital he was introduced to an evangelical Christian organisation, the Oxford Group, by a friend and former drinking companion who encouraged him to give up alcohol and live a life of sobriety. After initially struggling with the group's philosophies and finding himself tempted to drink again, Wilson struck upon an idea of building a community of reformed alcoholics who could help and support one another through their struggles and recovery. Teaming up with a fellow member of the Oxford Group, Dr Robert Smith, Wilson founded Alcoholics Anonymous the following year.

The drink he had on 11 December 1934 was the last of his lifetime.

abbozzo *(n.)* a rough draft or preliminary sketch

On 12 December 1980, the American businessman Armand Hammer purchased one of Leonardo da Vinci's meticulous handwritten notebooks for a record $5.12 million. Known as the *Codex Leicester* (in honour of Thomas Coke, Earl of Leicester, who originally purchased it in 1719), the notebook comprised seventy-two pages of da Vinci's notes – written in medieval Italian, and in mirror writing – as well as preliminary sketches, rudimentary drawings, charts and diagrams. Although much of the book is dedicated to lengthy discussions of the appearance and properties of water, da Vinci's characteristic butterfly mind darts between several subjects in the *Leicester*, from his thoughts on why fossils are found high in mountains to the luminosity and appearance of the moon.

A preliminary sketch or outline of a later written work can be known as an *abbozzo*, a term from Italian adopted into English in the mid nineteenth century. *Abbozzo* derives from an earlier Italian word, *bozza*, that originally referred to a lump of rock or roughly hewn stone. Likely in allusion to the early stages of an artist's sculpture, in the mid 1500s *bozza* ultimately came to be used of a first draft or rough outline of an artistic work, and it is from there that the word *abbozzo* developed in the early seventeenth century.

periplus *(n.)*   a written account of a grand expedition or circumnavigation; an epic journey

On 13 December 1577, the explorer and navigator Francis Drake set sail from Plymouth on the south coast of England on a journey that would last more than 1,000 days and take him 36,000 miles across the surface of the earth. Setting off with a fleet of five ships (he soon added a sixth, a Portuguese merchant ship captured off the coast of Africa), Drake headed south from England and reached the Moroccan port of Mogador, before heading south again to Mauritania and across the Atlantic.

Reaching Brazil, he headed south, around Cape Horn, and back up the west coast of South and Central America and on to what is now the USA – perhaps sailing as far north as Oregon. Heading west across the Pacific, he passed by the Philippines, Timor and Indonesia, before crossing the Indian Ocean back to Africa, rounding the Cape of Good Hope, and heading back home to England. Having successfully circumnavigated the globe, he arrived back in Plymouth on 26 September 1580.

An account of a journey like Drake's can be known as a *periplus*, a word derived via Latin from the Greek *periplous*, literally meaning 'a voyage around'. In its native Greek, a *periplus* was a logbook or description of the ports and coastal landmarks a seafarer could expect to see and could use to find their way while on a long sea journey.

As these accounts became more detailed, and often included descriptions of the entire coastlines of islands or seas, the word *periplus* came to refer more specifically to a circumnavigation. It was in that sense that the word first appeared in English in the early seventeenth century, but since then this meaning has weakened, so that today *periplus* can be used simply as another word for an epic journey or voyage.

Thule *(n.)* an extreme point, or the extreme point
of a journey or discovery

To the Ancient Greeks, *Thule* (which rhymes with *duly* not *rule*,
incidentally) was the name given to the northernmost inhabit-
able part of the world.

The earliest account we have of *Thule* comes from an early
Greek explorer and geographer named Pytheas, who wrote of
a journey to *Thule* in his travelogue *On the Ocean* in the fourth
century BC. Pytheas' work is sadly now mostly lost, but accounts
of his travels in the works of his contemporaries record that
Thule was so far north that:

> . . . there was no longer any proper land, nor sea, nor
> air, but a sort of mixture of all three, of the consistency
> of a jelly-fish, in which one can neither walk nor sail,
> holding everything together, so to speak. He [Pytheas]
> says he himself saw this jellyfish-like substance, but the
> rest he derives from hearsay.
>
> Polybius, *The Histories* (*c.*140 BC)

Here, Pytheas is presumably describing the slush-like sea ice found
in subarctic waters, but precisely where he travelled to is unclear.
Iceland, Greenland, the Norwegian fjords and even northern
Scotland have all been said to have inspired Pytheas' descriptions
of *Thule*. But no matter where he ended up, it is the general location (and somewhat evocative descriptions like the one above)
that ultimately led to the name *Thule* – or, as it is often known,
Ultimate Thule – becoming a byword for any extreme point.

It is also an apt word for today: on 14 December 1911,
Roald Amundsen and his team became the first people in history to reach the South Pole.

scurryfunge *(v.)*   to hastily tidy a house

A word worth knowing, both in the run-up to Christmas and in light of the events of this day in history, is *scurryfunge*. First recorded in the language in the late eighteenth century, *scurryfunge* originally meant 'to beat' or 'to lash', and later 'to rub' or 'to scrub clean'. These two apparently unrelated meanings are perhaps connected through allusion to someone working hard enough, or with enough power or elbow-grease, to wear away or abrade a surface. In that sense, etymologically *scurryfunge* may be in some way derived from *scour*, or else perhaps from the verb *scurry*, which has been used to mean 'to move rapidly' since the early 1800s.

From the mid nineteenth century, however, *scurryfunge* largely fell out of widespread use in the language, apparently surviving only in a handful of regional dialects:

> *Scurryfunge.* A hasty tidying of the house between the time you see a neighbor coming and the time she knocks on the door. This tends to be coastal.
>
> John Gould, *Maine Lingo* (1950)

On the subject of hastily tidying up, the world's first street-cleaning machine was put into operation on 15 December 1854. The brainchild of an inventor named Joseph Whitworth, the street-cleaner was horse-drawn, and comprised a large cart or carriage fitted with an elaborate system of chains and pulleys that rotated a series of brushes, which would then sweep debris from the ground as they moved. Whitworth patented his invention in 1843, but it wasn't until 1854 that the very first one was put into operation in Philadelphia.

passade *(n.)* a short-lived romance

Jane Austen was born on 16 December 1775. All six of her major novels have remained enduringly popular since they were written in the early nineteenth century, and her ability to challenge the idealistic, sentimental writing style popular among other writers of the day – replacing it with a more ironic and realistic tone – has established Austen as perhaps the greatest English authoress of all time.

But while her great literary heroines all eventually found love, Austen herself never married. She did, however, accept a proposal of marriage – albeit for only one day.

Shortly before her twenty-seventh birthday, Jane and her family were staying with her friends Elizabeth, Alethea and Catherine Bigg at Manydown Park in Hampshire. While they were there, the Biggs' brother, Harris Bigg-Wither, proposed to Jane and she accepted. Jane's niece Caroline later recalled that Harris, who was almost six years younger than Jane, was 'very plain in person' and 'awkward, and even uncouth in manner'. But as the heir to the Biggs' grand estate, 'the advantages he could offer . . . and her long friendship with his family, induced my aunt to decide that she would marry him'. By the following morning, however, Jane had reconsidered. Deciding that she could not marry someone she did not love, the engagement was called off almost as quickly as it had been arranged.

A short-lived romance is a *passade*. Borrowed into English from French, *passade* literally means a 'passing' and originally referred to a technique of walking a horse back and forward over the same patch of ground when it first appeared in the language in the seventeenth century. The romantic notion of a 'passing' flirtation or romance emerged later, in the early 1800s.

omnicide *(n.)*   the destruction of everything

In November 1919, the *Washington Times* and several other newspapers across the United States ran a grim story under the headline, 'Tremendous World Catastrophe to Happen on December 17?' Name-checking the Italian-born meteorologist responsible for the apocalyptic prediction, the article continued:

> Professor [Albert F.] Porta insists that the peculiar group-ing of the planets next month will produce a gigantic sun spot which will explode the earth's volcanoes, shake us with earthquakes and bury us with floods . . . There will be hurricanes, lightning, colossal rains. It will be weeks before the earth will regain its normal conditions.

Professor Porta's theory was that a rare alignment of all but one of the eight planets in the solar system (only Uranus would sit the occasion out) bunched together within an arc of 26° on one side of the sun would cause such a sizeable gravitational imbalance that an enormous sunspot would be torn open on the sun's surface. The result would be an unparalleled burst of solar energy, powerful enough to destroy the earth, 'much as Vesuvius might engulf a football'.

The destruction of everything – of an entire species or planet, or of the human race as it is today – can be known as *omnicide*, a word coined in the 1950s and derived from the Latin *omnis*, meaning 'all', and the suffix *–cide*, derived from *caedere*, meaning 'to cut'.

Needless to say, Professor Porta's prediction did not come to pass, and happily the world did not end on 17 December 1919.

bamblusterate *(v.)*   to hoax, to confuse

First used in the mid nineteenth century, to *bamblusterate* – a nonsense combination *bamboozle* and *bluster*, in the sense of hectoring, boisterous patter – is to hoax or defraud someone.

The word *hoax* itself is a century older. It first appeared in the late 1700s, and is thought to be a corruption of *hocus* or *hocus-pocus*, which was originally another name for a juggler or conjuror in seventeenth-century English, before it became the stereotypical mystical spell of a performer of magic. As for *hocus-pocus* itself, its origins are a mystery – although one theory claims it is a parody of the Latin phrase *hoc est corpus meum*, 'this is my body', lifted from the words of the Catholic Mass.

Returning to the topic of *bamblusterating* hoaxes, it was on 18 December 1912 that newspapers around the world famously proclaimed that the remains of the 'Missing Link' between apes and humans had been discovered, and that Darwin's theory of evolution was thus proved. Fragments of an ape-like skull and jawbone were unveiled at the London Geological Society the same day, and the species was tentatively named *Eoanthropus dawsoni*, 'Dawson's dawn-man', in honour of its discoverer, Charles Dawson, who had found the remains in a gravel pit in Piltdown, Sussex.

Dawson died four years later.

In 1953, his discovery was found to be a hoax.

The remains of the so-called Piltdown Man were actually an artful mishmash of a human skull and an orangutan jawbone which had been boiled, coloured and worn to make them look suitably ancient. Precisely who perpetrated the hoax is unclear, with suspicion ranging from Dawson himself to Arthur Conan Doyle, who lived nearby. The mystery remains unsolved.

master-daddy *(n.)* a wearisome or precocious child,
one trying to outdo their parents

On 19 December 1783, at the age of just twenty-four, William Pitt the Younger was elected to the first of three terms he served as prime minister of Great Britain in the late eighteenth and early nineteenth centuries. The son of William Pitt the Elder, who had served as prime minister from 1766 to 1768, Pitt the Younger's time in office greatly outdid his father's: he remains the youngest person ever to serve as prime minister, oversaw huge crises and change, including the French Revolution, the Napoleonic Wars and the Acts of Union, and served the second-longest term in prime ministerial history – a total of 6,917 days, equivalent to two-fifths of his entire life.

A precocious child that attempts to outdo or get the better of their parents is a *master-daddy*, a term defined by the *English Dialect Dictionary* (1905) as 'a troublesome child', especially 'one who tries to get the upper hand'. But that's not the only obscure, and fairly specific, term for a child found in the dictionary:

- *butter-print* (n.) a seventeenth-century word for a child who looks noticeably like their parents
- *barley-child* (n.) also known as a barley-bairn or barley-crop, barley-child is an old dialect word for a child born in wedlock, but tellingly within six months of the wedding
- *bessy-babs* (n.) a child that seems to cry for no reason
- *flattercap* (n.) a child that tries to get what they want through flattery or wheedling behaviour
- *mammothrept* (n.) a spoiled or overindulged child – literally, a child brought up by their grandmother

emption *(n.)* the act of purchasing something

Appropriate both in the weeks before Christmas and given the anniversary celebrated today, *emption* is the act of purchasing something. The word derives from the Latin verb *emere*, meaning 'to buy' or 'to obtain', which also crops up in the etymologies of a range of otherwise seemingly unrelated words like *premium, redemption, sumptuous, exempt, peremptory* and *impromptu*. Less familiar are a handful of related words like *emptory* ('a marketplace'), *pre-emption* ('the purchase of something before the chance to buy it is offered to other parties') and *coemption* ('the purchase of an entire supply of something').

An important *emption* occurred on 20 December 1803, when France officially ceded control of its Louisiana Territory to the United States, following a deal concluded the previous April. One of the largest territorial exchanges in history, the Louisiana Purchase saw an area of land now encompassing parts of fifteen different states (and two Canadian provinces) switch hands for the not insignificant price of $15 million. In total, some 828,000 square miles of territory was involved in the deal (bought at a price equivalent to 4 cents per acre – or about twice what America would later pay for Alaska).

The United States as a nation was instantly doubled in size, with the lands exchanged in the Louisiana Purchase still comprising just under a quarter of the entire USA as it is today.

unch *(n.)* an 'unchecked' square in a crossword puzzle that is used in one word

Although puzzles and riddles of interlocking words have been known of since antiquity, on 21 December 1913 the *New York World* published what is credited with being the very first crossword puzzle (although this original puzzle was actually called a 'word cross').

Compiled by British-born journalist Arthur Wynne, the puzzle's title wasn't the only difference between the crosswords we have today and the *World*'s original brainteaser. For one, Wynne's puzzle was diamond shaped, and comprised only words of three to seven letters. Nor were there any black squares in his design: all the letters in the grid, except those at the four points of the diamond, were used in two intersecting words. The crossword's clues weren't divided into the now familiar *across* and *down* columns, but rather were listed numerically from one to thirty-four, and required a bizarrely wide-ranging knowledge to complete: simple clues like 'the plural of is' (*are*) and 'what artists learn to do' (*draw*) were listed alongside near-impossible titbits of general knowledge like 'the fibre of the gomuti plant' (*doh*) and vaguer statements such as 'what we all should be' (*moral*) and 'what this puzzle is' (*hard*).

Despite these differences, however, Wynne's 'word cross' is nevertheless seen as establishing the modern crossword puzzle. Its popularity soon led to similar puzzles appearing elsewhere, and before long daily crosswords were appearing in newspapers and magazines the world over.

Nowadays, *cruciverbalists* – that is, crossword compilers and enthusiasts – have since developed their own vocabulary of crossword-solving terms, among them the word *unch*, which is used to describe an 'unchecked' letter that appears only in one word in a puzzle, either across or down but not both.

piper's-bidding *(n.)*   a last-minute invitation

According to the *Scottish National Dictionary*, a *piper's-bidding* is a last-minute invitation. Also known as a *fiddler's-bidding* or *invite*, the origin of the term is a mystery, but it has been suggested that it could allude to the fact that itinerant musicians may once have been invited to join a party, uninvited, in exchange for a tune or entertainment.

On the subject of all things last minute, on 22 December 1849 the Russian novelist Fyodor Dostoyevsky received a startling last-minute reprieve from Tsar Nicholas I – just moments before he was due to be executed.

In April 1849, Dostoyevsky had been arrested in St Petersburg alongside thirty-four other members of a socialist writers' and creatives' group known as the Petrashevsky Circle. Founded by a Russian political activist and theorist named Mikhail Petrashevsky, the group would meet each weekend to discuss art and culture, as well as issues of politics and inequality, and to read literature banned by the tsar's government. When the group's clandestine activities were discovered, Dostoyevsky and his fellow Petrashevskists were arrested, thrown in jail and eventually sentenced to death for conspiring to publish anti-government propaganda.

On what would have been the date of his execution, however, a drum was sounded to call off the firing squad just as they were due to fire, and a horseman galloped into the prison yard to deliver a last-minute pardon from Tsar Nicholas himself. The execution, it seemed, had been a ruse to terrify the Petrashevskists into falling into line with the tsar's regime.

Although not excused entirely (his sentence was commuted to four years' hard labour in a Siberian work camp), Dostoyevsky's life had nevertheless been saved. He later called on his experiences in his novels *Crime and Punishment* (1866) and *The Idiot* (1869).

love-drury *(n.)*   a love token, a gift of love

Derived from an ancient French word, *drut*, for a friend or lover, the word *drury* first appeared in the language during the Middle English period, when it was originally used to refer to love or courtship, or to a clandestine affair. Before long that meaning had developed, so that by the fourteenth century a *drury* was a sweetheart, a beloved person or treasured object, or else – in a sense that remained in use right through to the late 1500s – a love token or keepsake, or a gift from one lover to another.

As *love-druries* go, one of the most famous (and most peculiar) in history was arranged on this day. On 23 December 1888, while living at Arles in the south of France, Vincent van Gogh sliced off his left ear before wrapping the appendage up and allegedly delivering it to a local housemaid, with whom he was besotted.

Van Gogh had earlier moved to Arles from Paris in the hopes of establishing an artists' commune, and was later joined by his friend and fellow artist Paul Gauguin. After two months of living together, the pair had a violent argument that ended with van Gogh first threatening Gauguin with a knife, before turning it on himself.

The incident has since become one of the most famous in art history, but precisely how much of it is true is debatable. Some versions of the story claim the girl in question, known only as Rachel, was a prostitute not a housemaid, while others question whether van Gogh was indeed in love with her or merely experiencing a delusional fit of madness. Whatever the truth, in the aftermath van Gogh was hospitalised in a mental institution in Saint-Rémy to recover. Tragically, he died of a self-inflicted gunshot wound just two years later, in July 1890.

doniferous *(adj.)*   carrying a gift

A fitting word for Christmas Eve, if you're *doniferous* then you're bearing a gift. It dates from the seventeenth century in English and is derived from the Latin word for a present, *donum* – which also lies at the root of words like *donation*, *pardon* and *condone*. But as words that may prove useful on Christmas Eve go, however, *doniferous* is just the tip of the festive gift-giving iceberg:

- *drachenfutter* (n.) a German loanword literally meaning 'dragon-feed', a *drachenfutter* is a gift given to placate someone – especially one's husband or wife – who is angry at the giver
- *oblation* (n.) the act of giving or presenting a gift is *oblation*, a term derived from Latin that originally referred to the presentation or bequest of property to the Church
- *pang* (v.) is an old dialect verb meaning 'to palm off an unwanted gift on to someone else' – or, as the *Scottish National Dictionary* more tactfully puts it, 'to force an unwanted article on to someone'; in either case, it's likely derived from a local corruption of the verb *pawn*
- *present-silver* (n.) money given in place of a gift, a term dating from as far back as the fourteenth century; originally, it could also be used of money given to someone in return for bringing or giving out gifts
- *toe-cover* (n.) a slang term dating from the 1940s for an inexpensive and utterly useless present

One more word that might be worth remembering today is the Scots dialect term *Yule-jade* – defined by the *Scottish National Dictionary* as 'an opprobrious term for someone who leaves work unfinished before Christmas'.

yule-hole *(n.)* the hole you must move your belt
buckle to after eating Christmas lunch

The word *Yule* has been used to refer to the festive season since the Old English period, when it was adopted into the language – originally spelled *geol* – from its Norse equivalent, *jól*. Before we adopted the Roman names of the months of the year, December and January were known by their Anglo-Saxon names *ærra geola* and *æftera geola*, meaning 'before Yule' and 'after Yule'.

Referring to Christmastime as *Yule* or *Yuletide* is a fairly old-fashioned practice today, but the term nevertheless survives in a handful of fairly obscure words including *Yule-hole*, a dialect word the *Scottish National Dictionary* euphemistically defines as 'the hole in the waist-belt to which the buckle is adjusted to allow for repletion after the feasting at Christmas'. But beside *Yule-hole* and yesterday's *Yule-jade*, this time of year you might need to call on:

- *yule-blinker* (n.) a prominent star in the sky on Christmas night, also called a *yulestarn*
- *yule-crush* (n.) 'a Christmas feast', according to the *English Dialect Dictionary* (1905), after which you might have a *yule-gut*
- *yule-goad* (n.) a toy given as a Christmas present to a young child
- *yule-girth* (n.) the peace and time away from usual business that occurs at Christmastime, derived from a corrupted form of *grith*, an Old English word for peace, protection or sanctuary
- *yule-steek* (n.) a word from the far north of Scotland for a wide, quickly mended stitch that is unlikely to hold for long – a reference to, and hence used allusively for, the rush to complete work before Christmas Day

crapulence *(n.)* a feeling of sickness caused by overeating or drinking

'Surfeiting by overeating' is how the first English dictionary to record the word *crapulence* – Nathan Bailey's *Universal Etymological English Dictionary* – defined it in 1727. The adjective *crapulent* had appeared almost a century earlier in Thomas Blount's 1656 dictionary *Glossographia*, but was memorably picked up by the English herbalist William Westmacott in his divinely inspired *Theolobotonologia* or the 'Scriptural Herbal', a guide to traditional cures of a variety of ailments and sicknesses:

> The oil of wormwood by decoction, oil of quinces, and oil of mastic are reckoned by authors the three stomach oils, for outward use, to strengthen the stomach in vomitings, etc. Two or three drops of the chemical oil is convenient in a dose of stomach pills, in crapulent cases, and after a drunken debauch to prevent surfeiting, by cleansing the stomach of filth and ill humours.
> William Westmacott, *Theolobotonologia* (1694)

Crapulent derives via Latin from the Greek word *kraipale*, referring to the sickness or hangover that follows a period of overindulgence. If you're still feeling the after-effects of yesterday's overindulgence today, however, it might also be worth remembering a few more choice words for that morning-after feeling: *ale passion* and *barleyhood* are sixteenth-century words for hangovers or bad moods caused by drinking; *pot verdugo* was drunken light-headedness in the early 1600s; to *misportion* yourself is to make yourself feel ill by eating too much; and people have been feeling *cropsick* – that is, sick from eating or drinking too much – since the early seventeenth century.

ice-bolt *(n.)*   an avalanche

The word *ice-bolt* originally referred to a piercing sensation of cold, like a sudden chill or a literal 'bolt' of ice in the eighteenth century. From there it came to refer to icicles or hailstones, or other icy meteorological phenomena, but by the early 1800s another meaning had developed: in the sense of something that moves as swiftly or as suddenly as a bolt, *ice-bolt* became another word for an avalanche.

It is easy to associate avalanches only with remote mountainous locations, but on 27 December 1836 an avalanche devastated somewhere much closer to home: the market town of Lewes in East Sussex.

The winter of 1836–37 was notably harsh, with gales and snowstorms battering Great Britain for several weeks. On Christmas Eve the storm suddenly worsened, and an enormous blizzard blew in across southern England. In Lewes, the blizzard deposited a huge snowdrift, reportedly 20 feet deep, atop a hill above the town – beneath which was a small row of houses known as Boulder Row.

When it became clear that the snowdrift on the hill was unstable and liable to collapse (part of it detached and destroyed a nearby timber yard on Boxing Day), the residents of Boulder Row were advised to evacuate, but not all of them complied. Then, on the morning of 27 December, the bank of snow suddenly collapsed and the resulting avalanche swamped the houses below, pushing them out into the street and crushing them beneath its weight. Miraculously, seven people were pulled from the deluge alive, but another eight perished. The 'Lewes Snow Drop', as it is now known, remains the deadliest avalanche ever to have struck Britain.

scuddle *(v.)*   to wash dishes

Derived from its French equivalent, a *scuddler* is a scullery maid, and taken from that the verb *scuddle* emerged in the English language in the late sixteenth century to mean 'to wash dishes' – or, as one nineteenth-century dictionary defined it, 'to act as a kitchen-drudge'. Kitchen chores are hardly the most pleasant of household tasks, and perhaps as a result the *English Dialect Dictionary* also lists *scuddle* as a verb meaning both 'to do work, especially domestic work in a slatternly way' and, perhaps more usefully, 'to wander from home in order to shirk some duty'.

In the sense of washing dirty dishes, however, *scuddling* became that little bit easier on 28 December 1886 when an American woman named Josephine Garis Cochran patented the world's first dishwasher.

Far from being a humble *scuddler*, Cochran was a wealthy socialite who would often entertain friends at dinner parties, and wanted a device that could wash the dishes she had used faster than her staff could. When she couldn't find any such device on the market, she set about designing one herself.

She measured her cups and dishes in her home to produce a wire rack to hold them securely in place, and then designed a large copper drum with a wheel at the bottom, on to which the racks and dishes could be placed. From there, hot soapy water could be squirted on to the crockery, while an engine rotated the wheel to ensure they were fully rinsed clean. Cochran demonstrated her invention at the 1893 Chicago World's Fair, and after interest from local hotels and restaurants founded a company to manufacture her dishwasher – the first such device ever marketed.

morganise *(v.)* to assassinate someone to prevent them from disclosing information

On 29 December 1170, the Archbishop of Canterbury Thomas Becket was murdered by four knights loyal to King Henry II. Whether Henry had requested the archbishop's death or not is a matter of some contention, but whatever his comments or orders regarding the famously 'turbulent priest' were, they were nevertheless interpreted as a royal order and led to Becket's bloody assassination as he prepared for vespers that evening.

The dictionary provides us with quite a few words for assassins and assassinations (flick back to 15 March for more of those), as well as a number of words referring to the motives, methods or reasons behind them. Killing someone merely to obtain a dead body, for instance, is to *burke* them – a term from the early nineteenth century alluding to the murders committed by the infamous 'body-snatchers' William Burke and William Hare. To *bishop* someone is to kill for the same reason, supposedly derived from the surname of a man in London who drowned a boy in 1831 to sell his body for dissection.

To *kennedy* someone is to kill them with a poker, a word derived from a Mr Kennedy notoriously killed in Victorian London by precisely that means. And to *morganise* is to assassinate someone to prevent them from revealing secrets: *morganising* derives from the name of a New York writer named William Morgan, who disappeared and is presumed to have been killed in 1826 after threatening to publish a book exposing the secrets of Freemasonry.

mnemonicon *(n.)*   a device to aid memory

The Greek word for 'memory', *mneme*, is the origin of the word *mnemonic*, a term that has been used since the seventeenth century in English to refer either to something that aids the memory, or to the act of improving or aiding the memory itself. A *mnemonicon* is something that does precisely that – while *mnemotechny* (pronounced '*nee*-moh-teck-nee') is the art or science of improving your memory and *mnemonising* something is to commit it to memory using a *mnemonic* device.

Famous *mnemonics* have been invented to aid the recall of everything from the notes on a musical clef ('**e**very **g**ood **b**oy **d**eserves **f**avour') to the fortunes (*divorced, beheaded, died; divorced, beheaded, survived*) and names ('**a**ll **b**arons **s**hould **c**arry **h**eavy **p**arcels') of all of Henry VIII's wives. But the event that inspired perhaps one of the most famous of all *mnemonicons* took place on 30 December 1460 – when **R**ichard **o**f **Y**ork **g**ave **b**attle **i**n **v**ain.

The 'Richard' in this famous mnemonic (used to remember the colours of the rainbow) is Richard Plantagenet, 3rd Duke of York, who was a rival to the throne of King Henry VI in the early fifteenth century. After decades of wrangling with Henry's court and his queen, Margaret of Anjou, Richard finally secured an agreement that the throne would be his for the taking if Henry died before he did. The agreement was still not enough to settle the tumult, however, and on 30 December, Richard's Yorkist supporters fought the king's Lancastrian supporters at the Battle of Wakefield. In the fighting, Richard was killed – just weeks after securing his right to the throne.

handsel *(n.)*   a New Year's gift

A *handsel* is a gift given to wish good luck for the year ahead. In that sense, the word dates back to the late 1300s, but in a looser sense *handsel* was in use before then as a general word for any gift or presentation, or merely the act of handing something over to someone else.

Handsel derives from two fairly straightforward roots: *hand*, a word that has remained all but unchanged since the Old English period, and *selen*, an Old English word meaning 'gift' or 'donation' (and which is a none-too-distant cousin of our verb *sell*). Although its earliest meaning was fairly vague, it didn't take too long for *handsel* to develop: saying that you're doing something *for good handsel* began to refer to some superstitious practice done to ensure good fortune, while something that seemed ominous or inauspicious might likewise be described as *bad* or *ill handsel*. From there, a tradition of bestowing a gift on someone to ensure that good luck went with them – and in particular at momentous times of the year – gave us the word *handsel* as it is today.

As *handsel* continued to be pass down from century to century, it picked up a host of additional meanings referring to debuts and beginnings, so that a *handsel* can also be the first instalment of a payment or bond; a gift given at the start of a new job or new life stage; the first use of something newly bought or acquired; a morning's earnings or takings; and even the first customer or sale made by a business after opening in the morning. And, why not – a new word learnt at the start of the New Year.

SELECT BIBLIOGRAPHY

B. E. *A New Dictionary of the Terms Ancient and Modern of the Canting Crew*. London, c.1699.

Bailey, Nathaniel. *An Universal Etymological English Dictionary*. London, 1749.

Barrère, A., and Leland, Charles G. *A Dictionary of Slang, Jargon and Cant*. London, 1889.

Brewer, E. Cobham. *Dictionary of Phrase and Fable*. Philadelphia, 1887.

Cockeram, Henry. *The English Dictionary: An Interpreter of Hard English Words*. London, 1623.

Delahunty, A., and Dignen, D. *The Oxford Dictionary of Reference and Allusion* (3rd Ed.) Oxford, 2010.

Farmer, John S., and Henley, W. E. *Slang and its Analogues Past and Present* (Vols. 1–7). London, 1890–1904.

Grant, William. *The Scottish National Dictionary*. Edinburgh, 1931–41.

Green, Jonathon. *Chambers Slang Dictionary*. London, 2008.

Grose, Francis. *A Classical Dictionary of the Vulgar Tongue*. London, 1785.

Grose, Francis. *A Glossary of Provincial and Local Words Used in England*. London, 1787.

Halliwell, James. *A Dictionary of Archaic and Provincial Words*. London, 1855.

Jamieson, John. *An Etymological Dictionary of the Scottish Language*. Paisley, 1879.

Partridge, Eric. *A Dictionary of Slang and Unconventional English* (8th Ed.) London, 1984.

Partridge, Eric. *The Routledge Dictionary of Historical Slang* (Revised 6th Ed.) London, 1973.

Partridge, Eric. *A Dictionary of the Underworld*. London, 1949.

Rees, Nigel. *Bloomsbury Dictionary of Phrase and Allusion*. London, 1991.

Shipley, J. *Dictionary of Early English*. London, 1957.

Skeat, Walter. *A Glossary of Tudor and Stuart Words*. Oxford, 1914.

Wright, Joseph. *The English Dialect Dictionary* (Vols. 1–6). Oxford, 1896–1905.

Wright, Thomas. *Dictionary of Obsolete and Provincial Words*. London, 1857.

ACKNOWLEDGEMENTS

Many thanks as always to my superb agent, Andrew Lownie, and to Pippa Crane, Jennie Condell, Alison Menzies and all the team at Elliott and Thompson. Thanks too to Gav Howard, Chris Kirk and Louise Smith for their advice, encouragement and much needed distraction (that's what she said) throughout the compilation of this book. And to the followers of @HaggardHawks – a gracious and sincere thank you for your continued support and interest.

WORDFINDER

374